on track ...

New Order

every album, every song

Dennis Remmer

sonicbondpublishing.com

Sonicbond Publishing Limited
www.sonicbondpublishing.co.uk
Email: info@sonicbondpublishing.co.uk

First Published in the United Kingdom 2022
First Published in the United States 2023

British Library Cataloguing in Publication Data:
A Catalogue record for this book is available from the British Library

Copyright Dennis Remmer 2022

ISBN 978-1-78952-249-5

Typeset in ITC Garamond & ITC Avant Garde
Printed and bound in England

Graphic design and typesetting: Full Moon Media

on track ...
New Order

every album, every song

Dennis Remmer

sonicbondpublishing.com

Acknowlegements

Thank you to New Order (past and present), including Bernard Sumner, Peter Hook, Stephen Morris, Gillian Gilbert, Phil Cunningham and Tom Chapman. Your work is so very important to so many. Thank you to Prime Management – Andy Robinson and Rebecca Boulton – for your support, endorsing (along with the band) my original blog project with a 'Singularity' award, and for looking after myself and Anna on the band's tours down under.

For the original NewOrderTracks blog, which this book is based on, thank you to James Zeiter for his inner sight, and the many (many!) blog readers and New Order Online (NOOL) forum members who were kind enough to share their feedback, comments and love for the project – it is you who encouraged me to evolve the work into this book, and your support was truly overwhelming. Heartfelt thanks also to the various New Order fans who offered their precious gig photos and gave permission for their inclusion in this book.

Special thanks to collaborator extraordinaire Mark Reeder, for your wonderful contribution herein (which tantalisingly opens the door on some key influences and moments of New Order's history), and for all that you have achieved on your own music journey – huge respect!

Most of all, thank you to Anna – the love of my life – for your own music passion, partnering on Transmission Communications (Trans:Com: our record label), and producing music as The Isle with me. I'm glad my New Order mixtapes worked their magic whilst we were at college, because the journey we are on together is wonderful.

Dennis Remmer, September 2022.

Above: Gillian Gilbert and Bernard Sumner 19 April 1985 at Macclesfield Leisure Centre. (*Photo by Glenn Bennett*)

Below: Stephen Morris and Bernard Sumner at the Haçienda in Manchester, 10 June 1987. (*Photo by Paul Das*)

Preface

This book reviews every song New Order has officially released to date – from 'Ceremony' to 'Be A Rebel' – across every album from *Movement* to *Music Complete*, plus the many singles, compilations, soundtracks and other projects.

These reviews were originally published on my NewOrderTracks.wordpress.com blog, which took nearly three years to complete and has received well over 250,000 visits. I started the project around the time *Music Complete* was released – an album that had a significant impact on me by restoring not only my faith in New Order as an ongoing force to be reckoned with, but my passion for music in general.

I first became aware of New Order when the 'Blue Monday' 12" single was released by Factory Records in 1983. Packaged in Peter Saville's magnificent and enigmatic die-cut, colour-coded record-as-floppy-disk sleeve, it heralded life-changing electronic music – a driving, pulsating, futuristic, extended mix of genre-defining techno and dark electronica. I've heard it thousands of times, and yet to this day, 'Blue Monday' remains timeless, as if teleported from a future that we never quite arrive at. The song was an epiphany for the 14-year-old me, and was the foundation of a lifetime's exploration of indie, electronic and alternative music. I felt compelled to explore New Order's earlier work, connected the dots to their previous incarnation (Joy Division), grooved through their mid-1980s alt-dance material, and happily lost myself completely in *Technique* and the golden period of acid, house and rave music from which it emerged. By then, I was in a young synthesizer band, bringing these inspirations to my own creative output.

I started the very first online discographies for Factory Records and New Order (the latter with Rich Kernin), initially appearing in 1992 on the pre-WWW Usenet newsgroup alt.music.alternative. Over the following 20 years, these discographies expanded and evolved, eventually becoming definitive web references before being rehashed by others and surpassed by the excellent Discogs site. Out in the real world, I was making just enough money to help kick-start the electronic music scene here in Brisbane, where my hometown bands like Boxcar and Vision Four 5 (contemporaries of Severed Heads) previously had to exit from to find any support. So in 1994, my partner Anna and I set up Brisbane's first independent electronic-music record label Transmission Communications (Trans:Com), because we unashamedly wanted to be just like Factory Records: namely, a label whose primary mission was to support its city's bands. We celebrated our label's 20th anniversary by publishing a coffee-table book, and a USB music archive titled *BNE*, on the history and development of electronic music in Brisbane. To this day, our work continues because we love it.

The point is that all this endeavour can be directly traced to 'Blue Monday', New Order and Factory Records, through taking their incredible influences and putting them to good use. I owe my musical soul to these enigmatic Northerners from the other side of the world.

Anyway, around the time of the Joy Division *Plus/Minus* campaign, Prime Management's Andy Robinson invited me to prepare the discography for the official Joy Division website at joydivisionofficial.com, and it was this honour that got me thinking about evolving from the obsessive pursuit of discographies, to something more personal – moving on from 'what there is' to 'what it means'. The triumphant release of New Order's *Music Complete* album in 2015, was the trigger for a very personal project to revisit every New Order song and properly listen to it, think about it, write about it and share opinions with fellow fans. Creating the NewOrderTracks blog was a cathartic and hugely enjoyable experience, and you are now reading the compiled results of that work.

The band's history is well-documented, as is its place in the Factory and indeed, the Manchester story – not least of which by the band members themselves in their individual autobiographies. My aim here is not to rehash that story, but rather to delve into every song, offer some context and perspective, and above all, to share its personal impact. I wasn't there in the studio, I don't know them, I can't talk for them, but I know that (probably like you) I feel strongly about their music, and want to share why I think their work is amazing. You should definitely read this book while listening to the songs, and my hope is that this triggers a reaction, because isn't that what music is really about? Very importantly, all opinions are my own.

A quick note on the sequencing of content herein. A band timeline is supplied for initial context, then all the songs are discussed (generally following chronological release order, but may also factor in when the song was written). At the end, a detailed index of song versions and sources is provided, along with a core discography.

Foreword by Mark Reeder

My personal connection to New Order goes far beyond the handful of remixes which I've made for the band over the past couple of years. I am, first and foremost – like you – a fan. Since 1980, their music has moved me and inspired me. Yet, my association began even before their initial incarnation as Warsaw and then Joy Division, but that is another story.

After first representing Joy Division in Germany, Rob Gretton and Tony Wilson designated me as Factory Records' man in Berlin, and with the band's ever-increasing success, I had hopes of creating Factory Deutschland. But Ian Curtis' untimely death would change everything and bring us all crashing down to reality. Still traumatised from the devastating news only a few months before, I recall the moment when their manager Rob Gretton called me to ask what I thought of his suggestion for the band's new name: Man Ray. I told him that people might get confused with the photographer. He wasn't happy. A few days later, he called me again to tell me that they had finally decided on a new name and that the band were from now on going to be called New Order. Although Rob explained that this name supported the rearrangement of the original band members and their new musical direction, I still thought the name was a shade controversial and would almost certainly carry on the conversation surrounding the origins of their previous band name.

So, it was to be that their first single release under the New Order moniker was also a former Joy Division song, and through it, we got a glimpse into what we were going to be missing, or what could've been, yet at the same time, it was the sound of things to come. Musically, it sounded like a progression. It was haunting and beautiful, and it spoke to so many people. Bernard's vocals were drastically introverted and wrapped in reverb, almost as if he was trying to hide from something. A few months later, New Order released their first album *Movement*. Again, it was like the band had one foot in the past and one in the future. It fit perfectly with my melancholy, though, and I just couldn't stop playing it.

After this album's release, I managed to convince Bernard Sumner to come over to Berlin, as I wanted to expose him to the current club sound of the city that I was experiencing, mainly in the vague hope that it might inspire him too and perhaps guide him away from the sound of their past. I focussed especially on one club: the Metropol, which was Europe's largest gay disco at the time. The music they played there was mainly dark, pulsating, American, electronically-driven disco with a heavy trip flavour. Certainly not the tepid *Top of the Pops* style of disco that had diluted its name, this was disco music born from the driving sequencers of 'I Feel Love'. It was the same sound coming from the gay clubs of San Francisco and New York, and it was oozing with energy.

Bernard said the Metropol's music reminded him of New York, but it was also the club's atmosphere and vastness that captivated him. The huge imposing building, which dominates the Nollendorfplatz, already had a notoriously sordid past – formally a prestigious Jewish theatre in the Roaring Twenties, it was partially bombed during the war. In the early-1970s its blackened shell became a blue movie kino showing triple-X-rated porn films, then in the mid '70s became a middle-sized live venue for visiting rock bands, at weekends being transformed into the Metropol discotheque: Europe's biggest gay disco. We had nothing remotely like it in Manchester.

To keep the flames of inspiration burning, I sent Bernard all kinds of new electronic records that I thought might help to inspire him – like Kraftwerk's *Computerwelt* or Moroder's $E=MC^2$, and I recorded all the Metropol music that I was listening to onto cassettes for him. Bernard was a synth fan like me, and I secretly hoped these tapes would help to steer the band in a more electronic direction. 'Everything's Gone Green' and 'Temptation' were indicators that this kind of disco music was starting to have some effect on the band, but the formula had not yet been perfected. When the band went to London to record *Power Corruption And Lies*, I had the pleasure of being invited to the studio. While there, Bernard played me the rough outlines of a new track that he said had been loosely inspired by the music I'd been sending him. This track went on to become 'Ultraviolence'.

Yet, it was a new tape that I'd brought him on this trip, that would change everything. Out of the influence of these and 'Ultraviolence', came 'Blue Monday': the game changer. When I first heard it, I just knew it was going to be huge. I also knew that in my capacity as Factory's German representative, I wasn't going to be able to handle this all on my own, so our distributor – Rough Trade Germany – took on the task. The RTD Germany pressing of 'Blue Monday' was (and still is) outstanding – the reason being it was cut at Studio Nord Bremen from the original reel-to-reel stereo master, and it sounded louder and far more dynamic even than the original Factory pressing. It also had the first kick drum included, unlike the UK pressing, which was missing the very first kick drum beat due to a mastering error on their VHS Digital Master tape. The band had a vote – either go back to the studio and redo the VHS master, or leave it as it is (hence the 'out voted' quote in the run-out groove). 'Blue Monday' is one of the most iconic and influential tracks of the 1980s. It defined an era, and it brought the boys onto the dance floor and made dancing cool again. It paved the way for so many other bands to follow. With this one song, New Order went on to change the way young people viewed dance music.

In 1984, I was invited to support New Order on their European tour with my own band Shark Vegas. New Order had no idea what we were going to play, but we, too, had been inspired by the Metropol's music, and tried our best to mix throbbing bass-line sequences, tapes and drum machines with rock. Hooky was impressed enough with our first gig together, that he recorded all our shows thereafter, and shamelessly confessed years later that the tour together had resulted in the birth of the idea for 'The Perfect Kiss'.

My collaboration didn't end there. In 1990, I started my own label MFS, and helped build the careers of many now-well-known artists and DJs, one of which was German DJ Paul van Dyk. Paul was a New Order fan, and I thought it would be nice if one day I'd be able to fulfil his dream to remix a New Order song. 'Spooky' was to be the last single from *Republic*, and Bernard asked me who I could recommend to remix it. So I suggested Paul, and hoped he'd grasp this one-off opportunity. He went into the studio with Johnny Klimek, and barely finished before the deadline. He submitted two versions, neither of which I thought really worked as they could have (or should have). Out of frustration, I desperately edited both his remixes into one, but the deadline had passed and I was too late. However, I released my special extended 'Out Of Order' edit on the limited double CD of Paul's *45RPM* album: one for the completists.

By the late-1990s, New Order had been keeping things very quiet, with each member pursuing other projects. By this point, I'd also had some personal difficulties, and Bernard offered to help me out by writing a song for me: one that I could release on my MFS label. These were the bare bones of a song I eventually called 'Crystal'. I gave this to Corvin Dalek, and together we went into his little Berlin studio to make a demo. It wasn't long before we had our basic house track, which I sent to Bernard, and he loved it. He re-recorded the vocals, but pointed out that one of the last notes of the line 'shot me to the core' was a bit out of tune, and proposed we should just copy and paste the correct one. Bernard was impressed with these first results, and sent our demo to BBC DJ Pete Tong, who immediately called me and begged me to talk Bernard into releasing the song as a New Order single. I realised he was right, and I certainly didn't want to stand in the way of progress. I thought, if this opportunity can help bring the best band in the world back together, then I'll do it. So, I told Bernard what Pete Tong had said, and of my decision, and I even suggested that Mark Stent should mix it, and was so happy when I heard that the band had gone back into the studio to record what would become one of their most popular songs, and probably the best New Order song since 'True Faith'. It also rekindled the band's inner relationship, and helped heal the wounds that had torn them apart, and New Order rose like a phoenix from the ashes.

After a few more albums, Hooky left. The dark and difficult years following his departure saw the band forced to change their name to Bad Lieutenant while ownership of the New Order name was contested in court. For Bad Lieutenant's 'Sink Or Swim' video, Bernard asked me to film some Berlin footage, and I was given the opportunity to make a remix. Unfortunately, the postal service lost my video tape in transit, and by the time it had been retrieved, their video was almost completed. Using most of my refound Berlin footage, an alternative video was created especially for my remix, which I then released on my *Five Point One* album, along with my other remixes for the Bad Lieutenant song 'Twist Of Fate'. It was around this time that I also helped to bring Bernard and Blank & Jones together to create 'Miracle Cure', and as a thank you, they also asked me to remix it.

With their New Order name eventually intact, the band could venture forth and gig again, and a new album was planned. Around this time, I was making the documentary *B-Movie: Lust & Sound in West-Berlin*, and Bernard was so impressed when he saw it, that he asked me if New Order could use some footage from it to make the video for 'Singularity'. I was honoured, as it further cemented New Order's connection with Berlin. A few weeks later, I was in Bucharest when New Order's manager called and asked me how quickly I could make a remix for 'Singularity'. I was given a one-week deadline for my first New Order remix.

Their *Music Complete* album was a fantastic return to form. I was especially impressed with 'Academic' and 'The Game'. I told Bernard I had some ideas for both, and asked him if I could play around and see if they would work, really just as an experiment at first. My plan for 'Academic' was to make it more like a traditional indie-disco remix, as I thought it might also work as an electronically-driven club track. I also wanted to put Phil's guitar-playing at centre stage. 'The Game', on the other hand, just spoke to me. My idea was to strip it down and reveal its true beauty so that Bernard's wonderful lyrics could receive more focus, as they were serious and poignant. I thought they just got a bit overwhelmed by everything going on in the original version, so I wanted to enhance the song's emotion and get its point across. I decided to take the orchestra idea that comes in briefly towards the end of the original, and create my own orchestral version around a slowed-down beat and layered string melody, surrounded by a heavier, straight chugging and pulsating bass line. Also, I wanted to feature Tom Chapman's great bass work by putting it more up-front.

Mute Records released them both on the (digital) *Music Complete Remix EP*, and I released them on my *Mauerstadt* album. My shorter 'Akademixxx' version was released as a limited-edition 7" single with *Electronic Sound* magazine. My reworking of 'The Game' also indirectly gave birth to the idea of New Order playing a few gigs with an orchestra at the Sydney Opera House, which then evolved into the brilliant synth orchestra gigs for the $\sum$(No,12k,Lg,17Mif) New Order + Liam Gillick events.

Then, along came the pandemic, which had us all stuck at home and locked down. Bernard told me that during lockdown, he'd been working on a piece from the *Music Complete* session called 'Be a Rebel' – a song that hadn't been finished enough to be included on their album; but now, thanks to the Covid lockdown, here it was, and he asked me if I'd like to make a remix for it. I was told the deadline was three weeks and given a list of some of the other artists I'd be sharing the honours with, which included Arthur Baker and Paul Woolford. I immediately fell in love with this song. I could feel the message resonate around me. I knew exactly where Bernard was coming from lyrically – having been bullied at school for being a weirdo kid simply because I liked progressive music – and I knew I had stiff competition to do my best to make it more indie-club and electronic-sounding. As with 'The Game', I played some extra power-guitar, and embedded an additional guitar riff and a powerful driving sequencer bass line. As with all my remixes, though, I wanted to keep the essence of the original song, so I used as many parts from the original stems as I could so it remained recognisable while still sounding a bit different. I made two remixes of 'Be A Rebel'. One was really for all those who don't connect so much with techno, which I released on my *Subversiv-Dekadent* album. The other was a more up-tempo version, which became part of the *Be A Rebel Remixes EP*. Finally – with Eric Horstmann and my studio partner Micha Adam – we made an immersive Dolby Atmos mix of my 'Dirty Devil Remix', which may one day see the light of day.

This book is a devoted, in-depth and personal analysis of all New Order tracks – a collection of iconic works, many of which have undoubtedly shaped the lives of all the people who adore their music. Their music has certainly shaped mine. I hope you will enjoy this track-by-track review, and I also hope that New Order will continue to evolve and create more music for us in the future.

Mark Reeder, September 2022.

on track ...
New Order

Contents

Above: Stephen Morris performing on *Top of The Pops* in 1987.

Below: Bernard Sumner, Gillian Gilbert and Peter Hook performing on on *Top of The Pops* in 1987.

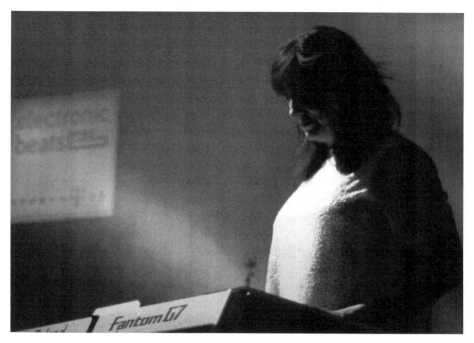

Above: Gillian Gilbert, 21 Jun 2012, Tempodrom, Berlin DE.

Below: Bernard Sumner and Tom Chapman, 3 Mar 2012, Future Music Festival, Brisbane AU. (*Photo by the author*).

Timeline

1980

Apr-May	Joy Division rehearse and demo 'Ceremony' and 'In A Lonely Place'; their final compositions post-Closer, and prior to Ian Curtis' death on May 18.
Jun	Recordings for several Kevin Hewick compositions at Graveyard Studios, Prestwich UK. Joy Division 'Love Will Tear Us Apart' single released.
Jul	Joy Division Closer album released.
Aug	Joy Division 'She's Lost Control' / 'Atmosphere' single released (US).
Sep	First New Order demo session: Western Works, Sheffield UK. 'Ceremony' sessions (I) incl. 'In A Lonely Place'.
Dec	'Ceremony' sessions (II). Mixing in March '81.

1981

Jan	John Peel (I) session: BBC Studios Maida Vale, London UK. Demo sessions: Cargo Studios, Rochdale UK.
Mar	'Ceremony' single (I) released, b/w 'In A Lonely Place'. 'Procession' sessions incl. 'Everything's Gone Green'.
Apr-May	Movement sessions incl. album tracks, 'Everything's Gone Green', 'Cries and Whispers', and 'Mesh'.
Jul-Aug	Movement mixing sessions at Marcus Music, and Basing Street Studios, London UK.
Sep	'Ceremony' single (II) released, b/w 'In A Lonely Place'. 'Procession' single released, b/w 'Everything's Gone Green'.
Oct	Joy Division Still compilation released.
Nov	Movement album released. Taras Shevchenko live performance at Ukrainian National Home, New York USA.
Nov-Dec	Xmas Flexi sessions.
Dec	'Everything's Gone Green' single released, b/w 'Cries and Whispers', and 'Mesh'.

1982

Jan	'Temptation' sessions incl. 'Hurt'.
Feb	'Video 5-8-6' sessions.
May	'Temptation' single released, b/w Hurt. John Peel (II) sessions: Revolution Studios, Cheadle UK. The Haçienda opens.
Oct-Nov	Power, Corruption And Lies sessions incl. album tracks, 'Blue Monday', and 'Murder'.
Dec	Merry Xmas From The Haçienda flexi released. Featuremist compilation incl. 'Prime 5-8-6' released.

1983

Feb	'Confusion' sessions incl. demo for 'Thieves Like Us'.
Mar	'Blue Monday' single released.
May	Power, Corruption And Lies album released.
Aug	'Confusion' single released. Taras Shevchenko live video released.
Dec	'Thieves Like Us' sessions incl. 'Lonesome Tonight'.

1984

Apr	'Thieves Like Us' single released, b/w Lonesome Tonight.
May	'Murder' single released.
Oct-Dec	Low-life sessions incl. album tracks, 'The Perfect Kiss', 'Sub-Culture', 'Skullcrusher', and 'Let's Go'.

1985

Apr	'Shellshock' sessions. 'State Of The Nation' sessions incl demo of 'As It Is When It Was'.
May	'The Perfect Kiss' single released. Low-life album released.
Sep	'Sub-Culture' remixed: Greene St, NY USA.
Oct	'Shame of the Nation' sessions. 'Sub-Culture' single released.
Dec	'Shellshock' remixed: Greene St, NY USA.

1986

Mar	'Shellshock' single released.
Apr-Jun	Brotherhood sessions incl. album tracks and 'Bizarre Love Triangle'.
Aug	Pumped Full Of Drugs live video released; performed 2 May 1985 at Shinjuku Koseinenkin Hall, Tokyo Japan.
Sep	'State Of The Nation' single released.
	Peel Session (II) EP released.
	Brotherhood album released.
Nov	'Bizarre Love Triangle' single released.

1987

May	Substance sessions, incl. re-recordings of 'Confusion' and 'Temptation'.
	'True Faith' sessions, incl. '1963'.
July	'True Faith' single released, b/w '1963'.
Aug	Substance compilation released.
Aug-Sep	Salvation! soundtrack sessions, incl. 'Salvation Theme', 'Touched By The Hand Of God', 'Let's Go', 'Sputnik', and 'Skullcrusher'.
Sep	'Touched By The Hand Of God' remixed: Shakedown Sound Inc, NY USA.
	Peel Session (I) EP released.
Dec	'Touched By The Hand Of God' single released.

1988

Jan	'Blue Monday' remixed: John Potoker.
Feb	Salvation! soundtrack compilation released.
Apr	'Blue Monday 1988' single released.
May-Oct	Technique sessions incl. album tracks, 'Fine Time', 'Round & Round', 'Run', 'Don't Do It', 'Best and Marsh', 'MTO', and 'The Happy One'.
Jun	Joy Division 'Atmosphere' single reissued.
Jul	Joy Division Substance compilation released.
Nov	'Fine Time' single released, b/w 'Don't Do It'.

1989

Jan	Technique album released.
Feb	'Round & Round' single released, b/w 'Best and Marsh'.
Apr	Academy live video released; performed 4 April 1987 at Brixton Academy, UK.
Jul	'Run' remixed: Ocean Way Recording, Hollywood, CA USA.
Aug	'Run 2' single released, b/w 'MTO'.
Sep	Substance 1989 video compilation released.
Nov	Revenge '7 Reasons' single released.
Dec	Electronic 'Getting Away With It' single released.

1990

Feb	'World In Motion' sessions.
May	'World In Motion' single released.
	Revenge 'Pineapple Face' single released.
Jul	Revenge One True Passion album released.
Oct	Revenge 'Slave' single released.

1991

Apr	Electronic 'Get The Message' single released.
May	Electronic Electronic album released.
Sep	Electronic 'Feel Every Beat' single released.
Oct	The Other Two 'Tasty Fish' single released.

1992

Jan	Revenge Gun World Porn EP released.
Feb	BBC Radio 1 Live In Concert live album released; performed 19 June 1987 at Glastonbury Festival, UK.
Mar-Nov	Republic sessions incl. album tracks, 'Regret', 'World', 'Ruined In A Day', 'Spooky', and 'Vicious Circle'.
Jun	Electronic 'Disappointed' single released.
Nov	Factory Records goes bankrupt.
Dec	New Order signs to London Records.

1993
Apr	'Regret' single released.
May	Republic album released.
Jun	'Ruined In A Day' single released, b/w 'Vicious Circle' (select formats only).
Aug	'World (Price Of Love)' single released.
Oct	The Other Two The Other Two & You album released.
Nov	NewOrderStory video compilation released.
	The Other Two 'Selfish' single released.
Dec	'Spooky' single released.

1994
Oct	'True Faith-94' single released.
Nov	The Best Of compilation album released.

1995
Jan	'1963-95' single released.
Feb	The Other Two 'Innocence' single released (US only).
May	Joy Division 'Love Will Tear Us Apart 1995' single released.
June	Joy Division Permanent compilation album released.
Jul	'Blue Monday-95' single released.
Aug	The Rest Of remix compilation album released.

1996
Jun	Electronic 'Forbidden City' single released.
Jul	Electronic Raise The Pressure album released.
Sep	Electronic 'For You' single released.

1997
Feb	Electronic 'Second Nature' single released.
	Monaco 'What Do You Want From Me' single released.
May	Monaco 'Sweet Lips' single released.
Jun	Monaco Music For Pleasure album released.
	The Haçienda closes.
Sep	'Video 586' single released.
	Monaco 'Shine' single released.
Oct	Electronic 'Until The End of Time' single released.
Dec	Joy Division Heart And Soul box set compilation released.

1998
Feb	Band members reconvene to discuss reforming for live performances.
Jul	First gig since 1993 at the Apollo Theatre, Manchester.
Aug	'Temptation 98' session.
Nov	John Peel (III) sessions: studio details unknown.
Dec	Gillian Gilbert's last live performances until 2011 in order to care for family.

1999
Mar	The Other Two 'You Can Fly' single released.
	Electronic 'Prodigal Son' single released.
Apr	Electronic 'Vivid' single released.
	Electronic Twisted Tenderness album released.
	The Other Two 'Super Highways' single released.
May	Rob Gretton dies.
Jun	Electronic 'Make It Happen' single released.
	The Other Two Super Highways album released.
Jul	Electronic 'Late At Night' single released.
Aug	Joy Division Preston 28 February 1980 live album released.
Oct-Nov	'Brutal' sessions.

2000
Jan-May	Get Ready sessions incl. album tracks, 'Crystal', 'Behind Closed Doors', '60 Miles An Hour', 'Sabotage', 'Player In The League', 'Such A Good Thing', and 'Someone Like You'.
Feb	The Beach soundtrack compilation incl. 'Brutal' released.
Aug	Monaco 'I've Got A Feeling' single released.
	Monaco Monaco album released.

2001

Apr-May	'Here To Stay' sessions.
May	3 16 live DVD released; performed 30 August 1998 at Reading Festival, UK. Also includes the Taras Shevchenko performance from 1981, and a performance from 21 September 1998 at Albert Square, Manchester UK for the 2002 Commonwealth Games bid.
	Joy Division Les Baines Douches 18 December 1979 live album released.
Jul	Phil Cunningham's first live performances with the band.
Aug	'Crystal' single released, b/w 'Behind Closed Doors' (select formats only).
	Get Ready album released.
Oct	BBC Radio Evening Session: studio details unknown.
Nov	'60 Miles An Hour' single released, b/w 'Sabotage' (select formats only).
Dec	'Someone Like You' single released.

2002

Apr	'Here To Stay' single released, b/w 'Player In The League' (select formats only).
Jun	'World In Motion' single re-released, b/w 'Such A Good Thing'.
Oct	International compilation album released.
Dec	Retro box set compilation released.
	5 11 live DVD released; performed 9 June 2002 at Finsbury Park, UK. Also includes various live excerpts from 1998.

2003

May	The Peter Saville Show 'Soundtrack' session.
Apr	War Child – Hope compilation incl. 'Vietnam' released.
Jun	The Peter Saville Show Soundtrack released.

2004

	Waiting For The Sirens' Call and Lost Sirens sessions incl. album tracks, 'Krafty', 'Jetstream', and 'Waiting For The Sirens' Call'.
Feb	Revenge One True Passion V2.0 album reissued.
Apr	In Session album released, featuring November 1998 & October 2001 radio sessions.

2005

Feb	Revenge No Pain No Gain (Live 1991) album released.
Mar	'Krafty' single released.
	Waiting For The Sirens' Call album released.
May	'Jetstream' single released.
Jun	Best Remixes digital-only compilation released.
Sep	'Waiting For The Sirens' Call' single released.
	A Collection video clip DVD compilation released. Also packaged with a re-release of NewOrderStory on DVD as the Item box set.
Oct	Singles compilation released.

2006

Feb	New State Recordings 12" reissues (x 12) released.
Sep	Electronic Get The Message: The Best Of Electronic compilation released
(Late)	Control soundtrack sessions.

2007

May	Peter Hook leaves the band.
Aug	Tony Wilson dies.
Sep	iTunes Originals digital-only EP released.
Oct	Control soundtrack compilation incl. 'Exit', 'Hypnosis', and 'Exit' released.

2008

Mar	Joy Division The Best Of Joy Division compilation released.
Jun	Live In Glasgow live DVD released; performed 18 October 2006 at Carling Academy, Glasgow Scotland. Also includes numerous 'rare and unseen' footage from performances in 1981 at Celebration - Granada TV and Glastonbury UK, 1982 at Rome Italy, 1983 at Cork Ireland, 1985 Rotterdam Netherlands and Toronto Canada, 1989 at Shoreline, Mountain View USA, and 2005 at Hyde Park Wireless, London UK.

2009
Apr	'Temptation' 7" single reissued for RSD.
Sep	Bad Lieutenant 'Sink Or Swim' single released.
Oct	Bad Lieutenant Never Cry Another Tear album released.

2010
Feb	Bad Lieutenant 'Twist Of Fate' digital-only single released.
Aug	Freebass Two Worlds Collide EP released.
	Freebass 'You Don't Know This About Me' digital-only single released.
Sep	Freebass It's A Beautiful Life album released.
	Freebass 'The God Machine' digital-only EP release.
Dec	Joy Division + - Singles 1978-80 7" singles box set released.

2011
Apr	New Order / Joy Division – 'Ceremony' / 'In A Lonely Place' 12" single reissued for RSD.
Jun	Total compilation released.
Jul	Gillian + Stephen 'Anna + Peter Swing Project 1' single released.
Sep	Band reunites (without Peter) for live performances, with Gillian Gilbert returning and Tom Chapman joining.
Dec	Live At The London Troxy live album released; performed 10 December 2011 at The Troxy, London UK.

2013
Jan	Lost Sirens album released.
Jul	Live At Bestival 2012 live album released; performed 7 September 2012 at Bestival, Dorset UK.
Apr	Peter Hook's autobiography Unknown Pleasures – Inside Joy Division published.

2014
Apr	Joy Division An Ideal For Living 12" EP reissued for RSD.
Sep	Bernard Sumner's autobiography Chapter and Verse – New Order, Joy Division And Me published.
(Late) -May	Music Complete sessions incl. album tracks, 'Restless', 'Tutti Frutti', 'Singularity', 'People On The High Line', and 'Be A Rebel'.
Nov	1981 - 1982 EP reissued for RSD.

2015
Sep	New Order announce signing to Mute Records.
	Music Complete album released.
Oct	'Restless' single released.
Dec	'Tutti Frutti' single released.

2016
Mar	'Singularity' single released.
May	Complete Music extended mixes album released.
Jul	'People On The High Line' single released.
Oct	Peter Hook's autobiography Substance – Inside New Order published.

2017
Apr	Music Complete: Remix digital EP released.
Jun	NOMC15 live album released; performed 17 November 2015 at Brixton Academy, UK.

2018
Aug	4'33" recording.

2019
Mar	'Ceremony', 'Everything's Gone Green', and 'Temptation' 12" singles reissued.
Apr	Movement definitive edition box set released, with Extras and a DVD with performances from 1980 at Hurrah's, New York USA, 1981 at Peppermint Lounge, New York USA, 1981 at Granada Studios, Manchester UK, 1982 at BBC Riverside, London UK, and others.
May	Stephen Morris's autobiography Record Play Pause – Confessions of a Post-Punk Percussionist: Volume I published.
Jun	Joy Division Unknown Pleasures LP reissued (40th anniversary).
Jul	$\sum$(No,12k,Lg,17Mif) live album released; performed 13 July 2017 at Manchester International Festival, UK.
Oct	STUMM433 compilation incl. (New Order's) 4'33" released.

2020

Jul	Joy Division Closer LP reissued (40th anniversary).
	Joy Division 'Transmission', 'Atmosphere', and 'Love Will Tear Us Apart' 12" singles reissued.
Sep	'Be A Rebel' single released.
Oct	Power Corruption And Lies definitive edition box set released, with Extras and DVDs with performances from 1982 and 1983 at The Haçienda, Manchester UK, 1983 at the Rosehill Hotel, Kilkenny Ireland, various TV performances 1982-1984, and others.
	'Blue Monday', 'Confusion', 'Thieves Like Us', and 'Murder' 12" singles reissued.
Dec	Stephen Morris's autobiography Fast Forward – Confessions of a Post-Punk Percussionist: Volume II published.

2021

May	Education Entertainment Recreation live album released; performed 9 November 2018 at Alexandra Palace, London UK.
Aug	'Be A Rebel (Remixes)' single released.

2022

Feb	Joy Division Still 2xLP reissued (40th anniversary).
Apr	Electronic 1989 Remixes 1992 compilation EP released for RSD.

2023

Jan	Low-life definitive edition box set released, with Extras and DVDs with performances from 1985 at Koseinenkin Hall, Tokyo JP, the Rotterdam Arena, NL, the Manhattan Club, Leuven, BL, the International Centre, Toronto CA, and The Haçienda, Manchester UK.
	'The Perfect Kiss', 'Sub-Culture', and 'Shell-Shock' 12" singles reissued.

Heaven Knows, It's Got To Be This Time: Movement +

New Order were Joy Division. Joy Division were Warsaw. Warsaw began as two mates that went to a poorly-attended but incredibly important punk gig in Manchester 1976, and decided that they could do it too. From 1977 to 1980, Bernard Sumner, Peter Hook, Ian Curtis and Stephen Morris – everyday young men creating serious art and reacting seriously to their time and place – wrote, recorded and performed some of the most incredible and important post-punk music that will ever be. Joy Division's two astounding albums *Unknown Pleasures* from 1979 and *Closer* from 1980 – together with a handful of singles including 'Transmission', 'Atmosphere', 'She's Lost Control' and 'Love Will Tear Us Apart' – exist forever in marble and stone. These works are flashpoints in modern music: stunning songs rendered iconic in their sleeves, as enigmatic as the musicians themselves.

Too driven by their craft to really bother with opinion, fashion or marketing, the bands' inner circle were all-important – from their manager Rob Gretton, to their producer Martin Hannett, to their record label Factory Records (i.e., Anthony H. Wilson and Alan Erasmus), to their designer Peter Saville. This was a planetary alignment of people and ideas that created very wonderful things, and whose influence (and myth) has only grown in the 40+ years since.

Ian Curtis' tragic destiny is well known, and it brought Joy Division as a creative force to an abrupt and shocking stop on 18 May 1980. Very soon after Curtis' suicide, Sumner, Morris and Hook decided that they wanted to continue making and performing music – understandably as a different entity since Ian Curtis could never be replaced. As 'a few musicians', they set out very tentatively, recording some backing tracks ('Haystack' and 'A Piece Of Fate') for Kevin Hewick, followed by a demo session of newly-written material at Cabaret Voltaire's Western Works studio. By September 1980, having settled on their identity, New Order played some low-key performances in Manchester, Liverpool and Blackpool, followed by a short tour of America originally planned for Joy Division back in May – all the while seeing some light at the end of the very dark tunnel that they'd so very recently found themselves in. Whilst in New Jersey, the three-piece band entered the studio to record a single, and upon their return to the UK, they found their fourth member in Gillian Gilbert. Now fully-formed, New Order began to accelerate away from what *was*, towards even more remarkable things.

Ceremony (Single, 1981)

Personnel: Bernard Sumner, Peter Hook, Stephen Morris, plus Gillian Gilbert for the re-recording.
Recorded September 1980 at Eastern Artists Recording Studio, East Orange, NJ, USA.
'Ceremony' re-recorded December 1980 at Strawberry Studios, Stockport, UK.
Producer: Martin Hannett
Record label: Factory

Original UK release dates: March 1981 (7", 12" (#1)), September 1981 (12" (#2))
Chart position: UK: 34

'Ceremony' (Curtis, Sumner, Hook, Morris)

'Ceremony' was written by Joy Division at the height of their powers but at the end of their tether, and was the last track captured by the band – just two weeks before Ian Curtis' death – at High Hall, Birmingham University on 2 May 1980 (and released on the *Still* compilation). Joy Division's 'Ceremony' can also be found as a rehearsal recording from the same period (at Graveyard Studios, Prestwich) on the *Heart and Soul* box set and the 2011 'Ceremony' RSD 12".

In many ways, 'Ceremony' is a parallel to 'Love Will Tear Us Apart' – rattling drums, melodic driving bass and processed guitar, with a powerful crescendo and deeply meaningful songwriting by Curtis. Listening to Joy Division's recordings of 'Ceremony' and 'In A Lonely Place' (see below) is difficult for two reasons – 1: they point to a creatively rich path beyond *Closer* (on which the band would've increasingly incorporated synths and electronics); but 2: unfortunately, Ian sounds completely spent.

Only four months later, whilst in the USA for their remounted tour, New Order entered Eastern Artists Recording Studios in East Orange, New Jersey, to properly record 'Ceremony' and 'In A Lonely Place' with Martin Hannett in the producer's seat. This original recording of 'Ceremony' – which is the one released on the 7" and initial 12" – closely resembles the Joy Division versions: more spartan, similar (slower) tempo, metallic in texture, vocals echoing back in the mix. The song is built around Hooky's commanding bass line, Morris' chattering cymbals and snares, and Sumner's melodic lead guitar and distorted chords. Tension builds as the track is progressively pared back – with Sumner singing Curtis' line 'watching love grow forever' over a beautiful, chiming three-note melody – before the song surges again towards a glorious end: always a religious experience when played live, with the crowd heaving as one.

The song was re-recorded in December 1980 at Strawberry Studios in Manchester (after Gillian Gilbert joined the band) and released as a different 12" in September 1981. This new recording is a little faster, and the performance is much tighter. Sumner sounds less tentative, Hannett was more subtle with the reverb and improved the balance, and – in my opinion – the overall recording sounds better.

Starting their new chapter by honouring the final creations of Ian Curtis was a deeply righteous act from Sumner, Hook and Morris – and regardless of which version from which band, 'Ceremony' is a towering track in the history of rock music.

'In A Lonely Place' (Curtis, Sumner, Hook, Morris)

Rarely has a piece of music sounded so bleak, brooding and final. The last and most unsettling song written by Joy Division. Darker even than 'Atmosphere',

'The Eternal' and 'Decades', much has been said of the lyrics, in hindsight so readily interpreted as prophetic of what was to come. How on earth New Order were able to subsequently record this (or even play it live) is beyond me. But clearly, closure and respect came into it. 'In A Lonely Place' is a remarkable, visceral track.

In 1980, with so much of the period's synthesizer music being of the cheap and nasty kind, 'In A Lonely Place' (originally titled 'Little Boy') delivered a majestic, almost funereal alternative – vast, sweeping chords of deep synthetic atmosphere over a slow march of drum rolls. Repeating, simple but beautifully-defined organ melodies played in combination with Sumner on melodica, and Hooky's discordant descending bass lines. In my opinion, this is one of Martin Hannett's finest productions, utilising his digital delay to remarkable effect, and cutting through with shards of manufactured electronic noise. The synths, cymbals, and even Sumner's hauntingly frail vocal, are all passed through a shimmering reverb, casting the whole track in a crystalline subzero mist.

Probably more so than 'Ceremony', 'In A Lonely Place' – with its emphasis on the darker shadows of electronic music (and recent Joy Division tracks in that context like 'Isolation', 'Heart And Soul' and the 'As You Said' instrumental) – informed what was to come on the *Movement* album. Caressing the marble and stone indeed.

Unique Demo Recordings (1980)
Personnel: Bernard Sumner, Peter Hook, Stephen Morris
Recorded September 1980 at Western Works, Sheffield, UK
Producers: Cabaret Voltaire and New Order

It's a marvel that in the space of only three months, Bernard, Peter and Stephen were able to regroup, reset and re-emerge (but not recover, understandably, from the horror of losing Ian) to the point of having a new set of songs in various stages of completion. By September 1980, New Order had written (at least) 'Dreams Never End', 'Truth', 'Mesh', 'Homage', 'Cries And Whispers' and 'Procession', and reworked the Joy Division songs 'Ceremony' and 'In A Lonely Place'. That the trio chose to draw such a firm line in the sand from their previous efforts (think of how recently they'd written and recorded all the songs on the masterpiece that is *Closer*), shows incredible tenacity and will. It's also a clear expression of their grief, which they have each admitted in their respective memoirs was otherwise suppressed and never really dealt with properly.

The Western Works studio session from 7 September 1980, whilst being what it is – namely a set of demos (of 'Dreams Never End', 'Homage', 'Ceremony', 'Truth' and 'Are You Ready For This?') – is hugely important in the band's history, being as it's their first recording as (and of) New Order, and predate the first 'Ceremony' session by about two weeks. It's at this stage that the band was still figuring out – in yet another marker of difficult recovery from tragedy – how to restructure, in the absence of a lead singer.

Who was going to reluctantly step into the role of frontman? It's these demos – and indeed the footage from their belated US trip – that so clearly document this intensely difficult transition period. Their inclusion in the 2019 *Movement* Definitive Edition box set is both generous and a much-appreciated gesture.

Recording at Western Works was a good idea. Working with kindred spirits in Cabaret Voltaire, away from Martin Hannett, and in facilities that bypassed convention (and cost), the band knocked out five tracks (two of them unique to the session) as a personal research -and-development exercise – never intended for commercial release or wider listening; not that this got in the way of bootleggers. The session must've been an affirming exercise, if not altogether successful.

'Homage' (Sumner, Hook, Morris)

Sonically, 'Homage' is a blend of early Joy Division-sounding bass from Hooky, some very Cabaret Voltaire-like (circa 'Nag Nag Nag') guitar riffs from Sumner, and a typically frantic drum performance from Morris. Bernard's lyrics – e.g., 'Father, please don't forsake me now' – make for difficult listening given the lack of paternal presence in his life. One feels so sympathetic for Bernard; his formative years would've been difficult.

'Homage' is a simply-structured song that looks backwards rather than forward, and I'm sure the band knew this, because the song disappeared from their live sets before the end of the month, never to be revisited again until made *official* by its inclusion on the *Movement* Definitive Edition. Not a great song, but a very important one.

'Are You Ready For This?' (Sumner, Hook, Morris, Gretton)

I suppose if you're going to try out every band member on lead vocals, you might as well give the manager a go. That this *song* gained an official release on the *Movement* Definitive Edition is remarkably magnanimous of Bernard, Peter and Stephen, and I suspect very much against their better judgement!

Clearly, this was only ever destined for a laugh, probably right at the end of the sessions, with the ale flowing freely, and yet there is something interesting going on here. First, the track sounds totally Cabaret Voltaire, and you can just imagine Stephen Mallinder on an alternative (more sensible) vocal, making this track sound right at home on their *Mix-Up* album. More importantly, it sounds like everyone just had fun messing around in the studio, offering some much-needed stress release from recent events. The sound palette is hilarious, particularly in the drum program (set to a ludicrous default pattern), with Morris adding 'pew' drum fills from his Synare electronic drums while Rob barks like a dog in the background. Mad!

How wonderful it would've been to see the band play this live (just once), perhaps on Rob Gretton's birthday, leading him against his will to the front of the stage while the other three made cacophonous noise in the background.

Procession (Single, 1981)
Personnel: Bernard Sumner, Peter Hook, Stephen Morris, Gillian Gilbert.
Recorded March 1981 at Strawberry Studios, Stockport, UK
Record label: Factory
Original UK release date: September 1981
Chart position: UK: 38

'Procession' (Sumner, Hook, Morris, Gilbert)
Producer: Martin Hannett
Though written later than songs like 'Dreams Never End' and 'Truth' (both of which emerged soon after the events of May 1980), the 'Procession' recordings preceded the *Movement* sessions, and the single was released before the album – which makes sense because 'Procession' is one of New Order's best tracks from their early period, with phased ARP Omni synth layers offering a dark yet strangely peaceful wash over the whole song, a cracking bass performance from Hooky (one of his best), restrained guitar highlights and a top vocal performance from Bernard (with backing from Gillian). Martin Hannett delivers a remarkable production filled with space, emotion and tone.

'Procession', bristles, and live outings of it from back in the day are a study in pent-up angst – all members showing little emotion from the neck up, yet delivering a channelled, intense performance like a band possessed.

One final comment. Just how remarkable is 'Procession'/'Everything's Gone Green' as a single: the band's actual first after the Joy Division-penned 'Ceremony', and a wonderfully eclectic release from Factory – issued in nine different sleeves: black, red, blue, brown, yellow, orange, green, aqua or purple design, each on a grey card background, and highlighting Peter Saville's futurist references of the time. Also, it's the first in a long line of New Order singles where you could toss the coin on whether the A or B-side is better, and this attests to their respect for their fans.

'Everything's Gone Green' (Sumner, Hook, Morris, Gilbert)
Producer: New Order
This track is just incredible – in my mind, the soundtrack to a late-night dash through the city, all lights green, no stopping. It's a metaphor for the band perhaps, speeding away from their connections to Hannett (critically, this is the band's first self-production), their prior approaches to songwriting, and any sense of convention. The track is a remarkable reveal of New Order's emerging *modus operandi* – extended sequencer-driven electronic backbone, Bernard's emerging lyric obliqueness (whoops of joy rising out of hurt, doubt, confusion, need for help, etc.), and a compelling new beat.

The chattering Dr Rhythm percussion is similar to that which threads through 'Truth' and 'Doubts Even Here' (see below). However, it's quickly overtaken by a guttural sequencer line and Hooky on prominent bass. Then the layers keep coming – cymbals and snares locking a disco groove, a metallic wash of effected guitar announcing the arrival of Chic-like chords, vocals doubletracked to add drama, and a lengthy instrumental break with the parts progressively breaking down before a final flurry of reverbed sequencer growl.

This was the new blueprint: dark, brooding, powerful alternative dance music. Few of New Order's contemporaries were close, and wouldn't break their shackles of twee electropop for several years, before discovering the more interesting edges of electronic music to which New Order had long staked their claim.

'Everything's Gone Green' has been the target of remixing over the years, the best of which is the superb 'Cicada Remix', which appeared as a B-side on the second of the three 'Waiting For The Sirens' Call' 7″ releases in 2005. The 'Dave Clarke Mix' from *The Rest Of* is five minutes of mindless techno purely for the hardcore dance floor, and has near-zero bearing on the original. For the completists' sake, there are also some outlier remixes that exist only on promotional or third-party issues, including the superb 'Martin Buttrich Remix', and a set of four extremely tedious mixes produced in 1996 by The Advent.

One final comment: I never quite understood Factory's original handling of this amazing and important song – only released domestically (in edited form) as a B-side (!) of 'Procession'; thereafter released in its entirety (but only on import) via Factory Benelux; not included on *Movement*, and not released as a single at all in the USA, but included on the Factory US *1981-1982 EP* which did belatedly bring the US fans up to date. The 2019 12″ reissue at the time of the *Movement* Definitive Edition box set campaign was very welcome.

Movement (Album, 1981)
Personnel: Bernard Sumner, Peter Hook, Stephen Morris, Gillian Gilbert
Recorded April/May 1981 at Strawberry Studios, Stockport, UK
Producer: Martin Hannett
Record label: Factory
Original UK release date: 13 November 1981
Chart position: UK: 30

'Dreams Never End' (Sumner, Hook, Morris, Gilbert)
Nearly a year had passed since the shocking events of May 1980, and by the time of their first John Peel session in January 1981, the band (now including Gillian) had developed a clutch of brand-new tracks – one of the earliest (in fact the first, according to Peter Hook) being 'Dreams Never End', which since its inception has featured Hook on vocals.

Had Factory approached things differently in the early-1980s and released singles from albums, 'Dreams Never End' would've been an excellent candidate. But I do like the notion that Factory (and the band) wanted to give maximum value to fans by only offering exclusive work across the releases, and this was certainly true for the Joy Division and early New Order albums. Later comments by the band – in the context of their financial position – lament the singles-not-on-albums issue as a detrimental one: a classic Factory art-vs-reality dichotomy.

The structure of 'Dreams Never End' gives it serious gravitas. Once the long intro builds up, it kicks into three minutes of speedy bass riffs, funk rhythm guitar and rapid-fire cymbals. Hooky's vocals (of which there are only verses) are underpinned by manic guitars and train-like drum patterns, with the space normally occupied by a chorus, replaced with the lead guitar cutting loose from its muted percussive form into a wonderfully emotive riff. Martin Hannett's production is on a high par with the 'Ceremony' recording, possibly because it's a similar style of song: no synths means less production experimentation (which could be hit-or-miss, e.g., 'Everything's Gone Green' vs 'Senses' (to be discussed later)).

The lyric remains in the shadow of Joy Division. However, Hooky does a great job on lead, and it's one of the stronger vocal productions on *Movement*, aided in part by Hannett's multitracking, using multiple takes at both high and low registers. Compare this recording with that from the first Peel Session, which has only a single higher-register vocal and sounds slightly weaker for it; though having said that, the Peel version still packs a punch.

The two demo versions included in the *Movement* Definitive Edition boxed set offer a fantastic insight into how quickly the band got *back to work* and strengthened over the course of six months, leading to the sessions for *Movement*. The Western Works demos, written and recorded so soon after Ian's death, are worth their weight in gold – not for their musical qualities (because they sound raw and tentative), but for their commitment to change. The Cargo studio demo shows further progression (including speeding up the track, which was necessary), and though the band isn't happy with *Movement*, I do believe the album version shows 'Dreams Never End' in its best light.

Over the years, Hooky's voice has gotten more resonant, lending itself to increasingly-better renditions of 'Dreams Never End' – the last New Order performance of which was in 1988, after which Hooky has kept the torch burning via Revenge, Monaco, and The Light.

'Truth' (Sumner, Hook, Morris, Gilbert)

Along with 'Dreams Never End', 'Truth' is one of the earliest tracks in the New Order canon, first recorded during the Western Works session. Sparse and dramatic, Bernard sings of a strange day where time passes slowly, to a sinister soundtrack with an incessant metronomic, electronic snare pattern interspersed with a repeating bass-drum sequence (all courtesy of the band's new Boss Dr. Rhythm) delivering the unnerving sound of someone knocking on your door, trying to get in.

People talk of Martin Hannett's approach to production as emphasising the space between instruments, and to these ears, tracks like 'Truth' illustrate this in spades. Yet, the track was in fact, mixed by the *band* (the only one on *Movement*), having clearly paid a lot of attention to Hannett's craft. The space in the track's minimal instrumentation is filled with reverb and electricity, and none of it feels comforting. The synths, guitars, bass, melodica, and indeed Bernard's vocal, weave in and out of the buzzing drum patterns like waves of locusts, building until the noise – as the lyric suggests – surrounds you.

When you really sit back and listen to New Order's early work, their artistic response to recent tragedy is remarkable. *Movement* is the band's visceral coming to terms; a very public outing of otherwise-private thoughts. For a band accused over the years of not communicating, what more do you really need than the music?

'Senses' (Sumner, Hook, Morris, Gilbert)

'Senses' is a strange track that doesn't quite gel, mainly because all the pieces seem to be trying a bit too hard. Hannett's production approach across much of *Movement* – that of emphasising digital delay to give atmosphere, with lots of tricky electronic overdubs – in this case, derails the song. Specifically, the rotating, phasing tom rolls, the low-end ARP synth and the main bass performances all sound separately loose because of the over-reliance on effects; on top of the main percussion and lead guitar, which are otherwise tight. Bernard's vocal – already overprocessed and mixed into the background – is flanged on the line 'no reason ever was given' in an attempt to add drama. The ending, however, is very atmospheric, and leads beautifully into 'Chosen Time'.

Overall, because of Hannett's production overkill, the album version of 'Senses' is not quite the sum of its parts. Look to the superior recording of the song from the 1981 Peel Session.

'Chosen Time' (Sumner, Hook, Morris, Gilbert)

There are times when I can't help but marvel at Stephen Morris. I can't think of another drummer who can sustain the sort of high-speed beat-perfect metronomic trance that you get with 'Chosen Time', and doesn't need to be plugged in! In fact, 'trance' is the right description for 'Chosen Time', because it aches for a full-blown 10-minute 12" single, with Morris's hypnotic rhythm combined with Hooky's incessant two-note bass line interplay with the synth bass. Has anyone thought to remix this gem? Stems, please!

Unlike the less successful tracks on *Movement*, on 'Chosen Time' (originally titled 'Death Rattle'), Martin Hannett has worked Sumner's reticent vocal into the mix really well, and he hasn't overworked the electronics – a very effective synthetic machinery noise rolling in like a digital storm over the track's last quarter. From the opening (and evocative) beat/chime, to the dissipating electronic chatter courtesy of Bernard's Transcendent 2000, 'Chosen Time' is an innovative, driving highlight in the early New Order canon. For me – particularly with Bernard's call-to-arms of 'believe in me' (lyrics by Morris) – 'Chosen Time' is the starting point for the forward-looking *beats & electronics*

New Order, and from here, the clouds rapidly cleared, towards tracks like 'Everything's Gone Green', 'Blue Monday' and 'The Perfect Kiss'.

'ICB' (Sumner, Hook, Morris, Gilbert)

Using the acronym of the transport company that handled the flight cases on the first New Order tour is a perfectly good inspiration for a song name. Of course, it's a bit perverse (and true to form) that the band (in fact, their roadie Twinny) turned that into the red herring that is 'Ian Curtis Buried'. Dark humour – a characteristic that permeates so much of New Order's output.

This is one of the top-three tracks on *Movement*, and according to Peter Hook, was first jammed as Joy Division. Among the highlights are the experimental guitar stabs playing tag with the electronic pings and sweeps, and the emphasis on tom and snare in Morris' rolling drum pattern. It's quite hypnotic, particularly when the track kicks into the chugging chorus and soaring instrumental close. The song is nicely structured, and it's probably Bernard's best vocal performance on the album.

On the strength of tracks like 'ICB', the *Movement* album – often placed low in the band's and fans' lists – needs some serious reconsideration. It's an inventive, brave, original and fascinating album. Stephen Morris' 'It seems to draw me in' line is very apt.

'The Him' (Sumner, Hook, Morris, Gilbert)

There's a sinister disquiet about 'The Him', which marks it as yet another distinctive track on *Movement*. The song has a ghostly, requiem feel, with Bernard singing about wasting life, penance, of being tired, and the need to experience a rebirth. Lyrically, I sense a line being drawn in the sand – the band has seen too much, felt too much and no doubt questioned too much. Emotionally and spiritually, they are peering into dark places in search of reasons, and yet it's a completely different darkness to Ian Curtis', which was personal, prophetic and tragic. The band's own mire – so clearly expressed across *Movement* – is more of the 'why?' variety, and the difficult path towards an optimistic future.

Musically 'The Him' feels like it has two distinct phases: fog and storm. The former is expressed through Peter Hook's plaintive bass played over washes of synthesized atmosphere, choral sounds, distant metallic guitar riffs and Morris on rolling toms and shimmering cymbals. There's an effective octave doubling of Sumner's vocals with Hooky's, and the overall mix is beautifully layered by Martin Hannett.

Then the weather really kicks in with a crashing of snare drum and guitars, and a dark synth line which sounds like an ill wind whistling through power lines. About three-quarters of the way through – for about 15 seconds – the eye of the storm passes over with a single note of synth, and then it all comes crashing in again as the band fights off their demons, tired as they may be. Visceral and revealing.

'Doubts Even Here' (Sumner, Hook, Morris, Gilbert)

I have doubts here. On the one hand, the minimal, quiet feel to (most of) the song is another successful exercise in less-is-more from New Order circa 1981, and Hooky's vocal works better here than Bernard's would if he was singing it. The song starts with a recall of the chirping percussion from 'Truth', but this quickly fades into the dark repeating three-chord synth motif, with some nice bass work and minimal guitar in the distance, sounding like chimes. Hannett has held back on the electronics, with only the occasional thunderclap to provoke the listener out of their hypnotic state.

It's after the third verse, when the song changes tone and gains momentum towards its conclusion, that I begin to disconnect with it. It becomes less melodic, rolling mainly around a single note that Hooky's bass (and his preacher-like vocal) holds manically onto, and though it's great to have her featured in a song, Gillian's spoken bible reading is hard to make out and might've worked better on its own in a more prominent mix. Overall, the 'Doubts Even Here' vocals sound like an unhinged couple careening downhill in an out-of-control vehicle. At night.

The song (originally titled 'Tiny Tim') disappeared from the band's live set after only a handful of outings in 1981, and it wasn't recorded for any radio performances. Overall, this is one of the less-remarkable tracks on *Movement*, and perhaps should've found its home as a curious B-side.

'Denial' (Sumner, Hook, Morris, Gilbert)

Admittedly not one of my favourite songs on the album, I find 'Denial' to be the most of-its-time of all the pieces on *Movement*. Bernard sings 'The answer's not there/It comes and it goes/It frightens me', which to these ears sounds like a final backwards glance to Joy Division, with the track's punk-sounding guitar, baroque-like organ sounds, fearful lyric and speedy bass and drums spine. 'Denial' wouldn't sound out of place on *Closer* or *Unknown Pleasures*.

That the song (originally titled 'Little Dead') closes *Movement*, is perhaps what jars most, because after an album of surprising experimentation and light, it seems to undo the efforts made in tracks like 'Chosen Time' (and other non-album songs of the period like 'Procession' and 'Mesh') – to progress away from the band's past.

I've been thoughtful elsewhere about Factory/New Order's approach to albums vs singles during this period. On the one hand, offering uniqueness across all releases (including B-sides that were great) was a considered gesture. But on the other hand, an album of stronger material would've led to greater acclaim and commercial strength, and perhaps *Movement* wouldn't be so relegated in peoples' estimation. With all tracks being contemporary to *Movement*, perhaps a stronger track list for the album could've been the following: 'Dreams Never End', 'Procession', 'Chosen Time', 'Mesh', 'ICB', 'Truth', 'Cries And Whispers', 'Senses', 'Everything's Gone Green'. But I digress. *Movement* as it stands is part of an endearing timeline marked by adversity and incredible creativity.

Everything's Gone Green (Single, 1981)
Personnel: Bernard Sumner, Peter Hook, Stephen Morris, Gillian Gilbert
Record label: Factory Benelux
Original Benelux release date: December 1981
Refer to 'Everything's Gone Green' details in 'Procession' single above.

'Cries And Whispers' (Sumner, Hook, Morris, Gilbert)
Recorded April/May 1981 at Strawberry Studios, Stockport, UK
Producer: Martin Hannett
One of my favourite B-sides, this is a wonderfully atmospheric piece, and crackles with electricity. At its heart lies a sci-fi synth motif curving randomly around Hooky's low-octave bass, lined with a simple but pulsing electronic 'boom-tish' beat variously effected by digital delay, and pierced-through on the instrumental breaks with snare riffs and shards of noise. Excellently produced, there's a depth and width to this track that's missing from some of the band's other 1981 output, and overall, 'Cries And Whispers' feels closer to *Power Corruption And Lies* than *Movement.*

Amidst this abstract modern music, Bernard shares what indeed seem to be cries and whispers from a dream state of flights, ships, assassins, ghosts, truth, light, hope and other worlds. Could this be Bernard reflecting on the events of May 1980?; how it impacted those 'left behind' – frozen and staring, needing light – and his hopes for (Ian?) arriving at a better place? Perhaps. But regardless, 'Cries And Whispers' is a period highlight that was only performed live about a dozen times in the early-1980s.

Subject over the years to a bit of naming confusion with its B-side partner track 'Mesh', 'Cries And Whispers' can be a bit tricky to find. On the original Factory Benelux 12" of 'Everything's Gone Green', 'Cries And Whispers' + 'Mesh' were the first and second tracks to appear (both music and roundel art) on the B-side. However, on the sleeve artwork (probably for aesthetics reasons), the track titles appear as 'Mesh' + 'Cries And Whispers'. The 1990 FBN CD-single reissue ordered the tracks on the CD per the artwork, but got the *actual tracks* mixed up. When the expanded editions of *Substance* were being compiled in 1987, 'Cries And Whispers' was included on the CD but was named 'Mesh', and on the UK cassette edition, both tracks were included, but each with the other's name. Finally, the digital edition originally listed the track as 'Mesh (AKA Cries And Whispers)'! Interestingly, though 'Cries And Whispers' was not included on the (Factory US) *1981-1982 EP*, 'Mesh' *was*, and was correctly named. A design call made back in 1981 created this storm in a teacup, resulting in years of serious debate amongst serious people!

'Mesh' (Sumner, Hook, Morris, Gilbert)
Recorded April/May 1981 at Strawberry Studios, Stockport, UK
Producer: Martin Hannett

'Mesh' is a curious thing. Caught up in the above misnaming saga, it is something of a rarity. Quite short at only three minutes, it still offers many subtleties – its *quiet* intro, mainly bass and snare drum with some high-note guitar picking, and in the background, a two-note synth motif which at the end of the first verse detunes to herald a brash, brassy noise as Bernard sings of making contracts in a field of snow. Perhaps that's how it felt signing to Factory!

Leading on with Morris' military snare patterns overlaid with metallic guitar chords and trebly riffs, and – almost hidden in the background – an electronic white noise not unlike gears and chains turning, the final verse comes into focus alongside extra-prominent synth:

What do they want with me?
I don't know
Nobody knows
Nobody even tries to find out

The track then curves down into the brassy brashness one final time, before dissipating altogether.

Like other B-sides of the time, 'Mesh' is inventive, left-field and a little bit odd, showing the band playing with form, sound and structure – the DNA of which will inform much of their mid-1980s output.

Temptation (Single, 1982)
Personnel: Bernard Sumner, Peter Hook, Stephen Morris, Gillian Gilbert
Recorded January 1982 at Strawberry Studios, Stockport; Advision Studios, London, UK
Producer: New Order
Record label: Factory
Original UK release date: 10 May 1982
Chart position: UK: 29

'Temptation' (Sumner, Hook, Morris, Gilbert)
This is extraordinary, epic dance rock full of soaring emotion that just brings me to my knees. As the most-played live song in the band's canon, 'Temptation' has led its own life, evolving and improving with time like a fine wine. It was first outed back in November 1981 in the *Taras Shevchenko* concert film, prior to being recorded (with Martin Hannett now permanently out of the production seat) as a stand-alone single. The song was re-recorded in 1987 for inclusion on *Substance* (which for me is the song's best studio recording), and then again in 1998 – all the while taking on new shades and colour for its many live performances, culminating in the glorious version currently heading the band's live sets around the world.

But let's take it back to 1982. The band was now going it alone in the studio, having learned all they needed from Martin Hannett in the four years since

1978, when – as Joy Division – they first worked with him recording 'Digital' and 'Glass' in Rochdale's Cargo Studios, for Factory's *A Factory Sample EP*. Not for a moment taking anything away from the extraordinary body of work achieved with Hannett, it's my contention that New Order are at their very best when in complete control of their own production, and 'Everything's Gone Green', 'Truth' and the 'Temptation' sessions are ground zero of this evolution. Having said all that, though the song itself is one of the band's greatest ever, the 1982 recordings suffer slightly in the production department – a situation the band wanted to correct by re-recording and updating 'Temptation' in 1987.

Regardless, this is a remarkable song for so many reasons. On 'Temptation', Bernard finally found his voice and his own unique songwriting style, and in doing so was able to at last step out of Ian's shadow as a frontman. Not overly verbose, Bernard sings about (his) emotions, relationships, hopes and desires, and with greater conviction than any of his performances on *Movement*. We're introduced to Sumner's emerging penchant for 'ooh's and tongue twisters. Peter Hook has pointed out how early New Order songs are special because they have long passages of music without vocals, and in 'Temptation', that music is wonderful. At its heart are the chattering sequencer lines, overlaid with Morris' metronomic patterns, Hooky delivering a muscular bass performance, and Sumner on guitar picking and chords. These layers weave in and out, building and falling gracefully before once again soaring to a closure. In this regard, the 1987 version is particularly majestic.

Remix-wise, 'Temptation' isn't strongly represented other than with the band's own revisions. For me, the best of the remixes is the 'Secret Machines Remix', which appeared as a B-side on the first of the three 'Waiting For The Sirens' Call' 7" releases in 2005. It takes on the original character of the 1982 recordings, to great effect.

'Tonight I think I'll walk alone/I'll find my soul as I go home', sings Bernard, and listening to this song, you *would*, wouldn't you? If I need to play to a newcomer just one song which represents everything magnificent about New Order, it has to be 'Temptation'.

'Hurt' (Sumner, Hook, Morris, Gilbert)

'Hurt' is one of the most unusual tracks in the New Order catalogue. It's a real mixed bag of experimentation, humour and unbridled weirdness. It's one of the early New Order tracks placing synth at the bass end of the spectrum, rather than being used mainly for noise flourishes, strings or high-range sequences: an important development.

After the vocoder-sounding count-in, the industrial-sounding synth-bass sequence is the first thing you hear, before Hooky – previously the caretaker of all things bass – rolls over the top. Then, beautifully delayed and reverbed chiming synth harmonies from Gillian announce the arrival of what can only be described as the most distorted clippety-clop drum pattern ever programmed. Bernard – who by now had thrown the shackles of deadpan – rips forth with his 'Give me, give me, give me' earworm, and shrieks of delight. Even his signature melodica makes a playful appearance.

There are other nice touches throughout – an incessant rubbery sequence line (particularly notable in the instrumental breakdown), Morris' distorted drum rolls, and the extra reverb used sparingly on particular noises to add flavour, including right at the end where the track clatters to its conclusion with an electronic background buzz.

'Temptation'/'Hurt' was yet another extraordinary single from the band, with a life-changing A-side and a fascinating B-side. I recall a comment by Tony Wilson on his tremendous pride at being able to facilitate remarkable works of art, referring specifically to Joy Division's 'Atmosphere' at the time. This single was another in a growing line of phenomenal New Order releases that must've been an all-consuming joy for Factory to represent.

Sound Formed In A Vacuum: Power Corruption And Lies +

In just two short years, New Order had taken significant steps away from their previous incarnation – initially still with Martin Hannett producing, but increasingly anxious to forge their own path. The band was adapting to new roles and a new configuration, and was experimenting with new technologies and new palettes of sound. The period finished with New Order in the studio, in full control of their sound for the very first time. Very soon, they were to find themselves at the leading edge of modern music, with their left-field blend of alternative and dance music, culminating in the release of one of the most important pieces of electronic music of all time. All while simultaneously opening The Haçienda – soon to become one of the most important clubs in the world – and lending their rapidly growing production skills to fellow Factory artists and bands, under the pseudonym BeMusic.

This is the band's first golden period: hugely creative, and certainly one of their most influential. *Power Corruption And Lies is* (in my opinion) New Order's masterpiece; an album, the quality, impact and influence of which fails to diminish, even after 40 years. Look to the beautifully-boxed Definitive Edition to capture it in all its glory.

Recording for the opening of the Haçienda and Feature Mist Compilation (1982)

Personnel: Bernard Sumner, Peter Hook, Stephen Morris, Gillian Gilbert
Recorded February 1982 (probably) at New Order's rehearsal studio, Cheetham Hill, UK
Producer: New Order
Record label: Touch
Original UK release date: 1 December 1982

'Video 5-8-6' (Sumner, Hook, Morris, Gilbert)

Not content with being one of the world's finest drummers, Stephen Morris – being somewhat of a walking sequencer – is obviously a dab hand with the synthesizer as well. He has sat behind the console for many of the band's most unusual excursions, not the least of which was a pure electronic instrumental composed in 1982 (primarily by Morris and Sumner) that was used as a soundtrack for the Haçienda's opening in May that year, and parts of which were also used behind the Haçienda construction footage on Factory's *A Factory Outing* video (FACT 71), and under the closing credits on the label's *A Factory Video* (FACT 56), both released later that year. In its miscellaneous forms and edits, this instrumental has been variously referred to as 'Primitive 5-8-6', 'Prime 5-8-6' and – most commonly – 'Video 5-8-6'. As the latter, the 22-minute track was cut up into 3 parts – the first and third of which featured on a cassette called *Feature Mist* (the first release by the venerable Touch label in 1982), and the second part turning up on the *Touch.Sampler* CD issued in 1996. Touch finally issued the track in its full form on 12" and CD-single in 1997: an eclectic release that actually charted.

'Video 5-8-6' is pretty brutal, and would make a great case study as a precursor to the EBM genre – harsh analogue synth layers covering an oppressive and incessant synthetic beat (courtesy of a Clef Master Rhythm and Powertran sequencer).

Unique Recordings for The Peel Sessions (1982)
Personnel: Bernard Sumner, Peter Hook, Stephen Morris, Gillian Gilbert
Recorded May 1982 at Revolution Studios, Cheadle, UK
Transmitted: 1 June 1982 on the John Peel show, BBC Radio 1
Producer: New Order
Record label: Strange Fruit
Original UK release date: September 1986

New Order's sessions recorded in 1981 and 1982 for John Peel's show on BBC Radio 1 included tracks recorded well ahead of their album recording sessions – highlighting works in progress equal-to and in some cases even better than their eventual album recordings. Furthermore, that the band chose to record some of their more esoteric works (as distinct from their singles) for their various Peel Session performances, is further evidence of their excellent disregard for convention. Of particular interest here are the two unique songs recorded for their 1982 Peel Session.

'Turn The Heater On' (Hudson)
Very occasionally, our Mancunian friends have been known to prise open a small window into their left-field listenings with the recording or performance of a cover version, including 'Sister Ray' and 'The Ostrich' by The Velvet Underground, 'When I'm With You' by Sparks, 'Anarchy In The UK' by the Sex Pistols, 'Vietnam' by Jimmy Cliff, and here with 'Turn The Heater On', which was recorded as a tribute to Ian Curtis for whom this song (originally by Keith Hudson) was a personal favourite. This outing from the band's rather wonderful 1982 Peel Session, is an intriguing, moody, electronic reggae trip. Who'd have thought, right?

The track is underlined by bass guitar tracked simultaneously with synth bass, with heavily echoed reggae guitar chops, some despairing melodica cries and a wonderfully odd percussion performance infused with Hannett-like electronic shrieks and burbles. Nice! With Bernard delivering a pared-back and quite-hypnotic vocal, the whole track is a fascinating insight into the band's readiness to experiment, to play with their influences (whilst adding to them), and above all, do anything but conform.

'Turn The Heater On' was a unique side track along the path of alternative electronic dance rock that New Order was forging in 1982. Ian would no doubt have enjoyed it had he – at the height of his powers – instead retired to a life of poetry and contemplation: perhaps, as some have suggested, in his own (*Black Books*-like?) bookstore, listening with satisfaction to his bandmates as they carried on the mission that he helped start. If only.

Too Late (Sumner, Hook, Morris, Gilbert)

It's a little bizarre that in promoting themselves on one of the UK's most important national music forums – John Peel's radio show – New Order would choose to record a brand new track that they'd never again play live, nor record for their upcoming album. According to Peter Hook, Bernard had a change of heart about 'Too Late'. Nevertheless, it's quite a good song, and would've sat happily on the looming *Power Corruption And Lies*. The track's first two-thirds are understated and ominous – a subtle, quiet heartbeat pierced with sharp white-noise-as-snare, several lines of deep modulated synth, and Hooky maintaining the melody on bass. The lyric is minimal: two verses expressing difficulty, devotion and chance. After verse two cuts back to Morris' reverbed snares, the track rises again to a grand close, with all drums firing, thick guitar chords, the bass guitar pitching up to hold time on a single manic note, and – way in the background – Bernard chanting indistinctly, before everything peters out via low tom drums and synth. This dark tone/rise-and-fall structure is central to so much of New Order's work; empires building and decaying in four minutes.

Merry Xmas From The Haçienda And Factory Records (Flexi disc, 1982)

Personnel: Bernard Sumner, Peter Hook, Stephen Morris, Gillian Gilbert
Recorded November/December 1981 at New Order's rehearsal studio, Cheetham Hill, UK
Transmitted: 23 December 1981 on the Granada Reports show, Granada TV
Producer: B-Music
Record label: Factory
Original UK release date: December 1982

This flexi disc numbered FAC51B in the Factory catalogue (FAC51 was the Haçienda itself) remains one of the rarest of things for collectors of New Order and/or Factory items. It was originally commissioned by Tony Wilson for use in a Christmas episode of *Granada Reports* taking an irreverent look at the Christmas season, which insiders have as being primarily Stephen and Gillian's creation. Subsequently, New Order's gift to Haçienda members for Christmas 1982 – with the club only six months old and the paint still drying – these tunes were never meant to be treated as anything other than farce: as lightweight as the flexi disc they were given away on. That they would ever be considered part of the New Order canon – let alone a single – is questionable, but people do, and so here we are. The tracks are actually attributed to B-Music (aka Be Music), which was the alias the band (and variously Bernard, Peter, Stephen and Gillian) used for publishing, production and remix work, roughly between 1982 and 1986. Refer to LTM's excellent *Be Music* compilations.

'Ode To Joy' (Beethoven)

I suspect 'Ode To Joy' (neither track is actually named on the disc) was programmed and recorded in about ten minutes; straight to tape in one take, with the eggnog flowing freely. The piece sounds like Christmas on Skaro (the Dalek home world, if you didn't know), with Davros (leader of the Daleks, if you didn't know) unwrapping his new Hornby train set, while Kraftwerk are held hostage by Daleks in the background, forced to play Beethoven's 9th on an oscillator. New Order should've licensed this to the BBC for *Doctor Who* – an obvious missed commercial opportunity, particularly as Stephen is clearly a fan.

'Rocking Carol' (Sumner, Hook, Morris, Gilbert)

...and after all the presents have been unwrapped, and Uncle Davros' senses have been dulled with sherry, turkey and pudding, all the little Daleks are shuffled off to bed to the gentle strains of their favourite lullaby 'Rocking Carol': perchance to dream of electric sheep.

Slightly less terrible-but-curious than 'Ode To Joy', 'Rocking Carol' is actually a little bit cute, with its flourishes of electronic hiss, dabs of drum machine, and plinky-plonk main melody, reminiscent of the soundtrack to platform games from early home computers. This would make a great tune for one of those audio greetings cards that play (for about a week before the battery runs out) a tinny little tune when you open the card. That would've suited the track very well – namely, to be able to listen to it (with diminishing quality) over the holiday season, and eventually be unable to play it ever again. This was a seriously under-explored release format by Factory. Shame on them for such lack of imagination and lack of innovation!

Blue Monday (Single, 1983)

Personnel: Bernard Sumner, Peter Hook, Stephen Morris, Gillian Gilbert
Recorded October-November 1982 at Britannia Row Studios, Islington, UK
Producer: New Order
Record label: Factory
Original UK release date: 7 March 1983
Chart position: UK: 9

'Blue Monday' (Sumner, Hook, Morris, Gilbert)

The biggest selling 12" ever? – Sure. The band lost money on each copy because of the cost of the sleeve? – For a short time. The band wrote it to have a machine-played outro that could be used instead of an encore? – Yes. The band are sick of playing it? – Well, you *would be*! All good mythological stuff.

Here's how I see it – 'Blue Monday' is the finest dance track ever recorded, and it single-handedly spawned a new generation of electronic music.

All roads led here – the band's work to that point; all they'd learned about space and depth in production; their tendency to the darker edges of sound; their increasing experimentation with sequencers, synths, and samplers; their flagrant lack of convention, and their soaking up of influences. To this day, 'Blue Monday' sounds like the future: and that's no mean feat.

It was originally released only on 12" vinyl, and was packaged in Saville's exquisitely stylish floppy disc cover, which itself spawned a new generation of modernity in sleeve design, where subtlety, colour, texture and suggestion, engaged the punter's intelligence and curiosity. On 'Blue Monday', Peter Saville designed an abstract coding system using colour to express information, which he used across several other Factory releases, including New Order's *Power Corruption And Lies* album and 'Confusion' single, and Section 25's *From The Hip* album. The decoder is found on the reverse of the *Power Corruption And Lies* sleeve. As with *Unknown Pleasures*, 'Blue Monday' was one of Factory's handful of perfect artistic statements that will exist forever.

With its classic Oberheim DMX bass-drum pattern, Moog Source synthesizer and Hook's bass melodies all driving the track's bottom end, 'Blue Monday' is beautifully minimal in its simple-yet-hypnotic arrangement. Pierced through with squelchy pre-acid sequence lines, rapid-fire snare patterns, synthesized choral lines and electronic strings, the track is an extended exercise in layering for maximum drama. Bridging the verses and breaks, we get the manufactured sound of a jet flying overhead (and crashing?) as Bernard delivers his classic abstract and deadpan vision of ships in the harbour, mistreatment, misfortune and being mistaken. Bernard may sing that he's finding it hard to say what he needs to say, but he manages to speak in volumes anyway. On a beach.

The product of pre-MIDI, pre-computer, and often self-soldered studio alchemy that was susceptible to mood swings, 'Blue Monday' was always going to be hard to replicate live: particularly for a band reluctant to use backing tapes (unlike OMD, for example). As such, live versions of the time (including the band's notorious *Top Of The Pops* performance) never quite sounded right. It wasn't until when the band reconvened in 1998, that the live version was reprogrammed to better match its original sound and form.

Of course, there are many remixes, including B-side 'The Beach' – an instrumental re-edit that I remember DJs using to extend the club experience of 'Blue Monday' into a 15-minute exercise in bliss. Five years later, the band's US label Qwest sought to re-release 'Blue Monday', with John Potoker remixing the track under the watchful eye of American producer Quincy Jones – emerging as 'Blue Monday 1988' in March that year. Though it charted very well, the 1988 version (and its flipside 'Beach Buggy') isn't nearly as good as the original, as it's lacking in depth, and is a bit too fussy with tricks and samples.

In the wilderness years of the mid-1990s – while the band members were focused on their various side hustles, and their new label London Records ransacked the back catalogue for new compilations, remixes and reissues – 'BlueMonday-95' emerged in various formats with many remixes. Most of them were pale imitations of each other, with the significant exception of one – the 'Hardfloor Mix': a superb contemporary interpretation, with an awesome video clip.

Remixed by many, covered by many, and in the musical and cultural DNA of many, 'Blue Monday' is a remarkable achievement of inestimable importance.

Power Corruption And Lies (Album, 1983)
Personnel: Bernard Sumner, Peter Hook, Stephen Morris, Gillian Gilbert
Recorded October-November 1982 at Britannia Row Studios, Islington, UK
Producer: New Order
Record label: Factory
Original UK release date: May 1983
Chart position: UK: 4

'Age Of Consent' (Sumner, Hook, Morris, Gilbert)
Power Corruption And Lies is my favourite New Order album. It's a definitive artistic achievement on so many levels – from the appropriated Fantin-Latour sleeve, which verges on the anonymous, to Saville's colour language and decoder, to the gorgeous soundscapes that lie within. It's beautifully produced by the band, and is a landmark album in their development. Absolute class, and its opener, 'Age Of Consent' is monumental. Like other songs on the album, it distinguishes itself with richness and depth; eschewing (for the time being) sequencers, drum machines and electronic noise for what is essentially a rock track with stunning interplay between bass and lead guitar, where the band rediscovers the drama and beauty of synth strings that have lain largely dormant since *Closer* and 'Atmosphere'.

The music – not unlike 'Ceremony' – rises and falls in waves, propelled powerfully by Hooky's driving bass line, Morris on frenetic-but-precise drums, and a broad wash of low octave synth; the beauty lying in the gorgeous strings and Bernard's vocal. Sumner's anguished lyric of relationship loss – delivered at full stretch – in combination with the track's *tour de force* of left-field rock, layers of strings, atmospheres and beautiful melodies, mark this as an awe-inspiring song. New Order combine beauty and power like no one else.

The song quietens as Bernard's despairing cries of 'I've lost you, I've lost you' fade into his fragile 'ooh's like a lullaby at the end of the line. Then just as the song reaches its most peaceful point, its crescendo rises like a juggernaut, with strings in full force and Bernard thrashing out percussive guitar chops. Hurt begets anger and regret amidst great beauty, which Joy Division understood very well. But New Order – and this is a big call – does even better. 'Age Of Consent' set the tone for this truly wonderful album, and – remarkably – the best was yet to come.

For completeness, I should remind you that 'Age Of Consent' was pointlessly remixed by Howie B in 1995 for London's *Rest Of* remix compilation, with all of the song's heart and soul ignored.

'We All Stand' (Sumner, Hook, Morris, Gilbert)

Neither mainstream nor conventional, 'We All Stand' is a fascinating and arresting piece, true to the whole album's remarkable inventiveness, and further evidence of this band's diversity and talent. The highlight here must be Stephen Morris' wonderful percussion, with its scattered rimshots and tom-tom flourishes. It provides the *trudge* on this march to the end of the road, over which Peter Hook slides his fretless bass guitar, and Gillian and Bernard weave melodies and motifs with keyboard and flanged guitars.

Lyrically, Sumner is compelled on a nightmarish rendezvous with a waiting soldier, with all futures ending down a bloody *cul-de-sac* (and there's always three miles to go). Not sure I'd want to reach the end of this road of torment either. It is interesting that Sumner will once again revisit the idea of a less-than-glorious soldier's destiny in 'Love Vigilantes', because – prior to the *urban regeneration* of historic Manchester neighbourhoods, which had such a profound effect on the young Bernard Sumner – wartime evidence remained long after 1945, and would've weighed heavily in the dark dreams of a thoughtful and artful young Salford lad. I'm still trying to decode the 'we' in the song title, and why it is that they are all standing. Perhaps in Bernard's dream, there are lines of bystanders silently observing his processional march down that hellish road. (shiver)

'The Village' (Sumner, Hook, Morris, Gilbert)

So, you're in your teens or early twenties, head over heels for someone, and finding it difficult to express those feelings without coming across as a complete tool. You're not in the A group, so you can't rely on your abs, tattoos, money or celebrity anecdotes to lay on the charm offensive. Your clear choice is the mixtape – the carefully considered sequence of music laid out on a shiny new TDK, that, on your behalf, speaks volumes on all those complex feelings, moods and admiration of beauty swirling around in your head and heart; even better if that music is completely atypical and unlikely to be anything that the focus of your affections will have heard before. Hand up if you ever poured your emotion onto tape and then passed it on with hope and trepidation.

My mixtape-as-bouquet of choice always featured New Order, and 'The Village' is one of those tracks – a soaring left-field love song sung imperfectly to a driving electronic beat, with gorgeous guitar riffs. Mind you, I just wish Bernard – having sung 90% of the track about the wonders of 'our love' (which is like the earth/sun/rain/sea/trees/flowers/hours etc.) – didn't close out the song with 'their love' dying years ago! Typical. A bit of a downer, which he does again in 'Thieves Like Us' – love, love, love, love, love, even more love… for everyone but us! I'm pretty sure I would always segue such tracks on my mixtapes before letting Bernard wilfully spoil the vibe.

A could've-been single, and long overdue for remixing or return to the live set, 'The Village' is five minutes of glorious upbeat alternative dance, from the synth bass lines flying the flag of the track's cousins 'Blue Monday' and '5-8-6', to Hooky's classic rolling bass work, to Morris' wonderful drum performance, to Gilbert and Sumner's chiming reverbed guitar riffs. The track peaks about three minutes in, when the sequencers go into overdrive and Bernard sings about being stuck in the same place and time for too long.

I hope that Gen-Z and beyond can find a modern equivalent to the mixtape-as-message as they discover the good things in life. I fear that a Spotify playlist (or its equivalent) will never quite be the same.

'5-8-6' (Sumner, Hook, Morris, Gilbert)

The essence of the 'Video 5-8-6' experiment – certain sounds, patterns and sequences – were rearranged in the writing of '5-8-6' as we know it (the naming of which apparently refers to the 'Ecstasy' bar structure), and first aired on the band's wonderful 1982 Peel Session. The Peel version has a grainy rawness which marks it as distinctly different to the album version but just as essential.

The album version of '5-8-6' – much like its ancestors – is quite experimental, utilising updated gear including the Oberheim DMX drum machine and Emulator sampler, and is significantly restructured: now taking the listener through several phases. The opening – spilled onto by the abrupt finish of preceding track 'The Village' – is a minimal exercise in very slow beats and snares, with a low-end synth riff pitched and modulated to sound tentative, metallic and sinister. Then, taking its queues firmly from 'Blue Monday', a choral sound (courtesy of the Emulator) heralds the arrival of the sequencers, firing rhythmic bass lines and drum patterns, with Bernard warning us of the dangers that he's sent, making us turn and run away. Emotionally it feels like a sequel to 'Blue Monday' – our day at the beach turning to darkness, with lots of running, calling and hiding. If ever there was a poster child for the dark wave genre, '5-8-6' is it.

There is much greatness in this track's darkness – the chattering sequence structure, the breakdown into snare flourishes and the sound of electronic crickets, Hooky's sliding bass, Bernard's emotional delivery, the synth pads and keyboard motifs of the closing third, and the tempo changes. With so much interest and variation crammed into seven minutes, '5-8-6' is really something to behold. Of all the *older* tracks that were candidates for revision in more recent times, this song was always at the top of my wish list, and so its rework and reintroduction into the band's live set in 2012 was a wonderfully-realised masterstroke.

'Your Silent Face' (Sumner, Hook, Morris, Gilbert)

I vividly remember when I first bought this album, being initially astonished by the sleeve with its classic-meets-ultramodern beauty – anonymous for those yet to break its code. Then the music hit me – one magnificent song after another, with depth and grace and atmosphere and gravitas. On this remarkable album, 'Your Silent Face' soars highest, and surely must be one of the most beautiful songs ever committed to vinyl in the modern era, on par with – if not even more special than – Joy Division's 'Atmosphere'. I've listened to it so often, and yet, every time, I still feel enveloped by its exquisite melancholy.

This is one of Sumner's finest lyrical efforts – abstract yet emotional; poetic without being pretentious; sad but soulful. Instrumentally, the atmosphere is layered in richness and beauty, its groundsheet laid out with a simple-but-beautiful arpeggiating sequence and electronic bass/snare heartbeat, across which the deep and powerful strings cast long autumnal shadows. The stars come out in these heavens, as Hook's signature bass and Sumner's melodica deliver note-perfect motifs and melodies. Chiming guitar chords add a curtain of northern lights, and you're left awestruck by the song's grace: 'No hearing or breathing/No movement or lyrics/Just nothing'.

'Your Silent Face' (working title 'The Kraftwerk One' ('KW1') apparently because the band was inspired by Kraftwerk's 'Europe Endless') is also one of the songs the band always nails when playing live, usually performed under an icy blue backlight with a single line of white light across Bernard's focussed face as he cuts through on his melodica.

If 'Your Silent Face' was the band being caught 'at a bad time' (that cold 1982 November at Britannia Row), then well may we 'piss off', leaving them to exorcise their misery through beautiful and majestic music like this. One of New Order's finest moments.

'Ultraviolence' (Sumner, Hook, Morris, Gilbert)

The clattering and hypnotic 'Ultraviolence' is yet another pearl in the eight masterworks collected on *Power Corruption And Lies*. Cut from the same cloth as 'Blue Monday', '5-8-6' and 'The Village' in its synth-bass-driven sequencer lines and electronic percussion (courtesy of the Syncussion SY-1), 'Ultraviolence' is almost industrial in its form and function, which makes sense, given the stated influence of *A Clockwork Orange, and* the song title.

At a time when MIDI and computer sequencing was still in its infancy, New Order delivered a new groove like few others. Recording live what would so often now be relegated to sampled loops, the band worked their rhythms via multiple layers of phasing and funk guitar arcing across the stereo spectrum (which we know is favoured territory for Bernard'), underscored by mechanical sequencer chatter and the mixing in-and-out of synthetic percussion, sounding like factory steam engines at full-tilt. Did I say this sounded industrial? 'Ultraviolence': dark disco for a deserted northern mill, perhaps.

BeMusic's head of hypnosis, Bernard Sumner draws you further into the swirling rhythms with his sensory lyric of dark eyes, cold hands and burning skin, delivered variously with outcry and gentle dreamlike tones. 'Everybody makes mistakes' – even Bernard apparently – but not on 'Ultraviolence'. It's terrific, and a further triumph has been its rework and readmission into the band's live set since the 2017 Manchester International Festival, as captured on the band's best live album ∑*(No,12k,Lg,17Mif) New Order + Liam Gillick: So It Goes*.

'Ecstasy' (Sumner, Hook, Morris, Gilbert)

'Ecstasy' is probably the album's most electronic-sounding track – notable for the Powertran ETI-driven vocoder vocal that blends seamlessly into several layers of pitch-bent synthesizer riffs (particularly around the halfway mark and in the run-out), with synth bass front and centre, Hooky providing the bridging and rolling background bass patterns, and of course, Stephen Morris drumming with exquisite precision on his disco-meets-slipbeat grooves.

There's a cleanness to the layers of 'Ecstasy' (originally titled 'Only The Lonely') that makes it sound very modern, even today. You can really sense the New York influence here and my ears are connecting the dots from 'Ecstasy' all the way forward to tracks like 'People On The High Line' and 'Tutti Frutti'.

I remember thinking to myself how remarkable it was, the dichotomy of sleeving music like 'Ecstasy' and 'The Village' within the romanticism of the album artwork – futurism meets fine art: a perfect visual metaphor for the music contained within. I think Peter Saville's a bit of a genius, and though the myth suggests that the band had a 'whatever' attitude to sleeve design, personally, I believe that little needed to be said, because all concerned were on the same wavelength – a synchronicity that would last throughout the Factory years. It has everything to do with the philosophy, creative ethic and sheer bloody-mindedness that were the foundation of independent labels like Factory and Mute.

'Leave Me Alone' (Sumner, Hook, Morris, Gilbert)

Apparently one of Stephen Morris' personal favourites, this is a dark song seemingly about an apocalyptic ending – a thousand islands in the sea where sailors once 'trod', people living underground, walking and falling in rows, visions from words in 'the book', and wanting to be taken away and left alone in these 'last few days'. Brrr…

Musically, 'Leave Me Alone' (working title 'Dark Nights') is one of New Order's finest guitar-driven pieces. Just listen as Bernard's repeated cries of 'Leave me alone' fade into glorious avalanches of reverbed guitar from Bernard and Gillian playing sublime harmonies, followed by guitars and bass intertwining through descending riffs that just sound so sad. The production – as per the whole album – is rich and deep, and at the end, you're left feeling emotionally drained, praying that this vision of the future is a path we never follow.

This song also makes me reflect again on Bernard as a lyricist, and how – even more so than Ian at times – he focusses on the impact on the self of the subject of his thoughts. Whether it's his observations on life, love, dreams, friends, the future or the past, he will often reference his (or his target's) senses, and here he is also at his tongue-twisting best with his head/toes/teeth/ nose lyric. The emotional and sensory context that he gives to his songs – often delivered sparingly – is one reason why we connect so strongly to so much of New Order's work. Elementary messages delivered powerfully.

Confusion (Single, 1983)
Personnel: Bernard Sumner, Peter Hook, Stephen Morris, Gillian Gilbert
Recorded February 1983 at Unique Studios, New York, USA
Producers: Arthur Baker, New Order
Record label: Factory
Original UK release date: 22 August 1983
Chart position: UK: 9

'Confusion' (Sumner, Hook, Morris, Gilbert, Baker)
The great 1983 New York experiment – co-writing and co-producing with Arthur Baker, hanging in New York clubs like the Paradise Garage, and osmosing the beats of the electro/ hip hop/breakdancing scenes when these genres were new. All three luminaries of the scene – Baker, 'Jellybean' Benitez and John Robie – had a hand in the production and recording of 'Confusion'. Apparently, the sessions at Unique Studios were strung out, with the song only taking shape at the eleventh hour, and the results (as we know from the video clip) tested almost immediately by Baker on the dance floor at the Fun House, using a reel-to-reel studio dub.

All good, and the resulting 12" is a fine thing – multiple mixes, dubs and bonus beats (with lots of handclap): everything that a 1980s DJ needed, except that there was always a niggling feeling that the recording could – given time and greater production attention from the band – have been much stronger. The original recordings suffer from a lack of dynamic range, hovering around the midrange beatbox drum patterns, midrange rolling sequencer line, and brightly reverbed synth riffs, over which Bernard lays down a midrange vocal. It's only when Hooky's bass kicks in near the end that we get some real bottom-end. The track opens up a little on the breaks and the 'Tell me you need me' verse, which isolates the bell-synth riff nicely.

I think the 'Rough Mix' and 'Instrumental' versions are the strongest on the original 12" – the former for having a raw edge to the bass and sequencer lines, and the latter for its interesting restructure. I can also understand – in compiling *Substance* – that the band wanted to re-record 'Temptation' and 'Confusion', because, in my opinion, the original singles suffer from weaker production. In the case of 'Confusion', the *Substance* re-recording is *harder*, and has a far better dynamic range, structure and vocal performance, whilst keeping the essence of the original in terms of melody and sequencing. The band also remixed a dub version, which is a terrific re-edit with lots of unique touches, perversely only found as a bonus track on the 'Touched By The Hand Of God' CD-single. Factory should've released a 'Confusion-1987' 12" as a second single (FAC 93R?), with the dub as B-side. It would've made a great second single off *Substance* after 'True Faith'.

But back to Arthur Baker. The guy has co-writing credits on 'Confusion', and he has taken every opportunity to revisit his first New Order love. His Streetwise label handled the US release of 'Confusion' in 1983, and then in 1990, he issued a slew of new remixes on his Minimal Records label. Some excellent mixes here, with the 'Con-om-fus-ars-ion' and 'Alternative' mixes being particularly good – and best of all, having way better range and depth than the 1983 original. Fast forward another 12 years, and Baker finally nails it when he again re-releases 'Confusion', this time on his Whacked label. Billed as Arthur Baker Vs New Order, and sleeved in a grainy 1983 in-studio picture of him with the band (so there's no doubt), the *Confusion Remixes '02* release includes one of the finest New Order remixes in their entire catalogue: the 'Koma And Bones' version. Absolutely superb. Dark, deep, faithful to the original, sublime beats and bass, and even a nod to 'Blue Monday''s choral sound just prior to kicking into an incredibly funky guitar-driven sequence.

Elsewhere, the 'Pump Panel Reconstruction Mix' from the *Rest Of* compilation bears no resemblance to the original, but was made popular by its inclusion in the *Blade* movie.

Thieves Like Us (Single, 1984)
Personnel: Bernard Sumner, Peter Hook, Stephen Morris, Gillian Gilbert
Recorded December 1983 at Britannia Row Studios, Islington, UK
Producer: New Order
Record label: Factory
Original UK release date: April 1984
Chart position: UK: 18

'Thieves Like Us' (Sumner, Hook, Morris, Gilbert, Baker)
The greatest quality of New Order's music is melody. Whether it's expressed in beautiful string-laden synths, Hooky's bass, guitar, the vocals or even melodica, New Order's music affects deeply because of melody, and 'Thieves Like Us' drips like honey with many gorgeous melodies. It's a beautiful song, and is one of New Order's great love songs, but it exists in Bernard's world where love is both light and dark. Accordingly, love belongs to us, everyone but us, every one of us; dies so quickly, and when it dies, it dies for good; grows so slowly; is the only thing worth living for; is found in the East and the West; when it's at home it's the best; is the cure for every evil; is the air that supports the eagle; is so uncool; has become unmentionable, and cuts your life like a broken knife.

Thanks, Bernard. This didn't help teenagers in 1984 deal with matters of the heart, which no doubt made 'Thieves Like Us' a perfect choice for inclusion in one of the great teen-angst movies of all time: *Pretty in Pink*. Though co-written/demoed with Arthur Baker during the 'Confusion' sessions, the song was recorded later at Britannia Row, and produced by the band. Distinctively post-*PC&L*, 'Thieves' has a warmer bass sound, and is one of New Order's most synth-laden tracks – full of pads, motifs and those melodic riffs. Look to the 'Instrumental' version to enjoy the music in all its glory.

In 2016 at the Sydney Opera House, I had the great pleasure of experiencing 'Thieves Like Us' performed live for the first time since 1988, with the band performing in conjunction with the Australian Chamber Orchestra. The performance was potent, and the song was still beautiful and still felt the love.

'Lonesome Tonight' (Sumner, Hook, Morris, Gilbert)

How can it be that this – one of the band's finest songs from their first five years – was relegated to B-side status? Could it be that New Order was riding such a wave of unbelievable creativity that 'Lonesome Tonight' was spare? Surely not – New Order don't do surplus.

'Lonesome Tonight' is one of those majestic and anthemic New Order songs that sends a shiver down your spine, through its combination of sad-yet-soaring soundscapes, beautifully intertwined guitars and very personal lyrics sung with honesty and emotion. The song is masterfully produced by the band. The various phases of guitar throughout are exquisite, with Hook's bass holding a slow and deep core alongside Morris' very fine drumming (note the emphatic snare). The lead-in reverbed guitar melodies turn to percussive picking before sliding gorgeously into the verse chord progression. The instrumental break sends the guitars and synth into cavernous melody before Bernard wills the song back into focus with one of his signature 'ooh's. His dark visions of empty thrones, empty beds, empty souls and eyes made of stone, lead us (questioning whether we believe in truth) into the second half – three minutes of sublime melancholy and atmosphere: the soundtrack to a soul-searching walk across a windswept field under a greying sky. Three minutes of pure gothic beauty.

I've mentioned this before, but during this early period it seems that releasing anything less than extraordinary was anathema to both New Order and Factory. Like 'Ceremony'/'In A Lonely Place', 'Procession'/'Everything's Gone Green' and 'Temptation'/'Hurt', 'Thieves Like Us'/'Lonesome Tonight' is a phenomenal single.

Murder (Single, 1984)

Personnel: Bernard Sumner, Peter Hook, Stephen Morris, Gillian Gilbert
Recorded October-November 1982 at Britannia Row Studios, Islington, UK
Producer: New Order
Record label: Factory Benelux
Original Benelux release date: May 1984

'Murder' (Sumner, Hook, Morris, Gilbert)

Can there be a more perverse offering on 12" single than New Order's 'Murder'? This instrumental experiment from the *Power Corruption And Lies* sessions – featuring disturbing samples from *Caligula* and *2001: A Space*

51

Odyssey – is a crawling, mind-bludgeoning soundtrack to a wrong turn down a very dark alley; full of sinister shapes, heightened anxiety and a primeval need to escape.

That Factory – notwithstanding via Factory Benelux (the label's low-countries outpost for the uniquely aesthetic and challenging) – had the notion that 'Murder' should be released as a single, is stupendously out-there. It illustrates in a nutshell Factory's *modus operandi*, particularly during this period – namely: this-probably-won't-sell-many-but-it's-important-and-artful-and-we're-going-to-package-it-beautifully-and-release-it-somewhere-unusual-for-those-who-care. This is why Factory was (and still is) of such peerless cultural importance.

New Order's 'Murder' is a challenging four minutes of music; the complete antithesis of its contemporary 'Thieves Like Us' (the aforementioned 'Instrumental' version of which was included here as the B-side) – a notion represented here not only via the music (its murderous tone the opposite of 'Thieves' love-in), but via the sleeve, described by some as the dark/negative to 'Thieves'' light/positive: both sleeves being based on abstract paintings by Giorgio de Chirico. Together, New Order's two 1984 singles are a triumph of the art form – from Morris' military beats, to the incessant guitar riff (which rings in your head long after burrowing its way in there), to the *Caligula* samples blended into *2001*'s Ligeti 'Requiem'. And then – to top it all off – HAL reminds us that his mind is going. He can feel it. I can feel it. What were they thinking?

We Believe In A Land Of Love: Low-life +

By the mid-1980s, New Order had already tasted significant success, with a top-5 UK album in *Power Corruption And Lies* and a top-10 single in 'Blue Monday' (unheard of for a 12"-only release), and both reaching number 1 on the UK independent charts. Though they had toured the USA several times already, and aligned with important producers, movers and shakers, broader commercial success in that territory remained elusive, so their signing to Quincy Jones' Qwest Records in the US was a game changer. From here, New Order's releases would receive greater overseas attention and support, also leading to their involvement in productions like *Pretty In Pink* – further growing their fan base, and firmly placing New Order at the global forefront of cool alternative bands for the subcultured youth to follow.

And so, the band dialled things up – still entirely left-field in their sound, intent and vision, but presenting their efforts with even greater style. *Low-life* – in its original tracing-paper LP sleeve designed to demystify the band – is New Order's most exquisitely packaged record and Peter Saville's finest hour. Saville himself refers to it as his 'zero hour' and a shift to an essentialist approach, as distinct from retrospective. An absolute masterpiece of monochrome, photography, typography and design. Iconic.

The music, too, was shifting and changing, with the band adapting to the rapidly-developing technology and techniques. Juggernaut electronic tracks like 'The Perfect Kiss' and 'Shell-Shock' signposted the times, and were entirely unique to New Order.

The Perfect Kiss (Single, 1985)
Personnel: Bernard Sumner, Peter Hook, Stephen Morris, Gillian Gilbert
Record label: Factory
Original UK release date: 13 May 1985
Chart position: UK: 46
Refer to other details per *Low-life* album and 'The Perfect Kiss' song entry below.

Low-life (Album, 1985)
Personnel: Bernard Sumner, Peter Hook, Stephen Morris, Gillian Gilbert
Recorded October-December 1984 at Jam Studios, London; Britannia Row Studios, Islington, UK
Producer: New Order
Record label: Factory
Original UK release date: 13 May 1985
Chart position: UK: 7

'Love Vigilantes' (Sumner, Hook, Morris, Gilbert)
'Love Vigilantes' is one of only a small handful of Bernard Sumner songs written as a story arc instead of an abstract insight into emotions and

observations. This anti-war tale of a soldier's spirit (or possibly alive but on leave) returning home from Vietnam to find his wife holding a killed-in-action telegram, is a pointed opener to New Order's third album.

Sonically the song is quite a detour from New Order's evolution to date through punk > indie rock > left-field dance > proto-techno, offering up a brand-new facet to their work: namely – of all things – country and western! Which is why 'Love Vigilantes' is one of the *Low-life* tracks that I often skip over, preferring instead songs like 'This Time Of Night' and 'The Perfect Kiss'. It was a vein to be mined again (perhaps more effectively) on *Brotherhood*, and later *Get Ready*, but woe betide them if they ever pick up a harmonica!

'Love Vigilantes' just feels a little overcooked in places; perhaps a verse/chorus too long; the percussion a little straightforward, etc. Conversely, the chunky guitar breakdown that closes the track is great, there are some fine melodies, and Bernard delivers his vocal with conviction and feeling – e.g., the 'I want to see my family, my wife and child waiting for me' chorus is beautifully pitched. I like the song, I just don't love it.

'The Perfect Kiss' (Sumner, Hook, Morris, Gilbert)

Oh, how I adore the video (FAC 321, produced by Jonathan Demme). Too young to have snuck into New Order's early tours to the colonies, and with live footage of the band thin on the ground in 1985, this video was the first time I really saw the band perform. I loved their reticence to look into the camera lens, with an apprehension and disdain that was the opposite to most other bands fighting over themselves for mid-1980s screen attention – a delicious attitude that reached its peak near the clip's end, with the can-we-go-now look across all their faces. I loved Bernard's singing – often flying too close to the sun of vocal discord, and all the better for it. I loved the cowbell, and I can picture the four of them at their Cheetham Hill rehearsal studios during the marathon session: 'We need something else… more cowbell!'. Can you picture Joy Division ever using a cowbell? I loved Gillian's demure coolness and grace, watching her turn dials on the sequencer like some sort of glamorous NASA mission controller, to herald those distinctive synth lines. I loved Hooky – all hair and leather jacket, with spare guitar pick in mouth – switching between his rollicking bass performance and bashing away at his bruised electronic pads (which he auctioned off a year or two ago *as is*: i.e., knackered). I loved Stephen's technical concentration and hint of amusement. I loved the frog and car crash samples. I loved the synths being performed live and with feeling, rather than as an overproduced and over-quantised backing tape. New Order always seem to give a human touch to the art of electronic music.

Apparently not about AIDS, but instead centred on a gun-toting American that the band met one night before going out, 'The Perfect Kiss' – in its epic nine-minute 12" version – is a *tour de force* of synths, metallic sequences, electronic percussion, samples, rolling bass, huge walls of sound breaking down into periods of forest-like ambience, and sheer energy. The song exists in various original forms, but, interestingly, has never been picked up for remix attention (excluding the Hot Tracks and Razormaid DJ mashups of the period) – surely an oversight to be addressed by an enthusiastic modern practitioner.

'This Time of Night' (Sumner, Hook, Morris, Gilbert)

My favourite track on *Low-life*, a highlight of their mid-1980s output, and in my top-10 New Order tracks of all time. 'This Time of Night' (originally titled 'Pumped Full Of Drugs') sparks and growls with its low-register sequencer bass lines, industrial flourishes, vocal edginess, guitar strikes, drum rolls and double snares, and that sinister-sounding four-note rotating synth/string riff sometimes forefront and sometimes just sitting back in the mix, adding drama. Hooky's bass – weaving in and out of the sequencer lines – is also a highlight, as are his intense backing vocals. The overall production is absolutely first-class.

In my opinion, this song contains some of Bernard's finest songwriting – particularly the incredibly honest, visceral and passionately-delivered 'Without you' callouts, the 'wooden heart'/'empty brain' lines, the sterling 'What good's a lie when you've nothing to hide?' and the 'Join our world and play our game' directive.

'This Time Of Night' – and it really does feel like the dark hours long after midnight – is one of a handful of New Order songs ('All Day Long' being another) that have as strong an emotional impact for me as anything Joy Division produced, and yet these songs continue to fly well under the radar, rarely finding room in the limited space of the band's modern-day live sets. Tracks like these must be eye-opening gems for newcomers to New Order, as they discover the classics and then delve deeper into the archive. Ageing Viking (certified hardcore New Order fan – FAC 383) to newbie: 'Of course, youngling, 'Blue Monday' is brilliant, but just listen to *this!*'.

'Sunrise' (Sumner, Hook, Morris, Gilbert)

Intense. Personal. One-way conversations with God gone unanswered, with a backing track that must be one of New Order's most furious (and is apparently Gillian's all-time favourite New Order song). Pop music, this isn't.

My main gripe with 'Sunrise' is that the opening synth chords – heavy with foreboding and malevolence – tease a depth of sound and atmosphere that disappears after Hooky's bass intro, lost to the crossfire of guitars that compel Bernard's baleful spleen-venting and fist-waving. The apocalyptic barrage of treble that marks most of 'Sunrise', keeps this song seldom played in my lists, but I respect its intent. It's not the first nor last track on *Low-Life* where Bernard is right on the edge with his vocals, and in fact, it's a key aspect of the album's overall sound. Had he delivered a pitch-perfect performance, it wouldn't have had nearly the same impact. Vocal auto-tuning is one of the great homogenising evils of 21st-century music, but I digress.

It's interesting to note how 'Sunrise' closes the album's A-side with such anger and fury, and how the B-side opens with such great beauty with 'Elegia'.

It's a perfect reminder of how we lost something with CDs (and to a much greater extent with music files) in terms of the considered and meaningful placement of tracks within the limitations of vinyl records. Physically turning a record over is like turning a new page in a book: you get a real sense of chapters changing.

'Elegia' (Sumner, Hook, Morris, Gilbert)

Fragile and beautiful, for me, 'Elegia' feels like the time-lapsed dawn of a new day; a warm sun breaking through the remnant clouds of last night's storm. More of a sunrise than 'Sunrise' in fact! Delicate arpeggiating synths from Gilbert and Sumner glisten, with Hooky's exquisitely-melodic bass the very rising sun itself. The light dips for moment behind a distant thunderhead (to the sound of ambient percussion from Morris, over a low electronic drone), and then breaks through in all its glory with a blast of harsh guitar. The track is also used to resonate one of the poignant emotional threads in John Hughes' iconic movie *Pretty In Pink*, with a desolate Molly Ringwald confronting the callow young men in her orbit. I've also heard 'Elegia' described as a lament – the band's elegy to Ian Curtis – and I get that. Perhaps 'Elegia' paints a completely different picture for you.

First written as a soundtrack piece to a planned (but unrealised) art film produced by *ID* magazine, the album version of 'Elegia' is tastefully edited-down from the best sections of its much longer parent recording; the full version of which was finally issued in 2002 on the *Retro* compilation (albeit on the limited-edition bonus CD). The full version is coarser, harsher, more impromptu; less of a sunrise, and more calm-before-the-storm, but still remarkable. Regardless of the version, New Order's elegiac instrumental is superb.

'Sooner Than You Think' (Sumner, Hook, Morris, Gilbert)

This process of listening intently to each track in sequence has been a revelation for many reasons, not least of which is that I'm reminded of so much beauty in New Order's music. They have a body of work that is remarkable. So much of it is extraordinary and a tribute to their collective creativity, but I'm also reminded that not all of it is perfect.

For me, other than its perfect sleeve, *Low-life* is quite a bipolar album – stratospheric highs in 'This Time Of Night', 'The Perfect Kiss' and 'Elegia', brought down to earth with less successful numbers. 'Sooner Than You Think' feels pedestrian, and probably includes the most mawkish lines in the entire New Order canon: 'To buy a drink that is so much more reasonable/I think I'll go there when it gets seasonable'.

Apart from the instrumental first minute (with its glassy synth riff) and the instrumental last minute (with the signature choppy guitars), I can pretty much leave 'Sooner Than You Think' well alone. It feels like a song that a band would be 50/50 about including on an album, and it seems – generally from the lack of B-sides (other than alternate mixes) on the *Low-life* singles – that the band were perhaps light-on for additional material circa 1985. Compare this with the bountiful and excellent non-album songwriting before, during and immediately after *Power Corruption And Lies*. You have to forgive New Order their occasional duff track – you know what I mean, yes you do!

'Sub-Culture' (Sumner, Hook, Morris, Gilbert)

I'm torn between my tendency to want to love everything that New Order produces – particularly most of their remarkable singles – and worrying that this may be hiding a truth that some of their tracks are just not that great. 'Sub-Culture' is like that for me. I don't have immediate love for it. Sometimes it hits the mark, and other times I reach quickly for the skip button. On the plus side, the album version is solid, with its intro synth sequence and mid-song bass line, Hooky's performance, and the strong finish. Gillian has been quoted (in the *Wayward Distractions* book) as saying she thought 'Sub-Culture' was 'trite', which is a fair call, because the pervy lyrics are a bit obvious: late nights, chains, shafting, 'a little bit' of hurting, submission, etc. Depeche Mode do 'strange love' better, and at least dress accordingly.

On the negative: John Robie's single remixes. Unlike his co-production on (the superb) 'Shell-Shock', he unfortunately overindulged here – the added backing vocals (and in particular the 'right' and 'shock' shrieks, and overuse of the 'One of these days' line), the noisy and overly-reverbed sequencer additions, the dodgy harmonising of Bernard's vocals, and the erratic cuts. Robie's 'Dub-Vulture' version loses the plot completely, with its ending sounding like he's tossed the tape deck into a washing machine. Legend has it that Peter Saville chose not to sleeve the 'Sub-Culture' single with his usual flair, because he hated the song, although the truth is he apparently wasn't commissioned for a full sleeve. Mind you, it still looks a little bit cool, though: almost like a white label. The only other mix that comes to mind is the obscure 'Record Mirror Exclusive Mix', which simply mashes up the album version. So it's curious that 'Sub-Culture' hasn't been approached by other DJs and remixers.

This was a song that promised great things as a remixed extended single but ended up being a textbook example of diminishment of the original rather than celebration. In this case, John Robie got it wrong, but thankfully he would bring the magic on other New Order tracks.

'Face Up' (Sumner, Hook, Morris, Gilbert)

One thing I love about Bernard's songwriting is that he doesn't mince his words. Most of the time, when he wants to express himself, he'll cut straight to the chase. To wit, in 'Face Up' – 'Oh how I cannot bear the thought of you': holding nothing back in his singing, right on the edge. Only Bernard can express his disdain with such unbridled joy, and 'Face Up' has some champion lyrics 'At the start, you had a heart, but in the end, you lost your friend'; 'As we get old we lose our place, reflecting back the world's disgrace' and 'We were young and we were pure, and life was just an open door', although I must confess to a little confusion when on the one hand Bernard is telling you to not let anyone get to you, and then expresses (repeatedly) how much he can't bear the thought of you.

I like the dramatic opening, revisiting 'Blue Monday''s low choral sample, but overlaid with a metallic, bleeping, chattering sequence vibe – found across *Low-life* tracks, and a defining sound of mid-1980s New Order: the Voyetra and Poly-Sequencer, in particular, getting solid workouts. Cut to a sequencer bass line with a pattern best described as 'giddyup', before cueing the synthesized horn blasts that herald Bernard's messages of confused passion.

Like 'This Time Of Night', 'Face Up' balances *Low-life*'s tendency towards the midrange with some decent bottom-end, and the song's freneticism is a great counter to the ambience of the side-B opener 'Elegia'. 'Face Up' closes well an album that temporarily lost its way but leaves a lasting impression of a record that forged new direction and left little in the tank. I can see how many consider *Low-life* to be *the* classic New Order album.

Sub-Culture (Single, 1985)

Personnel: Bernard Sumner, Peter Hook, Stephen Morris, Gillian Gilbert
Record label: Factory
Original UK release date: 28 October 1985
Chart position: UK: 63
Refer to other details per *Low-life* album and 'Sub-Culture' song entry above.

Shell-Shock (Single, 1986)

Personnel: Bernard Sumner, Peter Hook, Stephen Morris, Gillian Gilbert
Recorded April 1985 at Yellow Two Studios, Stockport, UK
Producer: John Robie
Record label: Factory
Original UK release date: 17 March 1986
Chart position: UK: 28

'Shell-Shock' (Sumner, Hook, Morris, Gilbert, Robie)

Frenetic and glitchy, 'Shell-Shock' is John Robie's strongest production effort for New Order, and in my opinion is vastly superior to his refit of 'Sub-Culture'. Lyrically it's a classic Bernard Sumner tale of problematic love, with the antagonist causing the protagonist shell-shock-level pain and suffering. But hey, 'It's never enough until your heart stops beating', right? It's unsurprising that the song was included (as an exclusive version with additional lyrics) on the *Pretty In Pink* soundtrack.

Musically, 'Shell-Shock' is pure (almost textbook) electro, focussed on crisp and punchy drum machine beats. It's all there: rapid-fire snare riffs, sample backtracking, *that* incessant ticking motif, brief flurries of bass, guitar strikes, stereo-panning, proto-house piano, bells, string sequences, etc. The full 12" version is quite a remarkable and complex piece of cutting and weaving, and it suits the track very well. The 7" and *Substance* edits are fine, but in their concision, they lose some of the interesting breakdowns (and an entire verse) of the full 12" mix. The B-side 'Shellcock' is a handy inclusion (I quite like how it starts 'in the middle'), but it perhaps finds Robie playing with his scissors just a tad overzealously, particularly on the vocal mashups, but there are some nicely-isolated sequences.

I vividly remember in the mid-1980s, a local breakdance crew using the electro vibe of 'Shell-Shock' to full effect, and I think the song is the ultimate expression of what both 'Confusion' and 'Sub-Culture' had set out to do: namely, sequence New York's genes into New Order's DNA.

State Of The Nation (Single, 1986)
Personnel: Bernard Sumner, Peter Hook, Stephen Morris, Gillian Gilbert
Record label: Factory
Original UK release date: 15 September 1986
Chart position: UK: 30

'State Of The Nation' (Sumner, Hook, Morris, Gilbert)
Recorded: April 1985 in Tokyo, Japan
Producer: New Order

Recorded in 1985 but not released until immediately prior to *Brotherhood*, 'State Of The Nation' is an interesting choice for a stand-alone single, being less of a pure dance number and incorporating a more caustic sound and social commentary. In fact, there are a handful of New Order tracks written during this period which pull no punches in their intent, and remain as relevant today as they were in 1986, even though the world may have changed. 'The state of the nation is causing death inflation': sadly true more than 35 years later. Whether they're aware of it or not, New Order can be quite the political band, but in their case, delivering their messages of conscience via the dance floor.

The video clip for this song – grainy and cut-through with flame and monochrome – reflects for me how the song feels: dissonant and densely packed. 'State Of The Nation' is underpinned by some excellent bass, metallic guitar sweeps layered with strident synth chords, and sequences that heighten the anxiety, all of which are a precursor to the track's cacophonous closing. It's an excellent production, which could've ended up a muddy mess, but didn't. The overall sound – particularly in the electronics and programming – had already evolved from the *Low-life* sessions just a few months earlier, and would flavour the band's output through *Brotherhood*, the *Substance* re-recordings and the *Salvation!* soundtrack productions.

Though completed in late 1985, the release of 'State Of The Nation' as a single was delayed to not interfere with the 'Shell-Shock'/*Pretty In Pink* promotions. Because of this, 'State Of The Nation' is afforded status as part of a terrific artwork trilogy by Peter Saville, that includes *Brotherhood* and

'Bizarre Love Triangle': like having sheets of metal in your record collection. It would've been a wonderful thing had Factory been able to deliver limited editions (of the album, at least) with actual sheet-metal sleeves, not unlike the Durutti Column's sandpapered *Return Of* LP. A ludicrously expensive proposition, but did Factory ever follow a budget?

'Shame Of The Nation' (Sumner, Hook, Morris, Gilbert, Robie)

Recorded October 1985 at Greene St, New York, NY, USA
Producer: John Robie
In between tours, the band returned one final time to New York and John Robie, to produce a reworking of 'State Of The Nation', the new name for which apparently came from the band's Japanese translator, who remarked that groupies following bands were the 'shame of the nation'. For me, the resulting new version – not unlike 'Sub-Culture' (but not quite as significantly) – is less successful and impactful than the original. To these ears, Bernard's lyrics and vocals absolutely need the intensity and instrumentation of the original version, and in 'Shame Of The Nation' they end up sounding hollow amongst the overcooked vocal overdubs and effects that Robie seems to feature in his productions.

The re-recording has pared the track back mainly to its synth bass line and a greatly simplified drum pattern, with various plinky-plonk synth-pad additions and flurries of fast editing to suggest original thought. Unfortunately, there's just far too much lost in the translation from the original. 'Shame Of The Nation's status as a double A-side suggests equal standing with the original. But I find the band's own superior production leads the way (as is so often the case with New Order), and indeed it's the one that finds its way onto the compilations.

Above: New Order performing on *Top of The Pops* in 1983.

Below: Bernard Sumner, 21 Jun 2012, Tempodrom, Berlin, Germany..

Above: Phil Cunningham, 21 Jun 2012, Tempodrom, Berlin, Germany.

Below: Gillian Gilbert, 6 Apr 2014, Lollapalooza, São Paulo, Brazil.

I Feel So Extraordinary: Brotherhood +

'State Of The Nation' is a line in the sand; a concluding chapter to New Order's first five years, in which their immediate post-Joy Division raids into dark-yet-primitive electronic territory were morphed and moulded by their evolving self-confidence, technical innovation and influences from Berlin and New York. From here, the next few years would see the band take the lead role in a new Eurocentric electronic dance sound, underpinned by two of the band's finest tunes, in 'Bizarre Love Triangle' and 'True Faith'. These and other masterpieces like '1963' and 'All Day Long' – together with song upgrades, a conceptual album and more soundtrack commissions – document a diverse, creative and hugely successful two years, enabled by the global breakthrough of the platinum-selling *Substance* compilation.

Substance collates all the New Order 12" singles from 'Ceremony' to 'True Faith', with their B-sides included on the cassette, CD and DAT editions. It was the perfect way to compile New Order's singles to-date, being that theirs were always first and foremost 12" versions. By my reckoning, it was the first 'best of' compilation by any band to be primed by extended versions, and it was a truly peerless collection of songs that highlighted just how remarkable and groundbreaking New Order were. There was no cooler release to own in 1987, and *Substance* was the starting point for millions of new global fans to come on board.

Brotherhood (Album, 1986)

Personnel: Bernard Sumner, Peter Hook, Stephen Morris, Gillian Gilbert
Recorded April-June 1986 at Jam Studios, London; Windmill Lane Studios, Dublin, Ireland; Amazon Studios, Liverpool, UK
Producer: New Order
Record label: Factory
Original UK release date: September 1986
Chart position: UK: 9

'Paradise' (Sumner, Hook, Morris, Gilbert)

After extensive research and one too many beers, I have concluded that 'Paradise' is not about drugs, but rather a murder-mystery sequel. Stay with me. If this song were a cheap novel, here's what the back of the book might read:

Hired by Tennessean good-ol'-girl Dolly to investigate the man-stealing escapades of the green-eyed gold-digging Jolene, Bernard Sumner – a tenacious PI from Salford, known for his motto 'There's no place you can hide that I can't find' – finds himself captivated by his target's incomparable beauty, casting hopeful what-if's about leaving town, finding a home, devastating the night and walking the earth, together. Torn between his professional duty and his darkening obsession, Bernard's world is turned upside down when Jolene's lifeless body is found. But what does he really know?

Opening the mostly-not-electronic side of *Brotherhood* (possibly the band's most underrated album), 'Paradise' is textbook New Order indie/alternative rock, driven by some sterling Hooky bass (and Prophet-5 synth bass), Morris' steady beats and some pleasant melodic guitar by Sumner and Gilbert. Not unlike their previous album's opener 'Love Vigilantes', 'Paradise' seems at once undemanding yet enthusiastic; marking time pleasantly enough before more challenging and innovative tracks come along, whilst still offering some *sha-la-la-la-la* sing-along potential, and the repetitious 'I want you, I need you' earworm, for lingering effect.

Worth mentioning here is one of the more obscure and interesting rarities in the band's official remix catalogue – namely Robert Racic's remix of 'Paradise' that originally appeared as a B-side on the Australian-only pressing of the 'True Faith' Remix 12" (FAC 183R), and later included in the *Retro* box set. Wanting to offer something unique, Factory Australia – run by the same team that operated the outstanding Australian label Volition Records – home to Severed Heads, Boxcar etc., for whom Robert Racic would provide (not unlike the Hannett/Factory axis) superb production and remix service until his untimely death in 1996 – requested clearance to produce an official and original remix, for which permission was given for (unusually) an album track. The resulting remix is excellent – faithful to the original, whilst giving it new dimensions, sounds and structure, and magnifying key parts to great effect. The way remixes should be done.

'Weirdo' (Sumner, Hook, Morris, Gilbert)

'Weirdo' is one of my favourite tracks on *Brotherhood*, and one of my favourites in New Order's rock catalogue. From its instantaneous stereo-panning jangle intro, to its long fade-out at the end, it features some wonderful guitar work, including outstanding bass-playing from Hooky, and Sumner's high-end melodic, chiming guitar, which nearly bends into discord against the bass (to glorious effect). Dare I say it, Bernard Sumner was giving Johnny Marr a serious run for his indie-guitar-cred money in 1986. The whole track is driven by Morris' drum performance that recalls classic Joy Division speed and power.

Sumner's in fine form vocally as well, sounding more and more confident (i.e., less frail and tentative than in times gone by), with an honest and emotive delivery at his classic high-end range, complete with requisite 'ooh's. The chorus lines are great to sing along with, and the mix of the backing 'just like, just like the ocean' (so subtly pitched off the main chorus) is perfect: much better than preceding tracks with backing vocals (e.g., 'Shame Of The Nation').

'As It Is When It Was' (Sumner, Hook, Morris, Gilbert)

I freely admit that I've never been one for country-tinged/slow-rock lullabies, and unfortunately, the first half of this song is mostly that. True to side A of *Brotherhood*, this song is all guitar, initially building on verses of gently-strummed melodies from Bernard on both acoustic and bass, bridged with flurries of waspish distortion. The second coda, however – heralded by a flare of feedback – is a terrific descent into chugging indie-thrash: a wall of fuzz, bass and percussion that nearly loses shape but just manages to hang on.

The three-part vocal harmonies (a featured technique across much of *Brotherhood*) in the closing 'The streets are so empty at this time of night' verse, are very effective, as is Bernard's little croon right at the end – much better than the crooning earlier in the song which is saved from dirge only by his emphatic, firm-jawed and snarling 'Whatever you think of me, you listen hard/I will make you see' lines.

'Broken Promise' (Sumner, Hook, Morris, Gilbert)

This is a straight-shooting piece of fast-paced indie rock, guitar-driven as with everything on *Brotherhood*'s A-side, but with some particularly interesting things going on. Highlights for me include Bernard's well-produced and well-considered vocal harmonies; the machine-gun-like snare rolls that pierce the track courtesy of our resident man-machine Morris; the unusual third track of instrumental/percussive-sounding 'oh oh oh' vocals behind the middle 'But what I think goes on in this world' bridge; the incessant pace of the bass; the buzzy lead guitar about two minutes in, plus the wonderful chord change that follows it, and the mad rock-out at the track's close, which collapses – fingers bleeding – into a very Joy Division-sounding last strum. And the track's final breath – a background tambourine that sounds like a rattlesnake, clearly annoyed at being woken up by the runaway freight train that has just blasted past.

Before embarking on this recorded-works journey, 'Broken Promise' was probably one of those tracks that I could take or leave, but now I find it has clawed its way back into favour. Why? It's New Order doing conventional rock very unconventionally: just the way we like it!

'Way Of Life' (Sumner, Hook, Morris, Gilbert)

It's interesting to note how New Order's rock has evolved over the years – from their post-Joy Division early phase, where the Hannett-produced sound is stripped back, gothic and with an emphasis on the space between the instruments, through the free-form post-*Movement* studio experimentations that lead into *Power Corruption And Lies*, where the atmospheric approach is all New Order's own. The rock songs that span *Low-life* and *Brotherhood* seem (with a few exceptions) to move distinctly towards the mainstream, with ballads, a nod to country, and straight-line production values being increasingly the norm.

Sometimes I feel, particularly in regards to post-Factory New Order, that – whether because of producer influence, label pressure, internal band politics or statistical inevitability – even the most innovative band will eventually find themselves writing songs that are middle of the road. New Order are at their most influential, their most powerful and their most important, when they ignore outside influence, and share their worldview through their own distinctive electronic/alt-rock lens, and not through trying to conform to others' expectations. It's why the New Order whole – when allowed to roam freely – is always superior to any of its parts, and furthermore is why *Power Corruption And Lies*, *Technique*, *Music Complete*, selected highlights from their other albums, and so many of their singles, are of such platinum-grade beauty and singularity. Straight rock just seems pedestrian in comparison.

But I digress. What of 'Way Of Life'? It's better than 'As It Is When It Was', not as good as 'Weirdo', and on-par with 'Paradise', but very much in keeping with the *Brotherhood* rock sound, with multitracked vocal harmonies, fuzz/acoustic leads, Hooky on continuous rolling melodic bass, and no-nonsense drums. My favourite part of the track is Bernard's emphatic 'That's the only thing about it' bridge, and pleasantly off-key 'Who do you think you're talking to?' chorus harmony. 'Way Of Life' also drifts to a dreamy acoustic close, tagged by a little Hook riff right at the end, before the needle unceremoniously (when compared to the equivalent moment on side B) lifts off from side A, leaving the listener feeling satisfied but perhaps a little underwhelmed. Thankfully, and by a massive margin, the best was yet to come.

'Bizarre Love Triangle' (Sumner, Hook, Morris, Gilbert)

I was in my final year at high school in 1986 when this gorgeous anthem emerged, with sweeping arpeggiating strings, Europop sequences, massive chords, layers of superb electro bass, and of course, Bernard's classic lines of love, sadness, regret and doubt, delivered in his inimitable boyish, slightly-sad-but-enthusiastic style. Thinking back to my early teens, I listened to some pretty questionable stuff, searching for meaning in those confused times and seeking one thing I could point to and say, 'This is who I am and this is what I like'. It was 'Bizarre Love Triangle' that called out to me like a titanium-sleeved treasure in the record store, and which rang out of every sound system in those mid-1980s clubs which easily accepted our fake IDs. Talk about heavy rotation – it set my musical compass to the alternative/dance genre, and I've never looked back. Not knowing it at the time, but my future wife was having a similar epiphany, and it's no coincidence that 'Bizarre Love Triangle' was A): the one piece of non-redneck vinyl in the DJ's record box at the only-club-in-her-village, and B): remains our go-to track when we're feeling the need to dance like no one's watching.

'Bizarre Love Triangle', for me, also defines a new phase in New Order's evolution. There's a new gloss to the sound – still firmly alternative, but driven by new synths and electronic kit, and new approaches to sequencing and production that are distinctly post-Hannett, post-Baker and post-Robie; a modern Euro sound which thankfully didn't tip over the precipice into the territory of Stock, Aitken & Waterman and others firmly of their time. This new phase of instrumentation and production would guide the band through 'True Faith', the *Substance* re-recordings and 'Touched By The Hand of God', before changing tack yet again somewhere on the island of Ibiza in the golden glow of 1988.

Version-wise, 'Bizarre Love Triangle' offers up some diversity. The album mix is the song in its purest form, as written, produced and recorded by the band. The sound is less crystalline than the remixes – rawer, with the bass and drum machine in particular sounding sparse and less processed. The synth sequences are gorgeous and distinct, and the crescendo is beautifully mixed. The single versions were remixed by Shep Pettibone – an American contemporary of Arthur Baker's with an ear for a more commercial sound. Pettibone's mixes are smoother and more fluid than the album version, and extend the song with breakdowns, vocoding and new patterns and sequences for club consumption: all of which are perfectly excellent.

Fast-forward to 1994, and London Records is cashing in on their investment with (yet another) *Best Of* collection, and for some reason, they feel the need to have Stephen Hague tweak several of the songs. Why fix what isn't broken? 'Bizarre Love Triangle-94' is okay, but doesn't improve on the original. Fast-forward another ten years, and Richard X takes aim with *his* remix. This is a decent update, paying tribute to the original Pettibone remix, but with a modernised drum and bass sequence at its core, some new instrumental overlays, choices of breakdown and rebuild, and variations on Bernard's vocals. There's a nice change in the closing as well.

A staple of the band's live set, to this day 'Bizarre Love Triangle' remains a huge live experience, and still seems to squeeze a little bit of joy from Bernard, offering whoops of delight, a sly bit of dad-dancing, and a roar from the crowd as that famous sequencer line kicks in. It's a beautiful thing when – stage awash with bolts of blue – thousands of people sing 'Every time I see you falling/I get down on my knees and pray'.

'All Day Long' (Sumner, Hook, Morris, Gilbert)

In my honest opinion, this is the finest song ever written by New Order. In an otherwise blinding set of tracks scattered across their canon, 'All Day Long' manages to ascend even higher. It's a work where the subject matter is of such incomparable darkness – set inside music that's quite simply, stunningly beautiful – that to this day, I find myself unable to listen to it or sing along with it without feeling a little bit overcome.

'All Day Long' is New Order's 'Atmosphere': it is that remarkable. Bernard was channelling something extraordinary the day he wrote lyrics like these:

So don't tell me about politics
Or all the problems of our economics
When you can't look after what you can't own
You scream and shout all day long

It's an exceptional and note-perfect production, combining once and for all the two poles of New Order's compass: alternative rock and electronic music. There's not one superfluous sound, not one questionable effect. Sung beautifully, the subject matter is handled succinctly and with great intent by Bernard, but in a way that incredibly (and in only two verses) puts you in the mind of both the perpetrator and – by way of warning – the rest of us. There is no such thing as an innocent bystander to child abuse, and – despairingly – it's a song that remains relevant to this day, in a world riven with darkness.

The song is so musically powerful. The synth bass keeps the main heartbeat with a wonderful depth of sound, allowing Hook to focus on his own exceptional bass. The percussion – though drum-machine based – is beautifully programmed, emphasising only when necessary, with a quick snare triplet or a single deeply reverbed strike to offer exclamation. The lead guitars add to the huge wall of sound with their thick chords and country-esque melodies. But it's the synths and strings (drawing so beautifully from the 'Prelude' to *Das Rheingold* – I'm sure Richard Wagner would approve) which turn 'All Day Long' into such a vehicle of grace. Those delicate chimes, the soaring cello sequences and arpeggios, the pizzicato violins… and they just keep coming, in layer upon unbelievable layer: all the parts perfect in isolation but sublime in their combination.

'All Day Long' is terrible and beautiful. It's an indictment and a rallying cry. It's this band's finest moment.

'Angel Dust' (Sumner, Hook, Morris, Gilbert)
A cacophonous beast of a track! I can sense the in-studio debates about its inclusion on the album or use as a B-side, but I'm glad it's on the LP, because it's the antithesis of 'Bizarre Love Triangle' – a raucous, discordant and industrial number, riddled with gunshots, distortion, brash piano, thrash guitar, wailing Middle-Eastern vocal samples and drum machine programming that switches from simple (and near-raw) to powerful. The synth sounds and sequences are textbook mid-1980s and seem to take one last look back to the influence of Baker and Robie in their tone and structure. A modern electro remix of 'Angel Dust' could be very cool.

'Angel Dust' shows that New Order hadn't sailed completely into the high seas of commercialism, and were still open to just going for it in the studio. The lyrics are typically obtuse, and I'm still trying to figure out if it's a tale of vampiric love and Bernard has gone all gothic on us – and who is the 'Master of Bourgeois whose life became illusion'? I need to know.

The track's evil mashed-up twin – issued only on the ultra-limited 'True Faith' CDV (and licensed to the great American tape label ROIR, and later the *Funky Alternatives* compilations) – opens the door a little wider so we can take in the fuller vocal samples. You have to admire Factory's willingness to brave media formats that were destined for obscurity (easy to say in hindsight), including Beta video, CDV (as distinct from VCD) and DAT.

'Every Little Counts' (Sumner, Hook, Morris, Gilbert)
I love the humour in this twisted love song, although I'm very sad for the target (estranged partner?) of Bernard's passive aggression. I love Sumner's cracking

up with laughter, and that it was kept in the final mix. I love the melodies and the swirling synths and strings. I love the slow buildup, the pause and the huge wall-of-sound finale. I also love live performances of this song, where Bernard usually chooses which of the band and/or audience is pig of the day and should be in the zoo. And finally, I love the bumped-needle effect at the end, which – and I imagine this was true for many others – had me that first time lurching towards the turntable, fearing a massive scratch on the vinyl. What a wonderfully subversive thing it would've been had Factory managed to follow through and incorporate a different defect on each media format: i.e., the bump/scratch on the vinyl, a chewed-tape effect on the cassette editions, and, of course, digital glitches on the CDs. A little is lost when listening via tape, CD or MP3.

'Every Little Counts' closes the B-side of *Brotherhood* with aplomb, underlining this side of the album's remarkable set of songs as some of the band's best – much more inventive, diverse and satisfying than the A-side, which are a little lacklustre in comparison. Having said that, *Brotherhood* is yet another wonderful New Order album and a stunningly packaged Factory artefact.

Bizarre Love Triangle (Single, 1986)
Personnel: Bernard Sumner, Peter Hook, Stephen Morris, Gillian Gilbert
Record label: Factory
Original UK release date: 5 November 1986
Chart position: UK: 56
Refer to other details per *Brotherhood* album and 'Bizarre Love Triangle' song entry above.

True Faith (Single, 1987)
Personnel: Bernard Sumner, Peter Hook, Stephen Morris, Gillian Gilbert
Recorded May 1987 at Advision Studios, London, UK
Producers: New Order, Stephen Hague
Record label: Factory
Original UK release date: 20 July 1987
Chart position: UK: 4

'True Faith' (Sumner, Hook, Morris, Gilbert, Hague)
One of New Order's greatest, and one of the greatest euro/alt/dance tunes of all time; sleeved in one of Peter Saville's most sublime designs, and partnered with an equally wonderful B-side that so nearly became the prime offering. To this day, 'True Faith'/'1963' for me remains New Order's finest single release, and it was the perfect rounding out of the *Substance* compilation. Cath Carroll put it beautifully in the booklet accompanying Factory's *Palatine* box: 'And ask not why this extravagant patch of pure blue, played first thing in the morning, can make you feel like Thatcher never happened. Here Stephen Hague introduced New Order to themselves all over again'.

Sonically, 'True Faith' is a leap forward from the *Brotherhood* recordings, and I think Cath was right on the money, because from this point forward, New Order's studio sound is richer and more spacious, although I have no doubt that advances in technology, greater experience, new gear, new influences and new ideas have something to do with it – not just the introduction of a producer, albeit a good one. I still maintain that New Order are at their best when self-producing, but this is the exception, and it's no surprise that 'True Faith' and *Substance* finally cracked the charts for New Order on both sides of the Atlantic.

It's such a wonderful song. From Bernard's exuberant lyrics (on feeling extraordinary, in motion, and a sense of liberty), to the huge snare sound pile-driving Morris and Hague's drum patterns, the interplay between Hook's excellent bass performance and the bass keyboard sequence, the glassy arpeggios, Gillian's melodic synth chimes, and more – all topped off with stellar guitar work from Sumner. Being of the discographer disposition, I have a tendency towards music lists, and there is a special one locked away in my brain that notes great moments in pop music – and by that, I mean actual moments in a song. Number 1 on that list has always been the high-octave synth solo at the end of David Bowie's 'Ashes To Ashes'. Number 2 is in 'True Faith' after the final verse, with Hooky maintaining his rolling bass for a couple of dramatic seconds before a massive chord change heralds the song's swirling outro. Momentous! At this moment during the (wonderfully bizarre) Philippe Decouflé video clip, there s a flaming explosion followed by Morris holding court over a pulsating crowd, and Sumner breathes steam out of his nostrils: so, I'm not alone.

'True Faith' was very well-represented in 1987 by various extended versions, dubs and edits – the best of which, in my opinion, is Shep Pettibone's 'True Dub' (aka 'Alternate Faith Dub'), which draws out, extends and emphasises the sequences from the original to nearly 11 minutes of joy. The middle section of the remix shines a spotlight on the crisp and beautiful arpeggiating synths. 'True Dub' achieves what John Robie had set out to do with 'Dub-Vulture', but rather than being driven off a cliff, Pettibone gives us a sweet ride.

Phase two in the life of 'True Faith' was its re-release as a single in 1994 via London Records, to accompany the (questionably titled) *Best Of* release. 'True Faith-94' is a tweak of the 1987 version, with some levels and effects shifted slightly to make it sound a little *tighter* – but why bother? The Perfecto mixes – unlike many of the other period remixes – remained true to the source, whilst adding value – with new drum, bass and glassy synth sounds, excellent glitchy patterns and modified sequences. To this day, the band incorporates the Perfecto arrangement at the core of their live performances of 'True Faith'. Noteworthy also is the Trannies With Attitude 'Grim Up North Mix', for its stripped-back patterns and quality gospel-like vocal additions.

Fast forward to 2001, and another set of remixes emerges on a double 12" via the band's US label Qwest. Richard Morel presumptuously adds his own vocal overdubs to his completely rebuilt 'Extra Dub' which focuses on a new sugary drum pattern, bleeps, Sumner samples ('Again and again I've taken too much' (repeat)) and synth flourishes. His other mixes are variations on that theme. Philip Steir's mixes start out okay – revolving around the main string chords and bass progression from the original – before careening off into their own worlds of glitchy drum and bass; occasionally coming back on target to something that sounds like 'True Faith'.

There are a couple of outliers as well – the innovative King Roc dubstep mix, which was included on the impressive 2006 12" reissue campaign by New State Recordings, and the 2008 'Eschreamer Dub' by Tall Paul, which bizarrely found its way onto the *Brotherhood* (Collector's Edition) bonus CD. It's terrible, complete with fake crowd noise – and on its inclusion, I turn to Paddy Considine's Gretton from *24 Hour Party People*: 'You've dropped a bollock, haven't you?'.

When all is said and done, there's simply no improving on the original. It's perfect.

'1963' (Sumner, Hook, Morris, Gilbert, Hague)

Quite the storyteller is our Bernard. His alternate JFK universe is a fine piece of songwriting, told from the perspective of Jackie – she being the one facing death (albeit in January 1963) at the hands of an assassin, but in this case arranged by (if not done by) John himself, in order that he could be with another (Marilyn?)! It's unique and heartfelt – particularly as it's told retrospectively in the victim's first-person. I might go so far as to say it's one of Bernard's finest songwriting moments, especially in how he portrays Jackie's desperation, sorrow and terror, and how he switches between the event itself and it being a distant memory, as her spirit begins to 'feel free'. The final lines in the original version are beautiful:

I just want you to be mine
And I don't want this world to shine
I don't want this bridge to burn
Oh Johnny, do you miss me
I just want to feel free

Even if not pitched on an alternative timeline, the song offers a poetic take on the real events of 1963.

The band and Stephen Hague did a wonderful job on this piece of alt/ electronic melancholy, particularly the many layers of strings and choppy synth bass. The vocal production is beautiful as well. Bernard has a strong sibilance in his singing, and Hague achieves a fantastic mix with his choices of reverb and delay. It's almost like Sumner's voice blends into the strings. Stunning.

As with 'True Faith', 'Round & Round' and 'Bizarre Love Triangle', '1963' was subjected to revision at the time of the *Best Of* compilation issue, being remixed and, finally, released as a stand-alone single. '1963-94' is structured per the original, with several major exceptions, not least of which is that the wonderful closing lines are excised completely, replaced for some reason with a repeat of the 'He told me to close my eyes' bridge, and ultimately fading out over a loop of the chorus. *Really?* The '94 version may be tighter and cleaner, but it's not better for it – e.g., there are quite a few subtle changes in instrumentation, and I think the power of the strings was diminished. For the 'Nineteen63' single release, it was accompanied by additional remixes from Arthur Baker, Justin Robertson (Lionrock) and Joe T. Vannelli, with Baker's '95 mix the best of these – faithful to the original but tastefully rebuilt with new melodies, sequences, sounds and ambience, and (importantly) respecting the original lyrics. Baker's version also underpins the accompanying (really odd) video clip: Jane Horrocks as an itinerant with a suitcase that grows (?).

Now, I have a soft spot for Justin Robertson. He produced some top gear during the 1990s, and I remember being excited at the prospect of his involvement. But how in any way do his mixes bear any resemblance to '1963' whatsoever? I'm even less enthusiastic about Joe T. Vannelli's mixes, which represent the low point of where the art of remixing went off-piste (and hit a tree) during this period. All this remix palaver detracts significantly from the original version of the song, which is superb and as fine a production as any from New Order.

Touched By The Hand Of God (Single, 1987)
Personnel: Bernard Sumner, Peter Hook, Stephen Morris, Gillian Gilbert
Recorded August-September 1987 at Pluto Studios, Manchester, UK
Producer: New Order
Record label: Factory
Original UK release date: 7 December 1987
Chart position: UK: 20

'Touched By The Hand Of God' (Sumner, Hook, Morris, Gilbert)
Unlike the polished gems that are the singles released immediately before and after it, 'Touched By The Hand Of God' rattles along in a darker electronic world of its own; closer in my mind to 'Shell-Shock''s bluster. Admittedly punched out at the eleventh hour from the *Salvation!* sessions (see below) at Pluto Studios in Manchester, the song is both cool and somewhat flawed.

The original mix – as released on the *Salvation!* soundtrack – feels like a rush job. Bernard's overtly breathy vocal overpowers everything else, and the editing is coarse, with certain vocal grabs cherry-picked and repeated *ad nauseum*. The song had potential, but it needed a rethink. Cue Arthur Baker, who, at his Shakedown Sound studio in New York, remixed the song into what we know as the single versions – enjoying much-improved sonic range, production and editing. They have a fantastic dark electronic backbone – EBM-like synth bass sequences and drum programming, with some funky guitar

New Order ... *On Track*

grooves, layers of synth riffs that play off each other, growling bass guitar and lots of orchestra hits. The dub versions are also particularly good.

The 'Biff And Memphis Remix' from *Rest Of* (as with other mixes on that compilation) is mediocre, but it at least retains some semblance of the original. Seek out Bias' remix from the *Manchester United* compilation, for an unofficial but far-superior revision.

By far, 'Touched By The Hand Of God' is at its finest when performed live, reaching its apogee on the excellent 1998 Peel session (released on *In Session*) where the song's core palette and programming have been fully upgraded, Bernard's vocals are much punchier and intense, and the song is hugely better for it. This version and (New Order's recording of Joy Division's) 'Isolation' from the same session, easily sit in my premier league of New Order recordings.

Lastly, I adore the 'Touched...' video clip. What a wonderful pisstake of late-1980s MTV hair metal – and to think so many thought it was the real deal. Ace!

Other Recordings for Salvation! (Original Soundtrack) (1988)
Personnel: Bernard Sumner, Peter Hook, Stephen Morris, Gillian Gilbert
Recorded August-September 1987 at Pluto Studios, Manchester, UK
Producer: New Order
Record label: Les Disques Du Crépuscule
Original UK release date: February 1988

'Salvation Theme' (Sumner, Hook, Morris, Gilbert)
Was there ever a movie soundtrack that punched higher above its weight than that of *Salvation*? For such a roadkill of a movie, that its soundtrack featured exclusive New Order works, two terrific pieces by Cabaret Voltaire, and Arthur Baker (amongst others), is a testament to whatever line of communication existed between the New York no-wave underground film scene and Factory Records. Did Michael Shamberg have a hand in joining these dots? That the *Salvation!* movie has never seen the light of day on DVD (not even as a bootleg), is probably sensible. I only ever saw it once, and that was enough – with televangelism not being something I'm drawn to: even in lurid satirical form. The soundtrack, however, is mostly excellent.

'Salvation Theme' is a short and sweet instrumental, cut from a similar cloth to 'Elegia' and again years later with 'Soundtrack' – namely an ambient collation of chiming melodies, mirage-like harpsichord motifs, organ chords to add drama, some languid Hook meanderings and a plucky rotating sequence. It's quite soporific, really, and I wonder if there is a longer version of it floating around on the studio tapes.

Whether it be for movie, TV, installation or otherwise, New Order have delivered on every soundtrack they've been commissioned for. It's an interesting branch off the main line of their creative output, and 'Salvation Theme' is a very good example. Long overdue is its inclusion as a box set bonus – watch this space!

'Let's Go' (Sumner, Hook, Morris, Gilbert)

This song has had a chequered history – a fully-formed *Low-life* outtake with vocals; performed live a few times as an instrumental; re-recorded and released as such for *Salvation*, and reanimated years later almost as a new song entirely.

'Let's Go' was first attempted several times during the *Low-life* sessions, at one stage, even included on an early draft of the running order for the album (apparently in place of 'The Perfect Kiss'). However, it never made the final cut. A leaked version complete with vocals, can easily be found on YouTube, as can instrumental live performances from the period. The song certainly feels contemporary to *Low-life*, reminding me a lot of 'Sooner Than You Think', and it was likely culled for space-vs-quality reasons when compared to the final album content. It's interesting to hear in the 1985 recording, the original opening bass line from Hooky, which, if I'm not mistaken, was re-used as the opening bass line of Monaco's 'What Do You Want From Me?'. The lyrics are also completely different to the 1994 re-recording, and although certainly not one of Bernard's better vocal performances, I think they work fine, and the song would've made a perfectly acceptable B-side for one of *Low-life*'s singles. Although, having said that, both 'The Perfect Kiss' and 'Sub-Culture' work better as singles with dub versions as their B-sides. In a parallel world, we all own a third (more rock-styled) single off the album – say, 'This Time Of Night' or 'Face Up' – with the original 'Let's Go' vocal recording as the flipside. No doubt the forthcoming (at the time of writing) *Low-life* Definitive Edition box set will have a surprise or two.

The 1987 attempt to record the track for *Salvation*, did in fact, include vocals (which also exists *out there* on a torrent somewhere but is very rough), but as we know, the band opted to finally release 'Let's Go' as an instrumental – likely because it made for a more-effective soundtrack piece, and because they'd probably gotten used to playing it live in this form. The instrumental works just fine – based mainly on a melodic bass core from Hook (one of his more *central* performances), with various layers and themes provided via jangly guitar, and the synths only there to add texture during the bridge. Overall, 'Let's Go' has a brash and metallic vibe to it, and it sits well among the *Salvation* soundtrack offerings. In this form, 'Let's Go' also ended up in an abbreviated form (why?) as 'Let's G...' on the rare fifth bonus CD from the *Retro* box set.

The song was then revisited at the time of the *Best Of* release, taking on board completely new lyrics, new production by Arthur Baker and Bernard Sumner, and additional programming by future manager Andy Robinson (formerly New Order's keyboard tech, plus engineer, producer, member of Factory band Life, and one half of the Primetime remix crew). This refit finally sounds complete, with a much clearer and smoother production than the brusque *Salvation* instrumental. The guitars have been toned down, there's a deeper influence from the re-programmed synth bass, and one's focus is shifted to the new vocal performance from Bernard. Though I'm not a huge fan of the 'la la la''s in the recording, I much prefer the new 'You did nothing for me, you did nothing' chorus, to the 'Waiting for so long, though I've been waiting for a chance to see you' lyric from the original 1985 outtake. It's also interesting to note that the main melody of the old vocal has become the opening guitar melody in the new recording – all very Frankenstein.

The handling of the 1994 version is a bit baffling – only released in the UK as a bonus track on the limited edition boxed '1963' CD single, and later the *Retro* box set; but in the US as the opening number (!) on that territory's issue of the *Best Of* compilation. Titled 'Let's Go (Nothing For Me)' in the US, the track even surfaced as a promotional single: so perhaps there was greater intent. The US *Best Of* release is notable in that it expands on all other editions by also including several additional early album tracks, in an attempt to provide a more representative 'best-of'. However, including 'Let's Go (Nothing For Me)' – particularly as the opening track ahead of 'Dreams Never End': where 'Ceremony' (also not included) should've sat – is a curious call, not unlike including 'Hellbent' on the *Total* compilation. More on that later.

'Sputnik' (Sumner, Hook, Morris, Gilbert)

Listening to 'Sputnik', I can visualise the spiky little Soviet sphere orbiting through the void in 1957; the first of its kind, with the paranoid West fearfully tuning in on shortwave radio. This instrumental piece is short and sweet but nonetheless dramatic as the music fades in and fades out, like the satellite coming in and out of range: receiving, transmitting and reflecting its crude signals. These low-register atmospheres and mid/high-range organ chords have a sinister melancholy about them, and their layering against a simple pulse beat is quite distinctive. Picture Rasputin as mad church organist at Baikonur Cosmodrome, with Yuri Gagarin on bongos! Cutting through this brief encounter, are two distinctive flourishes – one at about the halfway mark, sounding like an atmospheric collision, and the second near the end, with two rapid synth scales signalling the satellite to be on its way.

'Sputnik' is a minimal but affecting instrumental – not the first, and certainly not the last that New Order produced (as indeed did Electronic, who also crossed into *Soviet* territory on their debut album). It's a side to their output that remains quite special.

'Skullcrusher' (Sumner, Hook, Morris, Gilbert)

New Order certainly used the *Salvation!* soundtrack as an opportunity to get a couple of unused 1984/1985 outtakes *finished*. And like so many other tracks written during the band's Factory era, 'Skullcrusher' had its first airing live as a work in progress, with lyrics that were impromptu (at best). Gutsy!

Two things come to mind here. First – when you look over New Order's 1980s setlists, other than the occasional cover version, there's nothing played live that didn't eventuate on a release somewhere. In that respect, they are quite a lean band in that their archives hold few recordings that remain unreleased. Second (and conversely), there are few tracks released during the band's Factory period that weren't performed live at least once – with the makeup of a given set often being determined on a whim and incorporating more obscure or alpha-version tracks. Gretton's influence (or insistence) would've been key to this. There is a shift from the 1990s-on, where it's less common to get a new track tested live before it is released, and there are numerous studio tracks that have never been played live. Perhaps it's true to say that New Order used to be more experimental than they are now. But then, that's true of most bands with any sort of lifespan. It's also equally fair to say that experimental does not necessarily equal awesome.

Cue 'Skullcrusher'. Seemingly on the band's forward agenda during 1984, given that the track had several live airings that year – each time with Bernard ad-libbing extremely questionable lyrics. Easily found on YouTube, the Studio 54 live performance from Barcelona is probably the best quality recording that has lyrics, but good grief, they are dodgy: 'You heard me when I called you fat/You said that I was just a twat', etc. After that, it goes downhill fast, but the performance would've been a chuckle on the night. Words aside, the vocal melodies work okay, so it's a shame the song wasn't taken to its fullest conclusion.

As with 'Let's Go', 'Skullcrusher' was resurrected as an instrumental from the spares box for the *Salvation!* soundtrack. It's a frenetic piece revolving around a repeating Hooky riff, a simple tom-and-snare pattern and several layers of trebly guitar, with descending chords, Chic-like chugging and a blistering squeal at the top end. Parts of the track remind me of their label contemporaries Minny Pops and Section 25, and also hark back to some of Warsaw's earliest punk works. I can see why they pulled the track out a few times when they just wanted to thrash about a bit.

Blue Monday 1988 (Single, 1988)
Personnel: Bernard Sumner, Peter Hook, Stephen Morris, Gillian Gilbert
Record label: Factory
Original UK release date: April 1988
Chart position: UK: 3
Refer to other details per the original 'Blue Monday' single release above.

It Takes Years to Find the Nerve: Technique +

1988: the second summer of love; acid house, house music and warehouse raves; a new ground zero of youth culture that was on par with punk's impact in 1976.

Thank you, Bernard, Peter, Stephen and Gillian, for choosing your working (?) holiday in Ibiza – clearly having a huge time, returning home with at least one gem *in the can*, and (according to Stephen Morris) the backing tracks for about half of the other songs on *Technique*. I sometimes wonder if, at the time, you could sense – amongst all the revelry – that you were building towards the masterpiece that would become your first number-1 album.

The *Oxford Dictionary* defines a masterpiece as, 'A work of outstanding artistry, skill or workmanship', and, in my opinion, New Order (as distinct from Joy Division) can count two albums in their canon to date as true masterpieces – *Power Corruption And Lies* and *Technique* – and I've come to think of them (to paraphrase Martin Hannett) as two aspects of the same thing – *Power Corruption And Lies* all dark and brooding; *Technique* gleaming and ecstatic; yin and yang; winter and summer; entirely unique, yet linked in their sublimity.

Fine Time (Single, 1988)

Personnel: Bernard Sumner, Peter Hook, Stephen Morris, Gillian Gilbert
Record label: Factory
Original UK release date: 28 November 1988
Chart position: UK: 11
Refer to other details per *Technique alb*um and 'Fine Time' song entry below.

'Don't Do It' (Sumner, Hook, Morris, Gilbert)

I've always appreciated a unique B-side, along with a couple of quality remixes and/or dub versions, but I'm not convinced that offering a dozen remixes of the same track is a value proposition, particularly when they're spread (and duplicated) across multiple CDs and records, supposed *promos* and digital-only offerings. Factory seemed to find the right balance of quality-vs-quantity with its releases – usually one primary and one remix record, with little (if any) duplication. Things got a bit silly once the band joined London.

'Fine Time' was the first New Order single drawn from an album, that included an album outtake as its flipside, with 'Don't Do It' recorded during the *Technique* sessions but relegated from the LP. To these ears, the track's DNA – being a sample-driven instrumental with a darker tone – harks back to 'Murder' and 'Evil Dust', with a melodic core that reminds me a little of 'Thieves Like Us'. It's interesting to note that the band had enough outtakes and instrumentals from the *Technique* sessions, to populate all the album's singles.

I sense a strong Morris/Gilbert input on 'Don't Do It', from the harpsichord intro, to the many samples, the melodic string-strike motif and synth atmospheres. Hook's bass and Sumner's lead guitar meander underneath the mix where it feels like a verse vocal should be. Perhaps the track feels slightly unfinished, and was destined for more. However, the apparent *space* in 'Don't Do It' allows the samples to dominate – the (curiously emphasised) 'Don't put your finger on the button' line, lots of gunfire, creepy 'We're going to get you' and 'It's going to hound you' samples from the BBC's television play *Play On One* ('On The River' episode), and ending on a reversed sample from *The Exorcist*.

'Don't Do It' is a dramatic B-side that counters 'Fine Time's party, delivering an unconventional but wonderful single overall.

Technique (Album, 1989)

Personnel: Bernard Sumner, Peter Hook, Stephen Morris, Gillian Gilbert
Recorded May-October 1988 at Mediterranean Studios, Ibiza, Spain; Real World Studios, Box, UK
Producer: New Order
Record label: Factory
Original UK release date: 30 January 1989
Chart position: UK: 1

'Fine Time' (Sumner, Hook, Morris, Gilbert)

In 1988, I was your typical summer-of-love teenager, spending every night of every weekend clubbing, deeply immersed in S-Express, Stakker Humanoid, A Guy Called Gerald, 808 State, Baby Ford, Bomb The Bass and many more. My ears were tuned to house, acid and techno, and I would spend many an afternoon skipping Uni lectures to crawl Brisbane's record stores. Just before Christmas 1988, I'm downstairs (where the best record stores should always be) at Kent Records (now long gone), and there's a line of lurid yellow 12"s in the new-releases section, with purple dichromic pills all over them, with no band or title info on the front – 'Has to be New Order', I thought to myself, hoping they'd improved on 'Touched By The Hand Of God' and 'Blue Monday 1988', which hadn't seemed like much of an evolution compared with the new music changing my world. Now, all good record stores have listening stations, and I have a very distinct memory of putting 'Fine Time' on, and after about 30 seconds, I blurted out (with headphones on, and to no one in particular – certainly not the shoegazers lurking over in the corner), 'THIS IS F#%KING BRILLIANT!': actually shouted. Loudly.

With its unusual structure and distinctive club layering – rubbery techno bass at the forefront, punchy TR-909 programming, samples and an acid/house sound palette influenced by Detroit and Chicago (rather than New York) – 'Fine Time' is a leap forward from the industrial motorik of 'Blue Monday', the mid-1980s midrange sequencers and synths that define 'The Perfect Kiss' and 'Shell-Shock', and the alternative rock/dance crossover that is 'True Faith'. All the stars aligned because also peaking were Trevor Key (RIP) and Peter Saville, Factory Records and the Haçienda. Richard Heslop's video clip was suitably tongue-in-cheek: a kid (and his dog) dreaming of floating pills and opening his Christmas box of bliss! Even the choice of house pioneer Steve 'Silk' Hurley to remix 'Fine Time' was on point. Both his 'Silk Mix' and 'Messed Around Mix' honour the original (as all good remixes should), but strip the track back to a more rolling Chicago house beat, isolating sequences and melodies, and featuring – Lil' Louis style – more of Bernard's breathy expositions-on-love technique.

New Order once again found themselves at the forefront, and it's this capacity to jump to the head of the queue time-and-time-again with seemingly effortless cool, that's probably their most powerful quality. 'Fine Time' was the perfect single to herald the magnificent *Technique* album, and was the perfect soundtrack for a perfect summer.

'All The Way' (Sumner, Hook, Morris, Gilbert)

One of the reasons why I love *Technique* so much, aside from the strength of its dance tracks, is that its non-electronic numbers sound so exuberant compared with the previous album, and they are interspersed on the LP, rather than conceptually grouped together *à la Brotherhood. Technique* is a beautifully produced album that proffers the best of New Order's many facets in a much more cohesive body of work.

'All The Way' contains one of my all-time favourite lyrics from Bernard: 'It takes years to find the nerve to be apart from what you've done/To find the truth inside yourself, and not depend on anyone'. Over the years, Bernard has had – contrary to what he tells us (or at least his hairdresser on *NewOrder Story*) – various messages for the world, and sprinkled across *Technique* are various *bon mots* of wisdom that mean a lot to me, and which I'll explore through these reviews. These lyrics really spoke to me at a formative time in my life, and when combined with this song's lush backing track and performance, the track's impact was pronounced.

I reckon Bernard's vocal performances reached a peak across *Technique* and *Republic*. He found his voice, and the production values found him – emotive and with his own distinctively youthful tenor sound, using just the right amount of reverb and harmony, and with his nervy and endearingly-deadpan approach borne out of necessity during the early years, now a fond memory. Plus, he was still a decade away from teetering near the black hole of bluesy swagger.

'All The Way' is a lovely song, straightforward in structure, and a classic merging of rock and electronic sensibilities. The guitar work is gorgeous – listen for the Johnny Marr-like jangles in the chorus, which then morph into Sumner's quintessential percussive style during the verses and breaks. Hooky's bass, rolls up and down in his inimitable and wonderful way, but it's the sumptuous and uplifting string/synth/oboe/bass instrumental breaks and outro that reinforce 'All The Way' as a near-classic and a high point on an album of remarkable highs.

'Love Less' (Sumner, Hook, Morris, Gilbert)

One of the enjoyable aspects of *Technique*, is the track sequencing. The album is a terrific journey that offers both energy and respite, and 'Love Less' is of the latter disposition. Taking a moment after 'All The Way' to (literally) clear their throats, the band take us on a relatively short and straightforward acoustic/rock sing-along, full of melody and light that neither thrills nor offends.

The song features some great lyrics from Sumner, but the highlight is the bright instrumental work in the final break near the end, offering multiple layers of charming guitar alongside the downbeat vocals. Plus, it's some of the fine details and nuances that New Order (by now completely at one with the studio) slip into their productions that make the album's name so *apropos* – little things like the way 'Love Less' atmospherically ends on a Hook-note and some indistinct chatter caught on the mic. New Order start and end songs thoughtfully, and the bits in between aren't too shabby, either.

I agree with those that say (almost under their breath so as not to dislodge New Order's rightful standing in the pantheon of electronic music) that the band is, in fact, a great (and very English) guitar band. But it's when you add 'as well' to the end of that statement, that a measure of their remarkable creative breadth can be understood.

'Round & Round' (Sumner, Hook, Morris, Gilbert)

'Round & Round' is one of my all-time favourite electropop tracks, and a real gem amongst the rich pickings of *Technique*. Whereas for me, 'Fine Time' had a real brute-force impact and felt like a jet engine blast, 'Round & Round' – with its smooth production, structure, and refined sounds – is its cooler cousin. It is the sleek to 'Fine Time''s swagger.

In travelling through New Order's entire catalogue, I found myself thinking upon something that may seem patently obvious: that New Order – as purveyors of (in this case) electronic dance music – come at the task of songwriting, as a *band*. It's fair to say that the vast majority of dance music is produced by solo artists, a pair of gear wizards, or a small production team. But as we've always known (but maybe take for granted sometimes), New Order – with their roots in punk and their branches in post-punk, alternative/ indie rock, electronica and techno – come at the task of producing electronic music from a deeper body of experience and wider field of vision. And for that reason, their dance music has always been so distinctive.

'Round & Round' is a joyous and wonderfully-propulsive electro classic, the album version of which remains definitive, though the remixes are also particularly good. With reference to the *Technique* version, here's what glistens for me – A) the main electro bass line sequence, and particularly the verse pattern with its notes on the off-beat, and that little flurry before it dips down and then jumps up an octave; B) the drum programming is sweet: house meets techno meets disco, with lots of slip snares and the high/low tom combinations; C) the stripped-back, crystal-clear techno instrumental break; D) Sumner's vocals, and how the lyrics (apparently a commentary on his problematic professional relationship with Tony Wilson) are delivered with a subtle *slowness* over what is quite a high-BPM track; E) the orchestra-hit sounds in the intro, adding to the overall house texture; F) the bleep sound in the chorus and bridge was still relatively cool, and only later would define the *bleep* genre *à la* Tricky Disco, Sweet Exorcist *et al.*, and eventually find its way back into indie pop as a cliché; G) phasing the whole track to end the song with a flourish.

Stephen Hague was engaged to remix the song for single release, bringing on board additional synths, strings, ambient motifs and sequence variations, supposedly to make the song more radio-friendly. But it's only in his full 'Twelve Inch' mix that his efforts reach their full potential. I thought that Kevin Saunderson (one of Detroit's 'Belleville Three' techno originators, and Inner City's main man) being chosen to remix New Order was an inspired choice. But having said that, his 'Detroit Mix' just doesn't quite gel. Sure, there's a classic techno backbone of handclaps, backspins and echo, which work well with the original's electro-bass line and sequences, but I think the mix should've only sparingly sampled the vocals and kept Hooky's bass out altogether (sorry, Peter). It's like Saunderson's parts and New Order's parts were two jigsaw pieces which didn't quite fit together. Ben Grosse's '12" Mix' fares much better, emphasising the electro bass line and chatty sequencers in his version, and with a particularly great breakdown in the last third. Even better was his collaboration with Saunderson, which yielded the fantastic 'Club Mix'.

With my record label hat on, I find 'Round & Round' to be a fascinating case study. The band produced an ultra-cool, groove-laden, left-field electronic pop nugget, remixed brilliantly and marketed with one of their best video clips – only for the song to chart just outside the top 20, resulting in a spat amongst the label directors, with Tony Wilson resigning as Chairman of Factory Records (FAC 253 – March 1989). It's well-documented that the band preferred to have released 'Vanishing Point' as a single, and though I agree with Wilson that 'Round & Round' was a strong option for a single, I also agree with Gretton and co that 'Vanishing Point' would've been an excellent choice. They should've gone with it as the third single instead of 'Run'. Wilson's time *in the corner* was brief but symbolic.

With my fan hat on, I'm just glad to enjoy such a great song. I loved it at the time, and I still do. It makes me act like a child.

'Guilty Partner' (Sumner, Hook, Morris, Gilbert)

Standing among the triumphs of *Technique*, 'Guilty Partner' can best be described as a solid album track. There is some very fine guitar work, particularly the Spanish-sounding riff during the middle break. But the real highlight for me is the synth brought in between the final verses. It's a charming addition that adds much-needed depth, but regrettably appears and disappears all too briefly. Unfortunately, Bernard's lover-laden lyrics tend to swing between great ('To admit that I was wrong. It took me far too long') and iffy: 'I counted on you to give me a reason why the sun don't shine in the season' detracting from what's clearly a heartfelt and personal tale of relationship breakdown.

I mentioned above that one of *Technique*'s strengths is its sequencing, making for a wonderful journey across its tracks, and 'Guilty Partner' provides a respite in proceedings – grazing in the meadows between the snowcapped peaks of 'Round & Round', 'Mr Disco' and 'Vanishing Point'.

'Run' (Sumner, Hook, Morris, Gilbert, Denver)

'Run' starts sluggishly, and for the first half, the brashness of the guitars keeps the overall sonic experience – unlike most of *Technique* – firmly in the midrange. But halfway through, there's a gorgeous change, dropping down with a wind-chime flourish and a simple and mournful organ, harking right back to the synth sounds of Joy Division. It offers a sense of desolation, right in keeping with the nature of Bernard's lyrics, and suddenly 'Run' makes perfect sense. The song builds back up into a magnificent instrumental, before ending beautifully and with great atmosphere. For me, it's a song of two halves, and it comes to life midway through – not unlike the video clip, which also starts breathing once the little drummer girl starts pirouetting, and the moody gig footage captures the band in motion amidst the dry ice and lights.

There's some quality writing from Bernard, hinting at the social observations that feature so heavily in his future works: 'So what's the use in complaining when you've got everything you need'. But mostly, he's sharing personal thoughts on communication breakdown – all of which has F#%K ALL (to these ears anyway) to do with John Denver's 'Leaving On A Jet Plane', and to this day, I'm at a loss with respect to the lawsuit which derailed 'Run''s proper release as a single, and the ongoing need for co-writing credits. I can't think of a greater musical gulf than that which exists (sonically and geographically) between the protagonists in this case study of American litigation gone bananas.

'Run 2' then. I recall the excitement when the lads at Factory Australia presented me with one of the radio-only 7"s ('Here kid, enjoy'), bemusement at the often-played video, and then curiosity when everything went quiet because of the Denver debacle. In the end, I was forced to wire funds to an overpriced UK dealer for what was suddenly a limited-edition 12", but was 'Run 2' worth it? Given additional treatment to make the song more radio-friendly (apparently), for me the drums sound weaker, the overall mix a little insipid, and the edits, abrupt. American producer Scott Litt offers mildly entertaining alternative drum programming (except for the quack sound at the start of each bar), puts a spotlight on looped lead guitar riffs and Hooky's bass, but otherwise, his 'Extended Mix' doesn't add much.

'Mr Disco' (Sumner, Hook, Morris, Gilbert)

Many of the best New Order songs over the years never surfaced as singles, superior though they may have been to some of the actual singles selected at the time. Being spoilt for choice is a measure of *Technique*'s greatness. 'Mr Disco' is a classic example – platinum electronic pop, full of wonderful riffs and melodies, seamless production, and terrific house beats with a wonderful disregard for shame, that dials up the rimshots, handclaps, timpani, and (best of all) cowbell. The title says it all. The track's mainline is a muscular update on disco, which, in the hands of lesser mortals, would end up as retro as a cheese fondue. But unlike disco, the track is interspersed with intricate breaks and multilayered bridging sequences. Worth mentioning, too is the bass sequencing (tonally emphasised by Hooky) which delivers a great punchy bottom end. I also want to acknowledge (again) New Order's attention to detail because it's the sonic nuance and texture that make this gem of a track sparkle like it does – the delay and phasing on particular drum shots, the stereo positioning, the subtle synth pads just there in the background giving depth and atmosphere, the selective fade-in and dissipation of chattering sequencer riffs, and finally a terrific and thoughtful ending: in this case, Bernard whispering a final reprise before the track smashes to a halt like a Tron Light Cycle into a wall, splintering into a million shards of digital glass.

'Vanishing Point' (Sumner, Hook, Morris, Gilbert)

I reckon 'Vanishing Point' might be my favourite track on *Technique* (and is apparently Stephen Morris'), but 'Fine Time', 'Round & Round' and 'Mr Disco' are all completely sublime as well. Back in the day, 'Fine Time' would've been my preferred Friday floor-filler – raw and in your face, heralding the weekend with mischief and bustle. You're well into the weekend by Saturday night, and your senses are sharpened for some classy tunes, so bring on the silky brilliance of 'Round & Round' or the all-you-can-eat bliss of 'Mr Disco'. Sunday afternoon recovery needs clarity, so some unconfused beats and bass, beautiful melodies, and even a hint of ambient melancholy are required. 'Vanishing Point' is a superb expression of all of these, and having all four tracks together on the one album is simply remarkable.

Bernard excels himself – 'Grow up children, don't you suffer/At the hands of one another', and 'My life ain't no holiday/I've been through the point of no return/I've seen what a man can do/I've seen all the hate of a woman too' delivered in that upper-range and mournful tempo so typical of him, with a production-perfect amount of harmony, reverb and delay. 'Vanishing Point' also has another of Sumner's reprise vocals – in this case, the 'Whistle Down the Wind' reference: a form he applies on other tracks like 'Mr Disco' and 'Regret', unfortunately often lost when tracks get edited for single release, and partly explains why New Order's album versions are – almost without exception – definitive.

Musically, 'Vanishing Point' is gorgeous. I love the programming of the main bass line, melodically bouncing around on the 8ths and 16ths before slipping down into alternative keys, and then driving forward in a single line towards the vocals; all with Hooky adding much-appreciated texture. The drums are less complex than 'Mr Disco', being mainly variations on the huge 909 kick drum, snare rolls and clipped cymbals, but perfect in their classic dance-pattern simplicity. It's the evocative synth melodies and atmospheres which make the track shimmer and glide, and the instrumental break at the three-minute mark is wonderful – a stripped-back groove with Hooky delivering a thoughtful refrain, paring down completely to just reverbed bells, before the electro hi-hats lead us back one last time into a crowd-heaving full-on chorus, with Bernard reminding us again that he needs more holidays: because, you know, Ibiza was exhausting!

We can only guess at how successful 'Vanishing Point' could've been as a single. Potential remixers at the time? Mark Moore, Brian Dougans and Graham Massey come to mind. But – like 'Plastic' from *Music Complete* – there's nothing wrong with having a perfect dance track *only* on the album. The 'Instrumental Making Out Mix' was a welcome inclusion on the 'Round & Round' CD single, eschewing the vocals and emphatic dance mix of the original for additional melodies and an overall lighter feel. It works really well as the theme to its namesake TV production. And, is it me or does the show punch well above its weight having this as its theme?

One final note of admiration is how the band has recently refined and reintroduced the song into its live set – and in particular, how 'Bizarre Love Triangle' segues into it. Pure class.

'Dream Attack' (Sumner, Hook, Morris, Gilbert)

'Dream Attack' closes a near-perfect album near-perfectly, splendidly encapsulated in Bernard's lyrics:

Nothing in this world can touch the music that I heard when I woke up this morning
It put the sun into my life
It cut my heartbeat with a knife
It was like no other morning

Gillian's strummed acoustic guitar works so beautifully with the electric lead guitar, particularly during the verses, where it chimes and shimmers, and in the lead-in to the second verse, where Hooky's bass is in the spotlight. After the final chorus, we get this little flurry of orchestra hits (a sound much used across *Technique*), heralding a glorious instrumental outro – lead guitar balanced with the layered bass elements, merging into a wonderful (and exquisitely programmed, in terms of its simple notes yet unconventional meter and looping) synth melody. The long fade-out (one of the few times this is used on *Technique*) is also very effective, adding the dream-like quality that the song title hints at.

In their seemingly-unplanned evolution, New Order have passed through many doors (in some cases that they themselves constructed) – post-punk, electro, alt-rock, industrial, synth pop, house, techno, left-field, etc., but it's the tracks which intersect these genres that are often New Order's best. In many ways, *Technique* represents the summit of New Order's diverse approach to songwriting, and it was also the last LP on which the four original members would collaborate in relative harmony. What a brilliant album.

Round & Round (Single, 1989)
Personnel: Bernard Sumner, Peter Hook, Stephen Morris, Gillian Gilbert
Record label: Factory
Original UK release date: 27 February 1989
Chart position: UK: 21
Refer to other details per *Technique* album and 'Round & Round' song entry above.

'Best & Marsh' (Sumner, Hook, Morris, Gilbert)
This works so well as a B-side for 'Round & Round', don't you think? To me, the track sounds like The Art Of Noise meets S'Express, and yet there are the signature New Order touches, like the big string chords, Hooky's perambulations, the clipped electro drum patterns (harking back to their New York influences, but with better programming), the house piano and the numerous sweet synth riffs. Altogether, an upbeat and blissful tune.

Luckily, there's an unofficial upload of the Granada (and Tony Wilson-hosted) *Best And Marsh – The Perfect Match* (for which the track was produced) still on YouTube, where you can see that this piece works a treat as the theme. We all have a New Order instrumental playlist (don't we?), and 'Best & Marsh' is a true gem, making the whole 'Round & Round' package the best single off *Technique.*

Run (Single, 1989)
Personnel: Bernard Sumner, Peter Hook, Stephen Morris, Gillian Gilbert
Record label: Factory
Original UK release date: 28 August 1989
Chart position: UK: 49
Refer to other details per *Technique* album and 'Run' song entry above.

'MTO' (Sumner, Hook, Morris, Gilbert)
Producers: New Order, Mike 'Hitman' Wilson
'Much Too Old', you say? Before we explore, just a couple of clarifications: MT = Roland MT32 Sound Module, and thus 'MTO' (aka 'MT One' on early demo tapes) is a reference to this piece of kit, apparently used right across *Technique*. Also, 'MTO' isn't a medley (as someone suggests on Discogs), although the track's inclusion of 'You've got love technique' samples from 'Fine Time' could be the source of the confusion, and perhaps where the Much Too Young/Much Too Old association became a thing.

In my opinion, 'MTO' is New Order's poorest B-side. In fact, the demo version floating around *out there* is far more satisfying than the released B-sides as remixed by Mike 'Hitman' Wilson. The demo shows real promise, with several quality keyboard riffs unused by 'Hitman', a better synth bass sound, less cheap snares, and that fluid-sounding chime sequence integrating much better into the overall mix. If only New Order had worked the track more themselves, we could be enjoying a B-side on par with 'Best & Marsh'.

Hitman's efforts just never get out of first gear – all cheap snares, a muddled bass line and the repeated 'Fine Time' sample – trying really hard to be a jack/house/acid dance-floor nugget but failing dismally. The 'Minus Mix' is a poorly-cooked stew of cliche samples, mismatched styles and zero imagination. Maybe if Wilson had used only the last few acidy minutes of his 'Minus Mix' at the core, and relaid some of the original demo's more interesting synth and bass, perhaps he could've lived up to his moniker. But really, how the band could ever put their name to the 'MTO' mixes as released, is beyond me.

Technique outtake (1989)

Record label: Factory
Original UK release date: September 1989
Refer to other details per *Technique* album entry above.

'The Happy One' (Sumner, Hook, Morris, Gilbert)

I love the band's (or was it Gretton's) labelling of the *Technique*-era demos, usually with the 'One' suffix and differentiated by vibe. That they could tell which tracks were, respectively the Balearic, Disco, House, Funky, Happy and Dreamy ones, shows talent. Or perhaps their thoughts were elsewhere (It was 1988, remember): 'I'll have a dozen happy ones, Bez'.

'The Happy One' is an instrumental demo from the *Technique* sessions, parts of which were used between clips on the band's *Substance 1989* video compilation, and parts which were released (as 'Intermede Musical N°1' through N°6) on a 1991 Factory Records CD promo called *Palatine Lane* (FAC 303), which was offered to subscribers of the French music magazine *Les Inrockuptibles.*

Without over-analysing a demo recording, I can sense that – given more time – 'The Happy One' was headed in the same direction as 'Best & Marsh': a melodic and light-sounding instrumental which would've made a good B-side. Peter Hook also played solo over the tune as a backing track for Tony Wilson's *Other Side of Midnight* TV show, and it's interesting to hear the additional layers of instrumentation. Whether we ever get the complete recording as a bonus somewhere, remains to be seen, but let's hope it's no worse than 'MTO'. I tried remixing it once: https://soundcloud.com/the-isle/new-order-the-happy-one-the

World In Motion (Single, 1990)
Personnel: Bernard Sumner, Peter Hook, Stephen Morris, Gillian Gilbert
Record label: Factory
Original UK release date: 21 May 1990
Chart position: UK: 1

'World In Motion' (Sumner, Hook, Morris, Gilbert, Allen)
Recorded February 1990 at The Mill Studios, Maidenhead, UK; Mayfair Studios,
London, UK; Studios, Box, UK
Producer: Stephen Hague
Time-travel back to T. J. Davidson's rehearsal studio circa winter 1979, and play
this to four serious young men, and they'd have been inclined to push you
through the holes in the floor. Play this to Martin Hannett during the *Closer*
sessions, and you'd be locked in the stairwell. 'World In Motion' is not for
critical analysis; it is for dancing shambolically and singing along with the fans.
It was the right song at the right time by the right band on the right label, and
millions loved it.

The single version really is a very polished electronic pop song and it's no
wonder it reached number 1 (New Order's first and only single to do so),
being full of hooks, melodies, dance floor drums and bass, catchy lyrics and
football stars. I love the stylish sleeve, and it would be quite a while before
Saville was to return to this calibre of design for the band.

The remix versions are generally top-value as well, with the 'Subbuteo'
version by Pickering and Park, and the 'No Alla Violenza' mix by Farley and
Weatherall particularly welcome additions. I'm not so convinced by the
'Carabinieri Mix', though. Of these, the 'Violenza' mix is the most interesting,
with its loops, backmasks and overt house/rave feel, but the 'Subbuteo Mix'
was the floor filler back in the day.

New Order's final release on Factory Records was wonderful. Nothing too
serious, just one final joyous and celebratory sing-along (and a final nail in
the post-punk coffin). In 1990, Factory were at their most carefree, their most
sleek, their most loved-up. It was soon to career downhill, but right now – for
one last time – Factory and New Order had the world in motion.

'The B-Side' (Sumner, Hook, Morris, Gilbert, Allen)
Recorded February 1990 at Real World Studios, Box, UK
Producer: Roli Mosimann
Well-documented tales abound of 'World In Motion''s unconventional production.
That they ever got to the end product is remarkable and probably a testament
to Stephen Hague's organisational skills. Listening to 'The B-Side' is instructive,
because you get a more demo feel to the song from the Real World sessions versus
the Maidenhead/Mayfair sessions, including the non-Barnes rapping attempts,
additional verses and (a little too much) Keith Allen. You can sense just how much
work went into getting to the final single version, so Hague did remarkably well.

We're Dealing In The Limits: Republic +

I can't begin to imagine the chaos surrounding New Order circa 1991/1992. Label failing, club failing, money haemorrhaging, band weary. If there was ever an atmosphere within which to record a new New Order album with enthusiasm, coherence and belief, this wasn't it. Stepping back from the disarray to work on other projects was the right move. Eventually – against all odds and under extreme duress – the band recorded quite a good album in *Republic*, with at least one flare of brilliance ('Regret'), more than a handful of solid tunes, and it would be served by their new label London Records.

But first, some thoughts on the band's respective other projects, which were a significant force around this time. Consider the decade between the release of Joy Division's *Unknown Pleasures* (1979) and New Order's *Technique* (1989). What a phenomenal body of work. What a consistently stunning sequence of albums – almost year-on-year (not counting the singles, soundtracks and compilations in between), plus all that touring, the label and club, and their BeMusic production work. Ten years of peerless creativity and collective productivity, after which you'd want to take a break and change the dynamic, right? – branch out and work with other people; develop some ideas outside the inner circle. In hindsight, it's so obviously the right move, that I wonder why anyone challenged their (or each other's) motives at the time.

So, the *projects* in a nutshell (because this book is not about them). The *Electronic* album is simply brilliant in every way – a stunning release from Bernard Sumner, Johnny Marr, Neil Tennant and Chris Lowe, and the last-best album to come out on Factory. You can understand Peter Hook's consternation with Bernard wanting to fly solo for a while (and indeed the quality and his success in doing so), but – perhaps as a sign of things to come 15 years later – there's a bit of the puerile in Revenge. Aside from a few good exceptions across *One True Passion* and *Gun World Porn*, Revenge was lacking in quality songwriting and composition, and no amount of money thrown at the studio could make up for that. Monaco would be the real deal from Hooky seven years later. *The Other Two & You* was everything you'd expect from Gillian and Stephen – pure melodic electronic pop music, and how great was it to finally have Gillian singing lead! I've always felt that the solo works of 1990-1992 were, in some ways, the separate pieces of a lost New Order album that *Republic* didn't fully live up to. But then again, the album *did* top the UK charts, so what do I know! For the band, producing *Republic* probably felt like passing a watermelon, and it's a mark of their indomitable spirit that they were able to release such a decent album under the circumstances.

Regret (Single, 1993)

Personnel: Bernard Sumner, Peter Hook, Stephen Morris, Gillian Gilbert
Record label: London Records
Original UK release date: 5 April 1993

Chart position:UK: 4
Refer to other details per *Republic* album and 'Regret' song entry below.

Republic (Album, 1993)

Personnel: Bernard Sumner, Peter Hook, Stephen Morris, Gillian Gilbert
Recorded March-November 1991 at Real World Studios, Box, UK: RAK Studios, London, UK
Producers: New Order, Stephen Hague, except where indicated
Record label: London Records
Original UK release date: 3 May 1993
Chart position: UK: 1

'Regret' (Sumner, Hook, Morris, Gilbert, Hague)

The *Republic*-era releases sport some of my least-favourite sleeves in the New Order catalogue. The Malboro-men sunset thing seemed so far away from New Order and Peter Saville's representations to this point, that my first impression in the record store was, 'Oh dear'. I never quite got the hidden meaning in the choice and sequencing of the blended images used across these releases. However, the campaign was certainly distinctive (in particular, the lurid orange life-preserver-esque *Limited Run* CD), and it for-sure no longer looked like a Factory New Order release. Was it London that mandated spelling out 'A NewOrder Release' on all the sleeves? Things had certainly changed.

'Regret', however, is wonderful. If you were going to lead with your best shot, then this was a knockout. Huge synth calls and chunky guitar responses open the track and lead into Hooky's driving bass melodies. In my opinion, 'Regret' is one of Peter's finest performances, and his is the absolute backbone to the song. Bernard's vocal performance is first class – hitting his highs with confidence and force. Lyrically strong, I particularly love the opening 'Maybe I've forgotten' lines, the choruses and the final 'Just wait 'til tomorrow' reprise. The song is just so melodic – rising and falling in line with the intensification and easing of the regret in Bernard's voice. I've spoken before about the evolution of his songwriting and messaging, and 'Regret' felt absolutely like the right song at the time: a reflective, tuneful, powerful song that spoke volumes, and laid bare their recent past.

Remix-wise, the standout version is Farley and Heller's 'Fire Island Mix', which has a lovely laid-back feel with its loungey alternative bass line and additional piano work. The band's own 'New Order Mix' offers a different balance with respect to the original's guitars vs synths, with a greater emphasis on the latter, and an alternative outro (lacking the vocal reprise). The Weatherall/Sabres of Paradise 'Fast 'N' Throb' mix leaves me underwhelmed, largely because of its minimal connection to the original (something many of the London-era remixes suffer from), and it gets boring very quickly. Their 'Slow 'N' Lo' mix fares better for its echoey dub feel, vocal and bass inclusions, but the pseudo-harmonica sounds a tad cheap. However,

I actually prefer this excursion into reggae, far more than 'Ruined In A Day', but we'll get to that.

The video for 'Regret' is one of my all-time favourite New Order clips, with its postcards-from-Europe feel. As for the *Baywatch* version... lordy! I agree with Neil Tennant's assertion on *NewOrder Story* that 'Regret' is one of the band's finest singles up to that point. It's certainly in my top five of all time, and is easily the best song on *Republic*: proof-positive that you can't judge a book by its cover.

'World' (Sumner, Hook, Morris, Gilbert)

Solid electropop tinged with Bernard's headspace at the time (mainly frustration and caution), and an obvious choice as a single, 'World' drips with great synth, piano and organ riffs, peaking in the terrific Electronic-like instrumental break. Having said that, the mainly-electronic tracks on *Republic* seem to have a uniform sound to them, whether the result of adopting new kit, Stephen Hague having a more controlling hand production-wise, or a change in the balance of member input in the studio. 'World', 'Spooky' and others on *Republic* position themselves firmly in the sonic middle – the drum programming more loop-based and with an emphasis on cymbals, tambourine, shaker and hi-hats, together with the mid-toned electronic bass. It's perhaps this dimension to *Republic* which left me a little underwhelmed at the time, particularly with respect to its electronic music contemporaries like Orbital, 808 State, Future Sound of London and many others.

It's curious how 'World (The Price Of Love)' was handled as a single. The 'Radio Edit' – a decent and succinct edit of the album version – underpinned the video clip, but only led the 7" and cassingle releases: neither of which were primary formats in 1993 when CD singles were king, and 12"s were the most important supporting vinyl format (albeit mainly for DJs). It was a mark of London's approach that its primary formats (CD-single and 12") for New Order singles were in most cases *not* primed with the band's own version. It's one of my bugbears, because, for me, a single should always highlight, first and foremost, the band's creation, with remixes acting as bonuses and never the primary.

'The Perfecto Mix' is perfectly okay, but two things grate – the phasing glassy sequence, which opens the mix but suddenly sounds *off* once the beats kick in; the delay doesn't quite work, and to these ears, it completely throws the track. The backing vocals are a little overcooked as well. On the other hand, Oakenfold and Osborne's drum and bass programming is a great improvement. The 'Brothers In Rhythm' mix (and their associated 'Dubstrumental'), strips back the original's synth layers, emphasising particular tones and reverbed samples, and the overall effect is a lighter mix: cruisy even. Their 'Price Of Dub' version is more up-tempo, with some quality new beats and sonic layers, and would've aced the lot had they added full vocals to the mix. The K-Klass mixes are the least impressive of the set, bearing little resemblance to the original, either in beat, bass or melody. They frankly have nothing to do with New Order.

And finally, the clip – depressing in several ways. First, how separated the band are in their respective appearances – very telling, and of course, the subject matter *vis-à-vis* 'the price of love' for greying narcissists.

'Ruined In A Day' (Sumner, Hook, Morris, Gilbert)

It took me ages to find the right words to articulate just how I feel about 'Ruined In A Day', backspacing several times over words like 'bland' and 'innocuous'. Why on Earth it was ever considered for a single release, let alone what was done to it: Lord have mercy!

As an album track, 'Ruined In A Day' is okay, being a bit of a plod groove-wise, but saved by some melodic guitar, atmospheric synth and piano, and a swaying bass line. I like Bernard's delivery on 'I do the best that I can' and the opening 'listen' lines, but I just don't connect with the jade/shade, and cradle/wheel lyrics. The fade-out ending feels like a cheap exit, and I reckon they could've used a segue approach *à la* 'The Village'-into-'5-8-6', and blended 'Ruined In A Day' into 'Spooky', just to give it something more.

As a single, and particularly the remixes, gee, where do I begin? When I first put the needle to the 'Ruined In A Day' 12", my dislike for the 'Bogle Mix' and its near-equivalent 'Dance Hall Groove' and 'Rhythm Twins Dub' versions was surprisingly intense. The core groove was okay, particularly with the guitar lick at the start of each bar, but it was all quickly and comprehensively ruined by the god-awful *chats* and synthetic trumpet flares. The Reverend Badoo's performance is terrible. By four minutes, it all gets too much, so Sly and Robbie just fade the whole mess out. And this is the 12" A-side? The 'Live Mix' can't even claim the useful groove from the 'Bogle Mix', and is an exercise in pure irritation. Thankfully, the lead CD single included none of these, instead including the one remix with any real merit: K-Klass's 'Reunited In A Day' mix. The restructured groove – with additional background sequences and an effective repetitious guitar sample – offers without question the best rendition of 'Ruined In A Day'. The version is mixed really well, with a breadth of ambience and reverb that enhances the atmosphere of the original. Lastly, we have Booga Bear's tolerable 'Ambient Mix', which is just under six minutes of sweeping synths and subtle motifs following the main chords of the original.

'Ruined In A Day' is lacklustre and a too-soon comedown point on *Republic*, and should've sat further back on the album. Its remixes were – with certainly one and possibly two exceptions – appalling. A better option for a single would've been 'Young Offender' or even 'Everyone Everywhere', as both are stand-out songs and could've been reinterpreted by better remixers of the day, such as the Hartnoll brothers, Graham Massey, Mark Bell or Paul Daley.

'Spooky' (Sumner, Hook, Morris, Gilbert, Hague)

I've never really gotten out of the starting blocks with 'Spooky'. It's a satisfactory song with some highlights, but there are aspects that leave me flat, and I always found it a curious choice (if necessary at all) as a fourth single from *Republic*. Luckily, team Fluke gave the track some much-needed punch.

The very best part of 'Spooky' is its chorus – 'We could break every rule, any time we wanted to/Don't be afraid to live this way/Let's defend the things we say' – one of Bernard's best lyrics on the album, combined with a particularly funky piano pattern. The jangly off-key bridge leading into the chorus is also tasty, although the way it peters out in the middle eight is disappointing. The closing chorus is also particularly good because it's heralded by a bar of atmospheric strings that blend into a great background riff by Hooky. The chain keeping the album version shackled to the ground, is its insipid looped drum pattern, particularly when combined with its sampled overlay that sounds like the gravelly mating call of a toad. The pattern is an unending (and almost unchanging) spongy core to the track, which prevents some of the more-interesting motifs and textures from rising above the middle ground. There is actually a decent synth bass line in 'Spooky', but it's barely noticeable; the same with some reverbed guitar-picking in the second verse, but you have to listen hard.

Which is why the Fluke remixes are such a significant upgrade. Their 'Magimix' is amongst my favourite New Order remixes, with strong percussive buildup, excellent breadth with proper bottom end, techno squelches, chattering sequences, string-laden atmospheres, plus all of the important riffs, melodies and, of course, vocals from the original. The 'Moulimix' is a more-minimalist techno-driven take with ambient qualities: also really enjoyable. Fluke did very well.

Paul Van Dyk's mixes don't fare quite so well (as Mark Reeder mentions in this book's Foreword). His 'Out Of Order' mix starts outs okay with a moody arpeggiating sequence, but after incorporating Bernard's verse vocals, that's pretty much as far as the mix gets. It's in a permanent state of buildup! Sure, it speeds up in the last minute and a half, but it's just a sped-up buildup to nowhere. Tony Garcia's 'Stadium Mix' (and its instrumental sibling) is just boring – isolated samples from the original, shoehorned onto a simple disco pattern, and no amount of KLF-esque crowd samples will convince me that this mix would get a stadium full of people moving, let alone a near-empty bar. His Nightstripper Mix is probably the strongest of the non-Fluke versions, properly nodding to the original, but with flourishes and sequencing that remind me of The Shamen, The Grid and NJoi.

'Everyone Everywhere' (Sumner, Hook, Morris, Gilbert, Hague)

The biorhythm of each New Order album is different, and in my opinion, each side of *Republic* has a very distinctive journey of peak/dip/peak; side A starting with 'Regret' and 'World', closing with 'Everyone Everywhere'; side B opening with 'Young Offender' and closing with 'Special' and 'Avalanche'. One of the album's qualities is the lasting effect of this flow – i.e., open with your best shot and close it with style, regardless of what transpires along the way.

Which brings me to 'Everyone Everywhere': a real highlight and one of my favourites on the album. It's gorgeously produced, particularly how Hague and the band found such breadth and depth in the guitar mix, with quite a few layers of bass, lead and rhythm guitar interacting – starting with the rhythmic strumming under Bernard's beautiful vocals, the subtle additional textures that are added, Peter's integral bass riffs and the lush lead layers during the chorus. The primary bass line is synth-based and has a nice grain to it: a subtle but excellent touch of programming. Equal to the terrific guitar performances are the luscious and atmospheric synth layers. The last 30 seconds soar upwards to Bernard's repeated despair that 'This world is gone'. Sublime.

Unlike on 'Spooky', here Hague nails the vocal mix, not overdoing the phasing, yet emphasising Sumner's natural sibilance with the perfect amount of reverb. The song itself has some lovely lines, including, 'If we don't take a chance in our spare sideways glance' and 'When we kiss we speak as one/With a single breath this world is gone'. 'Everyone Everywhere' is another of those wonderful rock/electronic crossover songs that are such a hallmark of great New Order.

'Young Offender' (Sumner, Hook, Morris, Gilbert)
Producers: New Order, Stephen Hague, Pascal Gabriel

There are some gems on *Republic*, and 'Young Offender' is one of them. It should've been one of the stronger contenders for single release (and remix), and its quality may have more than a little to do with the fact that (as one of the earliest tracks written for *Republic* during Factory's dying days) Pascal Gabriel had a hand in its (pre)production, as he had with 'Regret'. I've got a lot of time for Gabriel – he having produced some of my favourite songs by S'Express, Bomb The Bass, Inspiral Carpets, and of course, The Other Two, and I sometimes wonder how *Republic* might've been shaped had his involvement continued. Rumours persist of a small handful of cassettes (of short instrumental demos) *issued* by Factory as FACT300 (which was the scheduled catalogue number for the New Order album had the label survived and the album been released on Factory). But it's likely this was, at-best, an informal listening tape shared among the inner circle and given posthumous Factory catalogue status. I'm told that the contents included 'Young Offender' (working title 'Identity'), 'Regret' and 'Times Change' (working title 'Heavy One'), which Gabriel had worked on at the early demo stage.

In my opinion, 'Young Offender' features some of the best programming on *Republic*, Bernard's vocal performance is excellent, and the overall production is top-notch. The band is firing on all cylinders, with Hook's contributions not completely lost in the mix (though I would've mixed him even higher to cut through), and, as with much of *Republic*, the track is dense with layers of fine keyboard. However, because the drum programming doesn't overpower in a *muddy middle*, the many synth melodies are given space to glisten.

'Liar' (Sumner, Hook, Morris, Gilbert, Hague)

Here's where *Republic* starts to lose me for a while. 'Liar' is just too middle-of-the-road; simply a mild album filler that's neither challenging or remarkable, and I can't think of a single New Order song up to this point, that I could pigeonhole this way. New Order were never ever MOR, and it's as if the whole studio production – instead of passing through a pipeline of interesting programming, workmanship and effects – has been passed by Hague and the band, through a teabag. Bernard's 'used up nearly all (his) love', Hooky's ten seconds of bass has been toned down as a courtesy to fellow patrons, and it's all so seemly.

The two or three highlights of 'Liar' – the 'If that's what it takes, I'll do it' coda, the chorus (and indeed Dee Lewis' backing vocals) and the string pads in the instrumental break – are all that remain in memory long after the song has sauntered by in its comfortable shoes.

'Chemical' (Sumner, Hook, Morris, Gilbert, Hague)

Because of their music, because of the way they present their art, because of their associations, and because of their coolness quotient, New Order loom very large on the soundtrack to my life. But just like when the weather turns south, or my favourite team has a losing streak, I feel genuinely perturbed when New Order delivers less-than-terrific: which is, of course, ridiculous and selfish; we all have our off days.

But in the interests of balance, honesty and constructive criticism, here we go: 'Chemical' is a bit of a pig. It carries the remnant DNA of a decent song (I quite like the chorus), but it has been bludgeoned in the studio until all its character, heart and soul has been neutralised. To wit, the god-awful mainline drum loop (What is it with the relentless chugga-swish programming on the album, typified by 'Spooky' and 'Chemical', the responsibility for which seems to fall squarely with Hague rather than Morris?); the irritable bowel that is the bass line; the faux-Depeche industrialism; the overall noise. And what a cheap fade-out!

The *payroll company* probably didn't care – it filled the CD space. But 'Chemical' should never have gone beyond a passable B-side. It's one of the three or four examples of why *Republic* feels below par.

'Times Change' (Sumner, Hook, Morris, Gilbert)

Like 'Chemical', 'Liar' and 'Ruined In A Day', 'Times Change' suffers from an identity crisis. These tracks – the weakest on *Republic* – are all an attempt to nudge somebody's ill-defined genre envelope, none of which succeed. My problem with 'Times Change' is that it sounds like a Frankensteinian experiment in that it has Bernard rapping to a completely derivative slip-beat drum loop interspersed with a melodic chorus. Then, as if giving Hooky something to do, the track drops to him noodling pointless nothings that bear no relation to the surrounding song. 'Times Change' is like a third-rate

Electronic demo spliced with parts of an unfinished New Order song, and cut with a studio mishap where the engineer accidentally records the bass guitarist in the kitchen tuning up... and I can't eliminate the mental image (from his opening rap) of Bernard lying Christ-like in a hay-filled manger, suffering yellow fever. That's some weird trip, and perhaps a throwback to the young lad in the 'Fine Time' video, dreaming of dirigible pills for Christmas!

'Times Change' – give me the chorus, the second instrumental lead-in with the interesting cuts, plus the melodic oboe instrumentals. Demolish the rest and rebuild, or just relegate it and move quickly on to 'Special' and 'Avalanche'.

'Special' (Sumner, Hook, Morris, Gilbert, Hague)
For a while there, *Republic* lost its way for me. I disliked disliking music from my favourite band, and I recall growing increasingly worried that New Order were going to end on a flat note, stuck in a funk of lacklustre songwriting. Thankfully, with 'Special' (and 'Avalanche'), the band took (in my mind) a collective deep breath, looked in the mirror, and remembered who they were – purveyors of original, alternative, melancholy, *Northern*, electronic/rock music – and with these two tracks, managed to close an imperfect album near-perfectly.

'Special' is superb for several reasons – Bernard's wistful singing of lyrics that sound so final, and the instances where his emotion rises above the central performance; the reprise verse at the end; the gorgeous strings and lush keyboard instrumentation; a classic Peter Hook performance where bass melody absolutely drives the song; the emphasis in the production, such as the slight organ phasing at the end of each verse line, and the thoughtful drum programming with some terrific drum rolls from Morris. Hague really nailed this recording.

It's 'Special' and 'Avalanche' (along with 'Regret', 'World', 'Everyone Everywhere' and 'Young Offender') that offer the kind of stirring stuff we've come to expect from New Order, and indeed makes *Republic* linger as one of the band's good (but far from great) albums. At the time – and certainly post Reading '93 when the band effectively split – I felt very strongly that the 'It was always special' line served as a poignant closure to New Order's incredible time in the light.

'Avalanche' (Sumner, Hook, Morris, Gilbert)
I love Gillian's voice. On 'Avalanche', she only repeats the word 'faith', so there's not much to go by, but I feel it important to take this moment to acknowledge a beautiful and highly underrated singer. We can complain about New Order's band members' divergences to their various projects, and the impact this had on the core band circa-*Republic*, but we can also celebrate the fact that we got to hear The Other Two. Gillian's humility belies an inspiring talent, because she and Stephen really know how to craft gorgeous tunes.

'Avalanche' has the most atmosphere, the most beautiful melodies and orchestration, and the most heart of any track on the album. It feels like the band put all their differences aside one last time to channel the sublime; drawing as they collectively did, some of their finest instrumental performances on *Republic* – the lovely interplay between bass and acoustic guitars, the washes of keyboard and reverbed piano, the deep tones and echoes, the simple but metronomic drum loop, and of course, Gillian's voice: as if it were itself a backing violin. 'Avalanche' has a melancholy cinematic quality to it, and that final held note is like a dimming light.

At the end of a challenging album, this song – and indeed Gillian's gentle call to arms – restored my (temporary loss of) faith in New Order. And if this was to be their swan song, then it was a fine ending.

Ruined In A Day (Single, 1993)

Personnel: Bernard Sumner, Peter Hook, Stephen Morris, Gillian Gilbert
Record label: London Records
Original UK release date: 21 June 1993
Chart position: UK: 22
Refer to other details per *Republic* album and 'Ruined In A Day' song entry above.

'Vicious Circle' (Sumner, Hook, Morris, Gilbert)

This is the only B-side as such from the *Republic*-era singles, although it was left off the vinyl issues, so I suppose it's less a B-side and more of a bonus. 'Vicious Circle' (working title of 'Icke One', although why is unclear) was one of the tracks worked on for *Republic*, and the only *spare* (so far) from those sessions to emerge fully formed.

The band's version of 'Vicious Circle' from the 'Ruined In A Day' cassingle is quite an interesting production with lots of ideas, closer to *Technique*, and sounding somewhere in between 'Mr Disco' and 'MTO' in its backbone, but with much better melodies and motifs than the latter. As a bonus, 'Vicious Circle' (a strong name for what is really a lighthearted instrumental; perhaps it was destined for a lyrically darker theme) is perfectly fine – a demo steered far enough along its course to be of good value, but needing much more work to fully form. The 'Mike Haas Mix' from the 'Ruined In A Day' CD-single seems more cohesive, running with particular ideas from the New Order version and sounding less *raw,* but perhaps losing some of the naïve fun of the original. Of particular interest is a short Hooky bass line motif right near the end of the Haas mix, that sounds a lot like a riff (re)used later on the Monaco track 'Sweet Lips'.

It's a mark of the time that 'Vicious Circle' was the only *leftover* from the 1992 sessions. *Republic* – with CD as its primary format – includes 11 tracks, whereas all previous albums (with LP as their primary format, and thus limited to 22 minutes per side) only featured eight or nine tracks. In a

Right: Bernard Sumner, 19 Dec 1980, College of Arts, Rochdale UK. (*Photo by Glenn Bennett*)

Left: Peter Hook, 19 Dec 1980, College of Arts, Rochdale UK. (*Photo by Glenn Bennett*)

New Order
Movement
Fact 50*c*

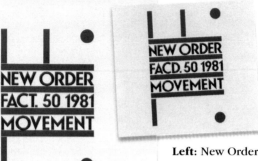

Left: New Order's debut album
Movement, Nov 1981. Sleeve
by Peter Saville, after Fortunato
Depero's Futurismo (note the F / L
shapes, representing Factory / 50).
Tape, LP and CD shown. (*Factory*)

Above: New Order's first single
'Ceremony' b/w 'In A Lonely Place' (both
written by Joy Division), Mar 1981. 7", 12"
and 12" reissue shown. (*Factory*)

Left: 'Procession' b/w 'Everything's Gone
Green' 7" single, Sep 1981. Released
in nine different sleeves, also based on
Futurist designs by Fortunato Depero.
(*Factory*)

Left: *Power Corruption And Lies* album, released May 1983. The sleeve is a reproduction of Fantin-Latour's A Basket Of Roses. CD, LP and Tape shown. (*Factory*)

New Order
Power, Corruption & Lies
Fact 75c

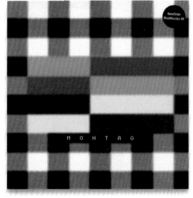

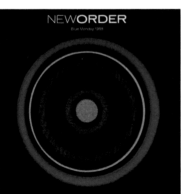

Above: The classic 'Blue Monday' 12"
single in its various incarnations: original
Mar 1983, 'Blue Monday 1988' (both
Factory), and 'Blue Monday-95'. (*London*)

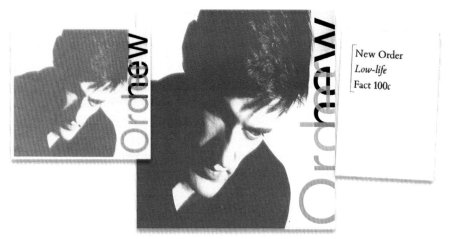

New Order
Low-life
Fact 100c

Above: *Low-life* album, May 1985. The first of Factory's 'linen box' cassette editions, all including unique artwork within. CD, LP and Tape shown. (*Factory*)

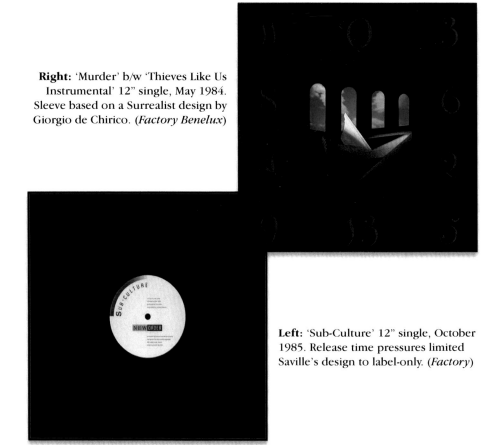

Right: 'Murder' b/w 'Thieves Like Us Instrumental' 12" single, May 1984. Sleeve based on a Surrealist design by Giorgio de Chirico. (*Factory Benelux*)

Left: 'Sub-Culture' 12" single, October 1985. Release time pressures limited Saville's design to label-only. (*Factory*)

New Order
Brotherhood
Fact 150c

Left: *Brotherhood* album, Sep 1986. Sheets of titanium zinc were photographed by Trevor Key for the sleeve. Tape, LP, and CD shown. (*Factory*)

Left: 'The Perfect Kiss' 12" single, May 1985. Saville could finally realise a 'reflective glamour' mirrored sleeve for the forthcoming *Low-life* reissue campaign. (*Factory*)

Right: 'Shell-Shock' single, March 1986. One of New Order's songs chosen for inclusion on the *Pretty In Pink* movie soundtrack. 7" and 12" are shown. (*Factory*)

shellshock

Left: Bernard Sumner, 27 Aug 1984, Heaven Ultradisco, London. *(Photo by Peter Petrou)*

Right: Gillian Gilbert, 19 Apr 1985, Leisure Centre, Macclesfield UK. *(Photo by Glenn Bennett)*

Left: Gillian Gilbert and Bernard Sumner, 19 Apr 1985, Leisure Centre, Macclesfield UK. *(Photo by Glenn Bennett)*

Right: Bernard Sumner and Peter Hook, 19 Apr 1985, Leisure Centre, Macclesfield UK. (*Photo by Glenn Bennett*)

Left: Gillian Gilbert, 10 Jun 1987, The Haçienda, Manchester UK. (*Photo by Paul Das*)

Right: Stephen Morris. 19 Apr 1985, Leisure Centre, Macclesfield UK. (*Photo by Glenn Bennett*)

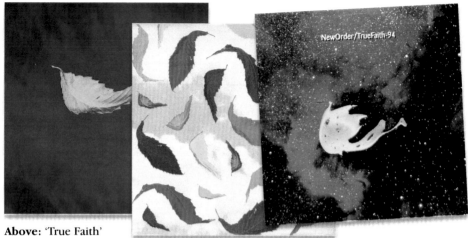

Above: 'True Faith' b/w '1963' 12" single in its various incarnations: original July 1987, remix September 1987 (both *Factory*) and 'TrueFaith-94' Nov 1994. (*London*)

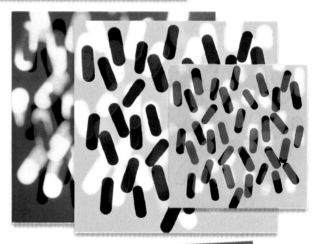

Right: 'Fine Time' b/w 'Don't Do It', Nov 1988. Dichromat sleeve by Key and Saville, after a picture by Richard Bernstein. 12", remix 12" and 7" shown. (*Factory*)

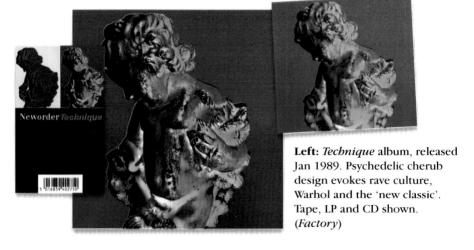

Left: *Technique* album, released Jan 1989. Psychedelic cherub design evokes rave culture, Warhol and the 'new classic'. Tape, LP and CD shown. (*Factory*)

Right: 'Round & Round' b/w 'Best & Marsh', Feb 1989. 'Little Louis' sleeve. 12", DJ 12", 7" and remix 12" shown. (*Factory*)

Left: 'World In Motion' singles. New Order's last release on Factory. 2004 CDS (*London*) and original remix 12" (*Factory*) shown.

Right: *Republic* album, released May 1993. The sleeve reflects the dichotomies of Saville's new Californian home. LP, CD (Ltd Ed) and tape are shown. (*London*)

Left: 'Regret' single, Apr 1993. Saville presenting a Hollywood aesthetic. 12" and tape are shown. (*London*)

Right: 'Nineteen63' single, Jan 1995. 'True Faith''s brilliant B-side finally given its own headline. 12" and (Ltd Ed) CDS shown. (*London*)

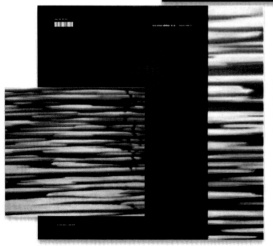

Left: Recorded in 1982, the 22-minute instrumental 'Video 5-8-6' was finally issued in its entirety on this eclectic release, September 1997. CDS and 12" are shown. (*Touch*)

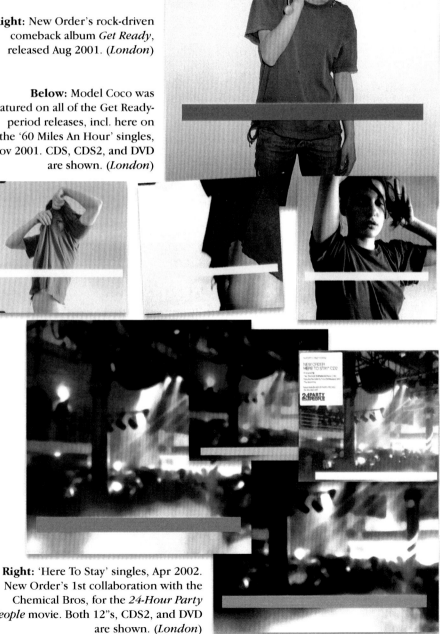

Right: New Order's rock-driven comeback album *Get Ready*, released Aug 2001. (*London*)

Below: Model Coco was featured on all of the Get Ready-period releases, incl. here on the '60 Miles An Hour' singles, Nov 2001. CDS, CDS2, and DVD are shown. (*London*)

Right: 'Here To Stay' singles, Apr 2002. New Order's 1st collaboration with the Chemical Bros, for the *24-Hour Party People* movie. Both 12"s, CDS2, and DVD are shown. (*London*)

No

Left: *Waiting For The Sirens' Call* album, released March 2005. Recorded with Phil Cunningham but without Gillian Gilbert. (*London*)

Right: 'Jetstream' singles, May 2005. Featuring Ana Matronic, and many, many remixes. CDS1, CDS2, and 12" are shown. (*London*)

Above: 'Waiting For The Sirens' Call' single, issued as 3x7"s (b/w remixes of older songs) + CDS. A limited-edition binder could be ordered from the label, October 2005. (*London*)

Right: *Lost Sirens* album, recorded during the WFTSC sessions, was eventually released in January 2013, after Peter Hook had left the band. (*Rhino*)

NewOrder Lost Sirens

Left: *Music Complete* album (+ companion *Complete Music* remix album), Sepember 2015 / May 2016. Feat. Gillian's return, Bernard, Stephen, Phil and Tom Chapman. (*Mute*)

new order. be a rebel

[REMIXES PART ONE]

new order. be a rebel

new order. be a rebel

[REMIXED]

new order.

Right: 'Be A Rebel' singles, September 2020. Released during the Covid pandemic, with many excellent remixes. Various digital editions and the 2nd 12" are shown. (*Mute*)

Left: Bernard Sumner and Peter Hook, 10 Nov 2005, Carling Academy, Brixton UK. (*Photo by Kevin Boyle*)

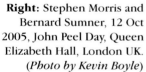

Right: Stephen Morris and Bernard Sumner, 12 Oct 2005, John Peel Day, Queen Elizabeth Hall, London UK. (*Photo by Kevin Boyle*)

Right: Phil Cunningham on 6 November 2021 at the O2 in London.

Left: Gillian Gilbert, 18 Jul 2019 at the Lloyds Amphitheatre, Bristol, UK. (*Photo by Kevin Boyle*)

Right: Tom Chapman 6 November 2021 at the O2 in London.

Above: Andy Robinson (Band Manager), Gillian Gilbert, the author, Stephen Morris, and Anna Petrou (author's partner), 3 Mar 2012, Brisbane AU. (*Photo by Dennis Remmer*)

Right: Mark Reeder – musician, producer, label founder, remixer, collaborator, and foreword author herein. (*Photo by Martyn Goodacre*)

parallel universe, I can see *Republic* as a tighter nine-track LP, with three great singles issued, each with a *proper* B-side and remixes – 'Regret' (single 1 b/w 'Chemical' plus mixes), 'World' (single 2 b/w 'Vicious Circle' plus mixes), 'Ruined In A Day', 'Spooky', 'Everyone Everywhere', 'Young Offender' (single 3 b/w 'Times Change' plus mixes), 'Liar', 'Special' and 'Avalanche'.

World (The Price Of Love) (Single, 1993)
Personnel: Bernard Sumner, Peter Hook, Stephen Morris, Gillian Gilbert
Record label: London Records
Original UK release date: 23 August 1993
Chart position: UK: 13
Refer to other details per *Republic* album and 'World' song entry above.

Spooky (Single, 1993)
Personnel: Bernard Sumner, Peter Hook, Stephen Morris, Gillian Gilbert
Record label: London Records
Original UK release date: 6 December 1993
Chart position: UK: 22
Refer to other details per *Republic* album and 'Spooky' song entry above.

TrueFaith-94 (Single, 1994)
Personnel: Bernard Sumner, Peter Hook, Stephen Morris, Gillian Gilbert
Record label: London Records
Original UK release date: 7 November 1994
Chart position: UK: 9
Refer to other details per original 'True Faith' single release above.

Nineteen63 (Single, 1995)
Personnel: Bernard Sumner, Peter Hook, Stephen Morris, Gillian Gilbert
Record label: London Records
Original UK release date: 9 January 1995
Chart position: UK: 21
Refer to '1963' details per original 'True Faith' single release above.

BlueMonday-95 (Single, 1995)
Personnel: Bernard Sumner, Peter Hook, Stephen Morris, Gillian Gilbert
Record label: London Records
Original UK release date: 26 July 1995
Chart position: UK: 17
Refer to other details per original 'Blue Monday' single release above.

Video 5-8-6 (Single, 1997)
Personnel: Bernard Sumner, Peter Hook, Stephen Morris, Gillian Gilbert
Record label: Touch

Original UK release date: 15 September 1997
Chart position: UK: 81
Refer to other details per the 'Video 5-6-8' recording above.

Keep It Coming: Get Ready +

With *Republic* seemingly the band's closing statement, completed under such duress after the Factory collapse, nightmares at The Haçienda, and band harmony at a low point, the mid-1990s was – on the one hand – a dark time for fans of the band, but on the other hand (and in hindsight), a good opportunity to let go of it all for a while. Electronic's *Raise The Pressure*, Monaco's *Music For Pleasure* and The Other Two's *Super Highways* are separately excellent albums.

London Records got some return on their investment by taking the easy path of (poorly-executed) compilations and (highly variable) remixes, and enough air eventually cleared to give Rob Gretton (having himself kept busy with his excellent Robs Records label) the opportunity to regroup the band in 1998: an admirable exclamation mark on his inestimable role in the story, which so tragically ended the following year. With only four (reportedly awesome) New Order gigs performed in 1998, I'm still sore (having travelled to Europe and the UK that year) that the Phoenix Festival was cancelled. It would've been my first New Order live gig (having inexplicably missed their *Brotherhood* tour down under in 1987). This wrong would eventually be righted at The Big Day Out, Gold Coast, in 2002 (inclusive of Viking investiture – thanks, team).

Get Ready was a welcome comeback that – by the late-1990s – I never thought would eventuate. It was a shift away from electronic dance, towards a more *mature* (largely guitar-based) formula that – though cohesive across the album – wasn't entirely to my liking. The band – for so long powered by self-belief, style-setting uniqueness, a seemingly unbreakable bond between the four original members, their situationist label, one top-class manager and their city – were now operating in a different form, for (and with) different people.

Recording for The Beach (Motion Picture Soundtrack) (2000)

Personnel: Bernard Sumner, Peter Hook, Stephen Morris, Gillian Gilbert
Recorded October-November 1999 at Real World Studios, Box, UK
Producers: New Order, Rollo
Record label: London Records
Original UK release date: 21 February 2000

'Brutal' (Sumner, Hook, Morris, Gilbert)

The stand-alone 'Brutal' sessions occurred in late 1999, sometime before the *Get Ready* sessions, though I'm told they also yielded an early version of '60 Miles An Hour' (with the imaginative working title 'The Beach'). The sessions afforded the band (at this time still the original four, but mainly Bernard, Peter and Stephen, with Phil Cunningham not yet on the scene) a chance to test the waters. Based on various peoples' books and interviews, the band weren't overly enthused with Rollo's production, let alone that the track was barely noticeable in the movie scene in which it was used.

So, what of it? To these ears, 'Brutal''s sound is unlike any of the rockier songs produced by New Order to-date, including tracks like 'Run', 'Way

Of Life', 'Love Vigilantes', 'Dreams Never End' or 'Ceremony'. It's an early indication of the palette to come over the next two albums, bordering on straight blues-rock with as much swagger as can be affected. It's particularly there in the drum production and choice of guitar effects: an unimaginative path that so many others had been on before. On a positive note, I really like the *eastern* string motifs, Pauline Taylor's backing vocals and Bernard's 'It's alright' assurances.

All things aside, 'Brutal' was a new recording from New Order: something most people had given up on. It was a glimmer of hope for more to come, and I figured at the time, I'd take it and see what happens.

Crystal (Single, 2001)
Personnel: Bernard Sumner, Peter Hook, Stephen Morris
Record label: London Records
Original UK release date: 13 August 2001
Chart position: UK: 8
Refer to other details per *Get Ready* album and 'Crystal' song entry below.

'Behind Closed Doors' (Sumner, Hook, Morris, Gilbert)
Producers: New Order, Arthur Baker
Being Arthur Baker's only production contribution of the period (except for the 2002 'Confusion' remixes), 'Behind Closed Doors' sounds quite removed from the context of 'Crystal' and *Get Ready*. It has a distinctive passive-aggressive tone, with Bernard's sinister whispers touching on domestic violence, lack of parental responsibility, not coping without drugs, and his slightly deranged 'Open up your eye' line – all placed alongside the near-hush of Hooky's bass, Morris' agitated snare/hi-hat patterns, reverbed wind chimes and the minimal piano and organ notes. 'Behind Closed Doors' really does sound like those very late hours when certain neighbourhood sounds leave you unsettled. Small wonder then that when the song shifts to a more-robust optimistic frame, Bernard's thoughts turn elsewhere, including (of all things) The Coors!

Some quality Baker beats and industrial sequencing close what's a very decent song; a track that – partnering, as it did, the incredible 'Crystal' – value-added to one of New Order's finest singles. Also notable was its unexpected inclusion in the live set for the Manchester International Festival in 2017.

Get Ready (Album, 2001)
Personnel: Bernard Sumner, Peter Hook, Stephen Morris, Gillian Gilbert
Recorded January-May 2000 at Real World Studios, Box, UK; Sarm Hook End, Reading, UK; Rockfield Studios, Monmouth, Wales
Producers: Various (See track details)
Record label: London Records
Original UK release date: 27 August 2001
Chart position: UK: 6

'Crystal' (Sumner, Hook, Morris, Gilbert)
Producer: Steve Osborne

What a cracking song this is, and a stunning comeback for New Order: for which we have Mark Reeder much to thank. 'Crystal' fizzles and sparks with real energy. The album version has a thrilling buildup, combining the opening bars of slightly distorted piano (with their unusual cycle and subtle volume fluctuation), emotive atmospheric synths and Dawn Zee's wonderful vocals. Dawn is an inspired choice, and with every collaboration, she has done with New Order, she's totally nailed the brief.

The sonic palette for 'Crystal' is completely different to *Republic*, particularly in the percussion – with a more acoustic-sounding performance that suits the track much better than would an electronic kit. And though I've spent more time in clubs than garages over the years, the jet-blast of guitars in 'Crystal' is a wondrous thing, with its mid-range assault well-balanced by both synth bass and Hooky's top-notch performance. Other terrific details include the locust-like spray of sound that backs the 'I don't know what to say' line, the brassy flare that emphasises the 'Here comes love' line, and the 'Keep it coming' lines that alternate between Bernard and Dawn. Finally, there's Crystal's signature piano break which loops around itself beautifully. It's one of my favourite New Order riffs ever, leading us into yet another break which runs the underlying gravelly keyboard textures through a panning phaser effect, before the track recombines and enters a long atmospheric fade-out. Stunning.

A quick comment on the design. I originally thought the artwork for the Japanese 'Crystal' CD-single – based as it was on the *3 16* DVD and Peter Saville's Waste Paintings of the same period – was going to be the design framework for the whole *Get Ready* campaign. Still, there's nothing wrong with the actual campaign using the various photographs of model Coco plus the neutral colour bands: certainly better than the *Republic*-era designs. I also must mention the video clip, which is terrific. I love the light-wall effect, and the younglings (supposedly the band) behind the juggernaut that is 'Crystal'. Still, The Killers tick the requisite look boxes, and pull off all the necessary moves. No dad-dancing here.

'Crystal' is very well-served by its remixes: some of the best from the London period. The 'Bedrock' mixes eschew some of the highlights I mentioned above, including the piano riffs, Dawn Zee's vocals, Hooky's performance etc.., but Digweed and Muir's alternative progressive house sequencing really rolls along, building and weaving with an incessancy that's very addictive. The 'John Creamer & Stephane K Remix' is less successful. By far the best of the bunch, in my opinion is the 'Lee Coombs Remix' – one of my all-time favourite New Order remixes, with its mainline sequencing driving forward with a real sense of propulsion. The core drum pattern pops and twitches, with flares of distortion and a low-end synth drone that adds breadth. Coombs takes his time layering the mix in true progressive house style, and honours all the important elements – particularly his use of the signature piano loop to rebuild the track from its midway breakdown. But rather than using it sparingly, it's blissfully sustained. Also worth mentioning are the original Mark Reeder/Corvin Dalek versions of 'Crystal', which are very good, with a harder techno edge and an earlier take of Bernard's vocal that sounds quite raw.

The band and Steve Osbourne are to be wholeheartedly congratulated on a stunning recording: one of New Order's all-time greats.

'60 Miles An Hour' (Sumner, Hook, Morris, Gilbert)
Producer: Steve Osborne
Driving well within the posted speed limits, our newly-minted rock gods keep it real and deliver a rollicking tune. '60 Miles An Hour' brought a grin to my face in 2001, and to this day, it still gets two thumbs up. The breadth and depth in Steve Osborne's production is excellent, with certain details giving the guitars room to shine through – including the deep synth tone that underpins the first verse, the subtle descending motif that (I think) Hooky adds to the second verse, and most of all, the storming instrumental break that really cuts through with keyboards and crashing cymbals, and leads into the final chorus with a phased and distorted guitar. Great stuff! Bernard gives it his all, standing by our side and being there when we want him to (Thanks, mate), but I'll politely decline his offer – not doubting his sailing skills – to cross some stormy sea to worship pagan idols.

The 'Supermen Lovers Remix' is not great, to be honest. It's quirky and different to be sure, but just too twee for me – large parts of the mix sounding like the background theme to an 8-bit Atari game, abruptly cut into some disco funk that unfortunately builds up and falls away too quickly. I'm also not sure about the video clip, particularly in the way the music frequently drops into the background for the sake of the on-screen panto-bear-wielding-mixtape-drives-himself-and-hitchhiker-into-a-tree silliness.

'Turn My Way' (Sumner, Hook, Morris, Gilbert)
Producer: Steve Osborne
Trigger warning: if you like the Smashing Pumpkins, I apologise profusely for the following. The early-to-mid-1990s was our post-Uni share-house period, and circa 1995 we enjoyed part of our rent being covered by a Dutch exchange student, who I remember for three main reasons: 1) True to his tribe, he and his mate cycled everywhere on some very uncool-looking bicycles they bought on the cheap; 2) His idea of dressing up for a Halloween party was to go as a self-described *fat Dutchman* (i.e., stuff a pillow under his orange t-shirt and wear clogs); 3) He persistently tried to turn me on to the Smashing Pumpkins. Try as I might, I just never clicked with the Pumpkins, bar one song: '1979', which is terrific. Fair enough that they were influenced by New Order, The Cure, Bauhaus etc., but their translation of these influences got lost on me via lengthy concept albums of sprawling styles and Corgan's nasally voice.

Whenever my flatmate pointed to his copy of *Melon*-whatever, I'd point to my *Technique* poster on the wall, and we'd agree to disagree.

Fast-forward five years, and when I heard that Billy Corgan was to be a guest on New Order's comeback album, I prayed that this appearance was to be limited to a guitar overdub. Some reports even suggested that his was to be a permanent joining of the band to replace Gillian, and I shuddered at the thought of our former Dutch exchange student chuckling over his stein of Oranjeboom.

It's an interesting phenomenon (post-millennium guest appearances on New Order albums – something which had previously never occurred), with Billy Corgan, Bobby Gillespie, Ana Matronic, La Roux, Iggy Pop and Brandon Flowers all getting a golden ticket. It's an eclectic mix of collaborators, and seems part of the band's concerted effort to be unlike they were before – i.e., break out of their previously impenetrable inner circle. It may also be in keeping with a prevailing trend in pop music these days: success by association.

To be brutal, perhaps it's Steve Osborne's mix, but Corgan's vocal just doesn't gel with Sumner's, and after a while, the distortion and reverse echo in the track's lead guitars just irritate. The percussion is basic, and though the sentiment of being free, true and individual is ace, some of the lyrics are pretty naff (e.g., not wanting to own keys or wash cars (repeat), the wheels of chance, and 'The sky will not be grey'). The song is saved by the chorus vocal melody, Hooky's bass and the synths on the intro and breaks.

'Vicious Streak' (Sumner, Hook, Morris, Gilbert)
Producer: Steve Osborne
I found myself listening to 'Vicious Streak' on a recent evening flight home, just as dusk's purples and oranges diffused the darkening sky. I hit play as we taxied to the end of the runway, and the song's subtle intro synths bled into Hooky's isolated bass riff. The plane accelerated to takeoff just as the song's strings opened into the uplifting guitar notes and Bernard's verse. That my partner kept hanging on (to me, that is, she's a nervous flyer), seemed to fit perfectly. As a soundtrack to an evening flight, you can do a lot worse than this.

'Vicious Streak' has great space – an overall quietness in the clipped and minimal percussion, the gorgeous strings, the reverbed piano and synth riffs and the expressive bass. There is restraint applied, which for me, marks the song as one of the real underrated highlights on *Get Ready*, and restraint is always harder to pull off than a wall of sound. Full marks to Steve Osborne. There's rocking-out to be had elsewhere on the album, to be sure, but 'Vicious Streak' is one of those New Order songs where subtlety reigns and there's real care evident. It's a lovely tune.

'Primitive Notion' (Sumner, Hook, Morris, Gilbert)
Producer: Steve Osborne
Sonically, this track is a blast, with the drum performance being one of the strongest on *Get Ready*. Seriously, there are extraordinary sections in 'Primitive

Notion' where the wonderfully clattering snare-loop pattern is bludgeoned with a bull-in-a-china-shop rush of cymbals. I already hold Stephen Morris in the highest esteem as one of the all-time great drummers/programmers, but productions like this are next-level. Hooky's excellent bass riff, wraps around the drum pattern like a snake around a branch, and there are just enough synth elements to mark the music as classic New Order.

But – and I can't help but look right at Bernard with my *critical smile* – it's the lyrics and the thin-sounding vocal that hold this song back from glory. Lyrically, the song suffers the same fate as many of the later-period Electronic productions, in that it sounds like Bernard has tried too hard and turns out clangers like 'Drink this magic potion … 'til the day that you, day that you die' and 'Not even a zoo would impound you'. And yet, Sumner redeems himself with a quality soaring chorus, sung with feeling rather than the in-store announcement delivery of 'Primitive Notion''s verses and bridges.

Had the band sent Bernard home for some minor rewrites, and even brought Dawn Zee in for some backing vocals, perhaps 'Primitive Notion' could've ended up as the true nugget that its potential showed.

'Slow Jam' (Sumner, Hook, Morris, Gilbert)
Producer: Steve Osborne

I can sense an expectation (on your part) of a hatchet job (on my part) on the next few tracks, but I may surprise you. In the lead-up to the album's release, I'd gotten myself ready for an album of genius proportions made up of unimaginably brilliant electronic and alternative rock originals, blowing my mind with the inventiveness of it all, justifying eight years of side projects to clear the air, and reinstating the band at the pointy end of the creative pyramid. Funnily enough, that didn't eventuate, and I convinced myself that it was the motley crew of producers and collaborators (riding on New Order's coattails) that were holding them back from greatness. It occurs to me now that one of my main blockages was that I'd never expected this group of pioneers – these self-taught champions of the synth, the abstract, the alternative and the left-field – to ever use words like 'jam', 'rock', 'shack', 'shake' or 'wild' in their song titles, let alone be caught singing about beer, getting high and the tribulations of Joe, Jack and Jehovah. They seemed to be straying into territory where a song called 'Railroad Whisky Blues' was a distinct possibility, and the producers were urging them on.

I've always really enjoyed 'Slow Jam', precisely for what its stupid name suggests: a head-nodding chug of a track with a cool groove. Bernard's enthusiasm and sentiment in lyrics like, 'I don't want the world to change/I like the way it is/To hit and not to miss/I can't get enough of this', really resonates, and counters the dodgy beer/sea/sick/arithmetic verse lines. But I'm willing to let them pass compared with similar turns in 'Primitive Notion' or 'Rock The Shack', probably because I'm enjoying his lower-than-usual singing register in the verses.

Here in Australia, we were treated to the song being used on a successful Ford television ad, resulting in 'Slow Jam' being issued locally as a rare promo CD and actually considered for release as the album's third single.

'Rock The Shack' (Sumner, Hook, Morris, Gilbert)
Producer: New Order, Flood

I freely admit, dear reader, to several reviews herein of the less-than-exuberant kind. This is unpleasant territory for the hard-core fan, and it rankles to cast aspersions on anything that these good people have worked hard to write, perform, record and produce, particularly as they've been variously at it for 45 years since Joy Division's 1978 debut *An Ideal For Living*. And yet, it's right to call them out when they occasionally put a fart to vinyl, because there is no success without failure. New Order are precisely the wonderful thing that they are because we can count on them to cough up the (very) occasional fur ball, as is the case here. Parking one of New Order's worst song titles for a moment, let's ride along and see what transpires.

00:00-00:20: Intro. 20 seconds of not-bad. Chunky rock beats with a nice little slip pattern, and guitars that hark back more than just a little to the band's Joy Division roots. I enjoyed these first 20 seconds very much. 00:20-00:50: first verse. Okay so far. Something bad sure happened in alt-Berlin: I wonder what it was? Nevertheless, we're with you, mate – this song's clearly a cry for support, so we've got your back (and your armour)! Before I continue, is there a proper term for the vocal style so prevalent in this track – you know, the one that ends in a nasal sneer/whine? In the absence of a proper adjective, I'm going to call it *swineing*, and it seems that our newly-minted rock pigs have picked up this highly irritating condition from their peers: Bobby Gillespie being particularly adept, but I digress. 00:50-01:05: first chorus. Oh, so the song's not a cry for help, it's an adrenaline-pumped affirmation and you believe in everything. Hang on, what was that? A baby crying? An old man dying? 01:05-01:20: what the f#%k, what the f#%k, what the f#%k, what the f##%%k? Sing that in your best swining voice: it works better than the actual lyric. Hands down, the previous half-minute of 'Rock The Shack' may be the most god-awful 30 seconds ever recorded by New Order. 01:20-01:33: instrumental respite. I enjoyed these 13 seconds tremendously; they were terrific. 01:33-02:08: second verse. I now have absolutely no idea what's going on. Lots of swining and irritable-guitar syndrome, and something from Gillespie about walking 100,000 miles and his head lying on his beating breast. What? A single mote of interest: the deadpan harmony right at the end of the verse sounds like something Brian Eno would do. 02:08-02:23: second chorus. Actually fine. The best set of lyrics in the song. 02:23-02:38: 'Get it right' (repeat). A hugely better name for the song right there, and we welcome back Bernard's whoops of joy, which have been missing in action for some time. 02:38-03:20: headache-inducing instrumental break. All guitar FX pedals dialled up to 11. 03:20-

03:50: third chorus. 10,000 years ago what? Who is crawling exactly? Jack? So much to answer for, mainly because you rhyme with shack. 'It's time to get up'… and press fast-forward. 03:50-04:12: never gotten this far. What's it like?

'Someone Like You' (Sumner, Hook, Morris, Gilbert)
Producer: Steve Osborne

Finally, a dance track. It's been so long! – which is not to say that 'Crystal', '60 Miles An Hour' and 'Vicious Streak' aren't terrific tracks. But so far on *Get Ready*, the New Order genre-ometer has been fixed firmly on rock, whereas historically, a twitchy gauge would be a truer visualisation of the band's biorhythms. It's always been this freestyle switching between electronic, dance and rock, that's been – for me anyway – the DNA of a truly great New Order album. I don't believe a pure rock album (or indeed a pure electronic album) is what our favourite band is about, and I was getting worried on my first run through *Get Ready* that something had gone terribly wrong. So, 'Someone Like You' – though not in the rarefied air of the band's finest dance tunes – is a gem, and it came along just at the right time (i.e., immediately after some song about shack-rocking).

'Someone Like You' brought some balance to the album, and was a decent choice as a third single, albeit only on vinyl, which for 2001 seemed an odd call given that A): It was a really strong song, had some decent remixes, and had it enjoyed a release campaign across all formats (with a promo clip), might well have seen some chart success; and B) vinyl sales were descending to their lowest ebb. Sometimes I find the business' handling of the New Order catalogue – from single choices to format to inclusions/exclusions etc. – a little perplexing.

The track grabs your attention right away, with its reverbs and jittery loops panning across the stereo in an extended intro that also features some great bass duality, with Hooky following the synth bass line, driving us towards the first verse. The singing here is a big improvement (performance-wise and lyrically) over many others on *Get Ready*, and I reckon Bernard genuinely meant it when he sang, 'We're having the time of our lives'!

The remixes were a mixed bag, with some standing the test of time better than others, and none surpassing the original. 'Futureshock's Vocal Remix' with its *scratchier* backbone loop and multilayered bottom-end, is a fine slice of tech house, making good use of Dawn Zee's sampled backing vocals and some mashing up of Bernard's lyrics, to great effect. Gabriel and Dresden's 'Voco-tech Dub' is interesting with its vocoder effects and additional riffs, but it's less recognisable as 'Someone Like You' than their '911 Vocal Mix' – noted respectfully on the sleeve as being recorded on '...Sept 11th 2001 and is dedicated to the men, women and children who senselessly lost their lives that day'. Neither 'James Holden's Heavy Dub' nor the 'Funk D'Void Remix' as featured on the secondary 12", bear much resemblance to 'Someone Like You', and the record can only tenuously be called a New Order release.

'Close Range' (Sumner, Hook, Morris, Gilbert)
Producer: Steve Osborne
The real sweet spot of New Order's output during this period was Bernard's songwriting shift towards positive identity, life perspective and a more-thoughtful social observation. You can feel it right across the post-2000 albums. The strength of 'Close Range' lies in Bernard's lyrics, with his message of getting back on your feet from a very dark place. Dawn Zee provides a lovely backing vocal, further reinforcing my opinion that in Dawn, the band found the perfect foil for Bernard.

Musically, 'Close Range' starts with a driving groove and phased loops that offer proper bottom-end missing elsewhere across the album. The percussion palette is excellent, the crisp piano stabs are a nod to earlier (loved-up) times, and unlike 'Rock The Shack', the guitars are well-balanced. Hooky is given room to flourish on the instrumental close, amongst nicely-produced ambience, flares of electronic signal and some lovely chiming guitar. Solid tune. Solid message. I need to play it more. I need to pull myself together, man.

'Run Wild' (Sumner, Hook, Morris, Gilbert)
Producers: Steve Osborne, Bernard Sumner
Oh, the sheer blandness in naming a song 'Run Wild'. In his autobiography, Hooky says, 'We used to take our titles from novels and arty foreign films and the *Sunday Times*. The more abstract, the better'. Must've been some Mills & Boon on Real World's coffee table that day!

And yet, there is much to admire in 'Run Wild'. The strings are properly gorgeous, and Sumner sings this beautifully, as does Dawn Zee. It's a very sweet song, and I don't think I've ever heard Bernard be more protective or in-admiration:

You're the kind of person that I always wanted to be with
Well, you're really cool
And you always say the right things to me
But now I'll tell you something
For my heart beats for you deep inside
You'll never be a burden
And my love for you will never die

Nice. I actually prefer Steve Osbourne's 'Original Mix', which sounds smoother than the album version, with its additional ambiences and electronic tones. Zee's vocals are more prominent in the mix, and there's a different reverb used on the acoustic guitar. Another excellent version is the iTunes Originals recording from 2007.

Setting aside the crystalline brilliance of its opener, I've concluded that – a couple of truly pants tracks aside – *Get Ready* is a very solid album, and is the clear break from the band's past that needed to occur. And as 'Run Wild' attests, 'Good times around the corner' were still to be had.

60 Miles An Hour (Single, 2001)
Personnel: Bernard Sumner, Peter Hook, Stephen Morris
Record label: London Records
Original UK release date: 19 November 2001
Chart position: UK: 29
Refer to other details per *Get Ready* album and '60 Miles An Hour' song entry above.

'Sabotage' (Sumner, Hook, Morris, Gilbert)
Producer: Steve Osborne
Another extremely worthwhile B-side, and very nearly album worthy. In fact, had the decision been mine, I think 'Sabotage' would've sat quite neatly on *Get Ready*, offering a sonic difference to the album's main threads of rock.

Aside from the verses – where I find Bernard's need to rhyme nearly every line (stay, play, anyway, etc.) a bit clunky – 'Sabotage' is really enjoyable. I love the subdued electronic intro and clear separation, which then crashes into a powerful, excellent chorus and a change to superior lyrics and performance from Bernard. Also particularly memorable is the instrumental break leading into the chorus reprisals, featuring (I think) Dawn Zee's emotive backing vocals and a terrific phased synth melody that follows the lead guitar, reminding me of Bowie's 'Ashes To Ashes'.

I look forward to the inclusion of 'Sabotage' on a future deluxe reissue of *Get Ready*, since it deserves – along with all the other B-sides of the period – to be brought back into the fold.

Someone Like You (Single, 2001)
Personnel: Bernard Sumner, Peter Hook, Stephen Morris
Record label: London Records
Original UK release date: 17 December 2001
Refer to other details per *Get Ready* album and 'Someone Like You' song entry above.

Here To Stay (Single, 2002)
Personnel: Bernard Sumner, Peter Hook, Stephen Morris
Record label: London Records
Original UK release date: 15 April 2002
Chart position: UK: 15

'Here To Stay' (Sumner, Hook, Morris, Gilbert)
Recorded April-May 2001 at Pulse Studio, Dublin, Ireland; Real World Studios, Box, UK
Producers: New Order, The Chemical Brothers

24 Hour Party People: what a wonderful book and movie. A decade since those dark days of 1992 when Factory went under, it was terrific to see the resurgence in interest. Having published the original online Factory Discography across those years, I remember being inundated with information requests from magazine editors, members of Michael Winterbottom's production team, and various people and band members from the inner orbit of the label itself. A highlight was chatting with Anthony H. Wilson himself, who sent me a signed copy of his book of the movie: now a much-treasured item. RIP Tony. The Factory Records arc from post-punk pioneers to purveyors of Madchester is such an important and inspirational tale, and here it was, told with great humour and tongues firmly in cheek. John Simm – already one of my favourite actors – worked a treat in Bernard's shoes, and his onstage appearance in the *5 11*/Finsbury set was great fun. 'Where's Ralf Little' indeed!

Which brings me neatly to 'Here To Stay'. It seemed the perfect time for a perfect plan – have The Chemical Brothers (fellow Mancunians and reigning big-beats premiers) pay their dues to the band which was such an influence on them, and indeed pay back Bernard's appearance on their 'Out Of Control' release a few years earlier. 'Here To Stay' is excellent – techno riffs, an homage to the 'Blue Monday' choral sound, sparkling acid-like arpeggios, cavernous snares, and (my favourite part) the stripped-down verse sequences. It's herein where the track has real depth, because I find other parts of the track seem compressed into the mid-range: very typical of Chemical Brothers, and possibly why I've always preferred Orbital. Nevertheless, the Chems bring some wonderfully quirky programming to the party, with lots of slip beats, atypical patterns, riffs and a solid intake of New Order's signature guitar work. Remix-wise, I'm not super-excited by either the Felix Da Housecat or Scumfrog offerings: neither of which are a patch on the original. However, the 'Extended Instrumental' offers some alternate breakdowns, but generally follows the original in most respects, perhaps with greater mix clarity so you can better pick out the tones and sequences, and appreciate more what The Chemical Brothers brought to the table.

For me, 'Here To Stay' is on par with 'Shell-Shock' and 'Confusion', as a supreme collaboration-driven dance single in New Order's canon. But above all, it's the 'We're here to stay' affirmation from Bernard that brought the biggest smile to my face – ringing true of the band and the Factory label, both of which will stay firmly – 'Like a bright light on the horizon' – in the Manchester (and beyond) consciousness forever.

'Player In The League' (Sumner, Hook, Morris, Gilbert)
Recorded January-May 2000 at Real World Studios, Box, UK; Sarm Hook End, Reading, UK; Rockfield Studios, Monmouth, Wales
Producer: Steve Osborne
It was nice to get a bonus track on the 'Here To Stay' CD single with this handy leftover from the *Get Ready* sessions. 'Player In The League' has some decent

sections in it, but overall the song feels only partially successful. The opening loops sound very Depeche Mode circa *Songs Of Faith And Devotion*, and the 'Don't want nobody, don't need nobody' vocal bridge, with its unusual key and backwards-sounding synth tones, doesn't really work. In fact, the bridge feels quite disjointed from the melody and rhythm of its preceding verse and following chorus. The lyrics are heavy in cliche – i.e., cry/weep, star/outer space, shine/sky/ golden eye, yeah-yeah, etc.. Also, the guitar production is way too muddy, as there are some choice chords, flourishes and melodies desperate for clear air, but they can't cut through the thickly-applied distortion. My final complaint is that the drum programming is so bland and insipid as to be completely inconsequential – this from a band that has its own unique and peerless human drum machine! A poor effort.

Having said all that, I really like the latter half of the song, and particularly where Sumner repeats the 'You've got everything you need' line, and where Hooky nails a terrific bass line (the best part of the track) that blends into some expansive synth. I reckon there was a killer version of 'Player In The League' lurking in the band's consciousness that never realised its full potential and just needed a critical eye.

World In Motion (Single reissue, 2002)
Personnel: Bernard Sumner, Peter Hook, Stephen Morris, Gillian Gilbert
Record label: London Records
Original UK release date: 3 June 2002
Chart position: UK: 22
Refer to other details per the original 'World In Motion' single release above.

'Such A Good Thing' (Sumner, Hook, Morris, Gilbert)
Recorded January-May 2000 at Real World Studios, Box, UK; Sarm Hook End, Reading, UK; Rockfield Studios, Monmouth, Wales
Producers: New Order, Steve Osborne
What is this football connection? With members not themselves particularly vocal about their football leanings, the New Order brand seems firmly embedded in football culture – not the least of which is due to 'World In Motion', 'Best & Marsh', 'Such A Good Thing' *et al.* Of course, Rob Gretton was a dedicated Manchester City fan, and then there are the connections to Adidas through Bernard and Peter Saville. Furthermore, Bernard reckons the main demographic of New Order fandom to be football hooligans. Could this be true?

For me, part of the greatness of New Order is that their music is embraced by a wide spectrum of fans who appreciate that the band conduct themselves outside the main manufacturing lines of pop. Here was a band for whom you didn't have to narrow your focus – accessible and meaningful to clubbers and ravers, indie alternates, tech-heads, goths and more: all of which had New Order as a point of mutual admiration and connection. But what does this have to do with football? I think Bernard's pigeonholing of fans is oversimplified, and is probably his way of expressing that the band's music has crossover appeal. If anything, I reckon the vast majority of New Order fandom consists simply of thoughtful non-posers that know a good thing but don't have to shout about it, unless, of course, you're at a New Order gig (not unlike a football game) where passionate support at volume is part of the deal! If that makes us wide-eyed football hooligans, then so be it: in which case, this song seems fondly directed right at us.

'Such A Good Thing' – used as the BBC Radio *Five Live* 2002 World Cup theme – has an energetic, positive groove, driven in no small part by Morris and Hook at their propulsive best. It's a terrific production too, with Steve Osborne and the band finding that perfect combination of synth and rock, and the spot-on choice of harmony and vocal reverb effects. I even acknowledge that 'Such A Good Thing' is the one New Order track in which Bernard uses that unmentionable vocal style to great effect. It's a gem of a song, sadly missing from live sets, and too long out of print. Bring on the *Get Ready* Definitive Edition.

Recording for *War Child – Hope* compilation (2003)
Personnel: Bernard Sumner, Peter Hook, Stephen Morris, Phil Cunningham
Recorded in early-2003; studio details unknown: possibly the Morris Farm, Rainow, UK
Producer: New Order
Record label: London Records
Original UK release date: April 2003

'Vietnam' (Cliff)
This is an amazingly faithful rendition of Jimmy Cliff's original 1969 anti-war song, and a welcome addition to the canon of covers by New Order – this one being offered up to help the hugely important War Child initiative. Respect to New Order for contributing to the good cause – something they've done on more than a few occasions over the years: usually without fuss and fanfare, which makes such gestures even more admirable.

An absolute highlight is Dawn Zee's lovely backing vocal, which counters Bernard's one perfectly – both of which honour the original with style and class. Stephen Morris nails the dancehall groove, and Hooky gives a good melody. It's a fine production.

I can't help but slot 'Vietnam' alongside 'Love Vigilantes' (and even 'We All Stand') in a small-but-notable selection of war-themed songs from Bernard, Peter and co., who were children during the Vietnam War. And though Great Britain weren't direct combatants in the conflict, I suspect the evening news of the 1960s and 1970s would've had an impact on our thoughtful future artists – we know that the spectre of World War II remained in plain sight throughout Manchester for a long time. Bernard's youngest memories of a still-scarred

111

Salford, and the war efforts of his grandfather and great-grandfather, are well-documented in his autobiography.

The Peter Saville Show Soundtrack (Soundtrack, 2003)
Personnel: Bernard Sumner, Peter Hook, Stephen Morris, Phil Cunningham
Recorded May 2003 at the Morris Farm, Rainow, UK
Producer: New Order
Record label: London Records
Original UK release date: June 2003

'Soundtrack' (Hook, Morris, Cunningham)
February 2004: my one and only Manchester pilgrimage to date. I was in London on business, and had a Sunday to spare. So – doing what we Aussies do well: driving vast distances on a whim – I thought a short trip up the road to Manchester was in order. The *Peter Saville Show* was in the midst of its run at the Urbis museum, and for me the whole experience was near-religious. Standing there in that fine building, with 'Soundtrack' resonating softly around the internal spaces, staring at the original source materials Saville used to produce genius sleeves like *Unknown Pleasures*, 'True Faith', the *Factory Sampler* and so much more, was sublime. John 'Cerysmatic' Cooper (fellow original archivist of all things FAC) met me there, and our conversation was rich with completist detail! It was a great day, and I also recall from the same trip, enjoying a few pints in London with Ian White of The Wendys, and catching a Re:Order gig with some of The Vikings. It's difficult to remember what business was conducted on that trip!

The *Peter Saville Show Soundtrack* was a perfect piece of ambience written by Cunningham, Hook and Morris for the exhibition. It doesn't sound like a repurposed session outtake, nor does it sound like it needs editing down (*à la* the 17-minute version of 'Elegia'). This is bespoke gallery music for wondrous things! The track's stereo-sweeping airs and synths, feather-light arpeggiating bells, bird-like tones, understated bass melodies from Hook, gentle acoustic strums and effected electric riffs from Cunningham, simple but melancholy piano, Morris' cymbal rides, and barely discernible sampled phone messages from/to Peter Saville, all blend and blur in a beautiful series of *waves*, that you lose yourself in.

This is 30 minutes of New Order that stands apart from anything else in their 2000s repertoire, and it showed that they were still able to experiment, be obscure, be artful and release something outside the operational parameters. There's also a nice symmetry at work here, in that New Order are supplying the art for Peter Saville, rather than vice versa: a reverse gesture of thanks for Peter having been so instrumental in the band's creative DNA. Imagine that: having your own personal soundtrack recorded by New Order!

Other People Made That Call: Waiting For The Sirens' Call +

Amazing really. In 1995, at a time when the band seemed finished, who would've thought that ten years hence, New Order would be, A) back together; B) touring extensively; C) so productive as to have released a quality comeback album, a slew of interesting singles, B-sides and soundtrack work, let alone follow that with recording sessions that yielded not one but two albums' worth of material.

It's a shame that not long after the release of *Waiting For The Sirens' Call*, that very same band would fracture along a tectonic line of personalities, opening the earth beneath it to expose much heat and poisonous gas. Hooky would announce his departure from the band, and the next decade would be awash with the most appalling, public and acrimonious bile-letting – horrible for fans to watch, no matter which side of the trench your allegiances lay. Many veils were lifted whether we wanted them to be or not, many notions were shattered and many reputations were damaged forever. Unreleased recordings from the album sessions notwithstanding (and which would emerge in 2011 and 2013), only the short *Control Soundtrack* motifs remained to be recorded. So, in 2006/2007, it was very much the case that New Order's ship – crewed by the core trio which agreed to set out on a remarkable journey in the months following Ian Curtis' death in 1980 – had finally been scuttled at sea, and it was a very sad time.

Neither Bad Lieutenant nor (to a much greater extent) Freebass, would have any major impact, and I only bought *Total* and *Lost Sirens* because I'm a completist. All of which points to the fact that the 2012 reformation (inclusive of Gillian), the signing to Mute, the release of *Music Complete*, the reinvigorated and hugely innovative tours, and even that Hooky found success revisiting old glories with The Light, was just so bloody remarkable.

All in good time. In March 2005, we had a new album on our hands, and of all New Order's long-players, I personally feel *Waiting For The Sirens' Call* to be their most inconsistent. There are some fantastic tracks that soar into the stratosphere alongside the band's timeless classics, but equally, there are songs which are, frankly, embarrassing. The LP design is hard to beat as the worst ever in their history – with little regard for thematic consistency across the campaign – and I'm still unconvinced by London's choice and handling of the singles. All to be discussed.

2005 also saw the *Singles* compilation released – intended to collate and remaster a complete set of all 7" radio edits of the New Order singles from 'Ceremony' to 'Waiting For The Sirens' Call', plus 'Turn': except that it didn't. Specifically, album versions and other edits were used variously for 'Confusion', 'The Perfect Kiss', 'Bizarre Love Triangle', 'True Faith', 'Run', 'Spooky' and '1963'. And so, in 2015, *Singles* was remastered (again) and reissued the following year, this time also as a 4-LP edition, with a number of fixes so it properly represented the correct 7" radio edits, 'Turn', and additionally, 'I'll Stay With You'. The available digital release reflects the revised 2016 edition, which *is* now truly *the* definitive New Order singles compilation across the Factory and London Records eras.

But wait, there was more! The *Total (From Joy Division To New Order)* compilation issued in 2011, wasn't too bad an idea, particularly as it was specifically designed for newbs who may have had their interests piqued by the *Control* or *24-Hour Party People* movies, and for which a *best-bits-of-both* selection from Joy Division and New Order was handy. For the rest of us, it was simply yet another compilation, and we'd already hoarded *Best Of, Rest Of, Retro, International, Singles* and *The Best of Joy Division* in very-recent memory. The main issue I have with *Total*, is that I can't quite believe that Rhino Records abandoned – on a compilation supposedly offering a *total look* at Joy Division and New Order – tracks like 'Heart And Soul', 'Everything's Gone Green', 'Confusion', 'Shell-Shock' and 'Here To Stay', for 'Hellbent'! This was a cynical choice, purely designed to also get existing fans to buy the compilation because, you know, the song was *previously unreleased:* wow! But I'm being ungracious because with the real possibility of the *Lost Sirens* tracks being forever lost in a world of legal red tape (not unlike the Ark of the Covenant in *Raiders Of The Lost Ark*), giving us a previously-unreleased song was tantalising – although, 'I'll Stay With You' would've been a much better choice.

Krafty (Single, 2005)
Personnel: Bernard Sumner, Peter Hook, Stephen Morris, Phil Cunningham
Record label: London Records
Original UK release date: 7 March 2005
Chart position: UK: 8
Refer to other details per *Waiting For The Sirens' Call* album and 'Krafty' song entry below.

Waiting For The Sirens' Call (Album, 2005)
Personnel: Bernard Sumner, Peter Hook, Stephen Morris, Phil Cunningham
Recorded 2004 at the Morris Farm, Rainow, UK; Real World Studios, Box, UK; St Catherine's Court, Bath, UK
Producer: Various – see track details
Record label: London Records
Original UK release date: 28 March 2005
Chart position: UK: 5

'Who's Joe?' (Sumner, Hook, Morris, Cunningham)
Producers: New Order, Jim Spencer
As an opening track (which on every previous New Order album had been reserved for something magnificent), this – the first in Bernard Sumner's

soon-to-become-tedious *wotcha doin* trilogy – is pretty mediocre, and when followed by yet another mediocre *wotcha doin* track, had me checking if I'd actually bought the band's new album. Why didn't they lead with 'Krafty'? Anyway, welcome Joe – the latest member of Bernard's J Gang, joining Jack, Johnny and Jolene in his jet stream of people with issues. Due respect, though, for writing a song about the plight of the homeless.

The opening minute of 'Who's Joe?' promises drama, through a buildup of darker-toned strings, clanging keys, rumbling tones and finally some signature brash guitar and percussion, but then the verse falls completely flat. The MOR backing, lyrics and singing just lack colour and punch, and it's only when the 'I'll look for you' chorus kicks in that the song finds some heart. This pattern of ordinary-verse/quality-chorus is a frustrating formula across many of the tracks on *Get Ready, Waiting For The Sirens' Call* and *Lost Sirens*. Perhaps they were trying too hard, or perhaps having five producers on the album wasn't the winning idea that it seemed on paper.

Unlike all New Order albums to date, I'd have to slog through lacklustre tracks before the hoped-for *aha* moment would arrive, and – sadly, unlike all New Order albums to date – I wouldn't be able to pass the time by being transfixed by the graphic genius of the album artwork.

'Hey Now What You Doing' (Sumner, Hook, Morris, Cunningham)
Producers: New Order, Stephen Street
Part II in the *wotcha doin* series, and to be perfectly honest, I'm struggling because it's all starting to taste like chicken. The one admirable highlight in this song is Bernard's nicely-sung chorus and its interplay with Hooky's bass. The chorus vocal has quite a range (for Bernard), and there's a subtle harmony applied that works well.

Otherwise, the track is, at best, fine and safe and well-engineered; there are many layers of guitar, to which many effects have been applied (tremolo anyone?), and they're all recorded by a big name producer of British guitar music; 'closer' rhymes with 'shoulder holster'; and they think it sounds fresh (and not too New Ordery); and *God I'm bored*. This lies at the heart of my discontent with (a large percentage of) millennial New Order – that they were actively trying to *not* sound like themselves but ended up sounding like so many others.

Maybe I've just hit a wall and I need to push through, because some of my favourite New Order songs are close by.

'Waiting For The Sirens' Call' (Sumner, Hook, Morris, Cunningham)
Producers: New Order, Jim Spencer
Reading Peter, Bernard and Stephen's autobiographies (and specifically their recollections of this period), it's remarkable that another album ever saw the light of day, let alone two albums' worth of material. In any other reality, the

115

toxic combination of creative friction, alcoholism, rehab, family pressures, illness and egos etc., could've so easily killed any creative spark, stopping the *Sirens'* sessions in their tracks. And yet, here we have one of their finest songs ever – 'Waiting For The Sirens' Call': a stone-cold New Order classic.

There's a pattern to many (if not most) of my favourite New Order songs because they all feature human-condition themes from Bernard, an exquisite blend of electronics and rock (that they should never lose sight of, or feel indifference towards), melody (usually led from the front by the bass line), beautiful soaring strings, and driving percussion. It's no surprise that this is the one track from the album that consistently features in live sets to this day and was included in their 2007 iTunes Originals set. And given the band's state of affairs at the time, I thought its release as their final single was a great way to go out. The single campaign was quite unusual – a series of 3 x 7" records with a collectable sleeve to house them all (and each featuring terrific contemporary remixes of much older singles), a singular CD single with only two tracks (neither of them the best of the available remixes), and no London-issue 12".

The 'Rich Costey Mix' follows the album version structurally but sonically sits differently, being to my ears *lifted* and *clarified,* particularly around the non-electronic parts. I prefer the ambience and atmosphere of the album mix and 'Band Mix', the latter of which would've been a better choice for inclusion on *Singles*. The 'Jacknife Lee Remix' is serviceable, offering only a new main-synth sequence to pique interest, but suffering by shifting Hooky's excellent riffs way too distant in the mix, and substituting Morris' quality performance for some fairly featureless drum programming.

I'm not sure how the various remixes were commissioned at the time, because the best of all – the 'Planet Funk Remix' – should've been the primary mix on a dedicated London-issued 12" single, and yet, didn't appear until New State Recordings delivered their (somewhat oddly-collated) 2006 12x12" remix reissue program. By my reckoning, 'Waiting Of The Sirens' Call' was the first New Order single ever *not* to have a primary-label 12" – which for this band (a pioneer of the format) seems completely and utterly sacrilegious! This version is wonderful: one of the finest remixes in the entire New Order canon.

'Krafty' (Sumner, Hook, Morris, Cunningham)

Producers: New Order, John Leckie

For me, there's something sweet about a whole bunch of New Order's/ Bernard's songs this millennium, and it's largely to do with his *It'll-be-okay* stance – a subtle shift from his youthful concerns and abstractions, and seemingly directed at mentoring the younger generations (likely with his own kids front of mind, or perhaps in hindsight his younger self). These themes of turning things around, living life well, finding meaning, making sense of the world ('a beautiful place'), second chances and love being precious, prevail right across New Order's most recent albums (and indeed Bad Lieutenant's). These songs seem to come from a place where much water has passed under the bridge, many miles have been travelled and hard lessons have been learned that need to be passed on. Uncle Bernard has things to say (contrary to his 30-something attitude in *New Order Story*), and what better way to do it than to wrap it all in the fabric of finely-honed Mancunian dance rock.

'Krafty' was a solid opening single to herald the album, and should've been its lead track. I thought the titular nod to Kraftwerk was cool (and right on the money: the intro/verse percussion palette has that ultra-clipped electro vibe), and the hazy lens-flared freeway sleeve image is a great visual representation of the song's opening verse. I was also keyed up by the strength of interplay between Hooky's bass and the electronic bass sequences (always a signature of quality New Order). I also love the strings that rise behind the 'This is where I wanna be' line, though I would've enjoyed them if they were a bit louder in the mix or perhaps drawn-out and highlighted in one of the remixes (Andy Green's notwithstanding: see below). My only negative (and it's a minor one), is that I find the main choruses to be a bit of a mid-range sonic slush, in comparison with the more-spacious verses and breaks.

'Krafty' is served by a swathe of versions and remixes (15 if I have the count right, which frankly is a bit silly) – from The Glimmers, Phones, Andy Green, Eric Kupper, DJ Dan, Riton, Passengerz and Richard Morel – few of which are that great, to be honest, which emphasises my point about quality over quantity, as demonstrated during the Factory era. It's also notable that there seemed to be a period in the mid-2000s when the US label made a distinct effort to commission its own remixers – something which neither Factory US/Qwest before, nor Mute US since, have done. It makes you wonder if issue was taken with the UK label's choices at the time

The 'Glimmers 12" Extended Mix' is bland, and why it served as the primary London-issue 12" A-side is beyond me. Seven minutes of main vocals, looping the same bass line, and a few sonic motifs to add colour does not a great remix make. For my money, the real knockout Krafty remix is the 'DJ Dan Vocal Remix'. Though relegated to the US B-side (but, curiously, chosen for the *Best Remixes* digital compilation), it's by far the most innovative and interesting, with its driving electro bass line and disco patterns, new acid tweaks and arcing sequences, and depth of bass. I love the mid-track breakdown and soaring recovery: very atmospheric. 'DJ Dan's Dub Remix' (obscure and only available on the US Jetstream CD-single) takes the party into high-speed acid-meets-disco-meets-D&B territory. In my opinion, a stand-alone DJ Dan-mixes 12" similar to (but better than) the green-striped second 'Someone Like You' 12" would've been a terrific offering.

'I Told You So' (Sumner, Hook, Morris, Cunningham)
Producers: New Order, Jim Spencer
I'm way more content with New Order grooving in the dancehalls of reggae with 'I Told You So' than 'Ruined In A Day', though both still fall short of the band's best dub-style moment: their cover of 'Turn The Heater On'.

Nevertheless, 'I Told You So' is perfectly pleasing, from the moment it washes up on the shore to the sounds of radio static, through its rolling beats, electro toms, shout-outs, groovy percussive guitars, Bernard's calls to arms (to go out every night and 'get high down the old west side'), and some fat loops that underpin Dawn Zee's backing textures. The mixed-up-guy/no-good-girl together-in-a-crazy-world missives from Sumner are also endearing. There's a swagger to this song which I really enjoy, and the track has excellent beat-driven sonic breadth and layers of distinctive guitars that neither compete nor cancel out. I sense Phil Cunningham, in particular, having fun here.

'Stuart Price's Remix' (from the New State Recordings 12"), aka the 'Crazy World Mix' as it appeared later on *Lost Sirens* (although being on this album, it wasn't actually lost, was it), doesn't really add much. The reggae stylings have been forsaken, and the whole mix has a buzzing/droning pitch to it. You can better hear Hooky's performance in the mix, but it's only for a few bars. The mix builds up as it motors forward past the 3/4 mark, but it drives into the garage rather than the dancehall, which for me, is not what makes 'I Told You So' special. I think the sonic plane crash at the remix's end is entirely suitable.

Having started so poorly, the album is on a roll at the moment. 'Waiting For The Sirens' Call', 'Krafty', 'I Told You So' and 'Morning Night And Day' form a terrific quartet.

'Morning Night And Day' (Sumner, Hook, Morris, Cunningham)
Producers: New Order, Jim Spencer

This is a fantastically produced, beautifully balanced and brilliantly programmed piece of signature New Order electronic rock. Like 'Mr Disco', 'Vanishing Point', 'Age Of Consent' or 'Plastic', 'Morning Night And Day' is delicious because it was never released as a single and subject to remix interference (and possible corruption), but it's a missed trick for the very same reason. Put simply, I reckon this would've made a great single, but I'm glad that it wasn't!

Right from the outset, there's so much to love about the track, opening as it does with soaring arcs of synths, and choral tones that could be the start of something large and foreboding very nicely. These elemental tones quickly converge onto the main electronic bass sequence and pile-driving drums. Man, those snares and rolls: Morris in jackhammer mode! I'm not sure if it's Bernard or Phil, but the metallic guitar stabs that precede the verses, also work a treat.

Lyric-wise, it's on public record that Bernard has had many (many) nights on the tiles, and for someone so apparently reluctant to *share*, here he offers in no uncertain terms a private view, through Pernod-goggles, of his rock-star life – blameless though he claims to be.

The real genius of 'Morning Night And Day' lies in its second half. The instrumental break is so propulsive, due mainly to the classic combination of Hook and Morris. Peter is given the spotlight to solo with a driving bass line that seems to be racing alongside Morris, who has shifted his own performance/program into high gear. It all careens into a final chorus with guitars at full tilt, then drops down into some pure electronica with dirty bass and sparkling synth arpeggios, more rapid-fire drum rolls and guitar stabs, finally ending on some isolated cello. Just stunning.

'Dracula's Castle' (Sumner, Hook, Morris, Cunningham)
Producers: New Order and John Leckie

'Dracula's Castle' is one of my least-played New Order songs. Why? The name for a start. Horrible. I get that the song was partly recorded in a place Bernard found spooky, but I reckon the lyric 'We Once Stood High' might've suited much better as the song's title. The faux misery lyrics are pure cringe (with all the stay/leave, love's not real, on my knees, took my heart, running away, etc.). But the biggest problem I have is with the song's sonic palette, and in particular, the terrible preset-sounding keyboards. The acid squelches during the breaks are awful, as are the strikes/plucks and added keyboard melody at 4:30. I struggle to think of another instance where New Order have resorted to such an obvious set of sounds. Can we blame John Leckie?

The two saving graces are the opening and closing piano, and Peter Hook's bass. I can imagine a version of this song stripped back completely to its acoustic elements, and slowed right down into a heartfelt and melancholy piece befitting Bernard's heartache; free of the electronic layers that are (shockingly) so poorly produced. It's not often that one can suggest a New Order song be made better by removing the electronics!

'Jetstream' (Sumner, Hook, Morris, Cunningham)
Producers: Stuart Price, New Order

I'm a simple guy, and to this day, I struggle to grasp the nefarious goings-on in this song, so here's my considered interpretation. Bernard's involved. There's a woman involved, possibly two (at least one of which seems to be an air hostess), and maybe even three. I'm pretty sure there's a milkman involved. Perhaps Bernard is the milkman, whistling happily because he's finished his last run and is heading off on holiday tomorrow, probably to Majorca, probably on a budget airline, and probably to spend his hard-earned on lager and chips. 'It's only one more day', says his lady customer, who may or may not be his travelling companion. On board the freedom flight, the air hostess – per budget-airline reputation – is a light-dimming floozy. However, contrary to budget-airline policy, she fails in her sworn duty to charge huge excess-baggage fees. Our milkman's female friend – who may be his lady customer, or may be the hostess, or may be someone else altogether (I'm not sure because I think there may be a fourth woman waiting 'at the gate') – is dreamily watching clouds drift by whilst our hero practices his spelling; both opining that they should try something naughty whilst in flight, because, you know, 'It's been so long since (she) made (him) cry'. Clearly, he's for up it though, because a) it's 'so good for (them)'; b) he's 'coming back for more', and c) it's 'how (they)

119

wanna be'. In a nutshell, he can't get enough of her, yet he needs more thrust from the 'J-E-T' to take him home to her. What?

And the music? Plodding and uninspiring, and no amount of *du jour* guest vocalist inclusion can improve it. Ana Matronic is no match for Dawn Zee or Denise Johnson, I'm afraid, and I'm sure Matronic's involvement was considered on point, and a gateway to chart-topping riches, except that it wasn't. And the many remixers which lined up to polish the proverbial – including Arthur Baker, Richard X, Jacques Lu Cont (in particular, which is a crying shame, because I love what he did with Depeche Mode's 'A Pain That I'm Used To' and more recently London Grammar's 'If You Wait'), Tom Neville and Peter Heller – all failed in their mission, except for a couple of the dub versions. Perhaps there's some nuance in 'Jetstream' that I've missed, and it's actually a killer track that I've wronged terribly.

'Guilt Is A Useless Emotion' (Sumner, Hook, Morris, Cunningham)
Producers: Stuart Price, New Order

This is a very welcome return to form at a point on the album where the plot was very nearly lost. Aside from Bernard's unhelpful bipolar view – 'Real love can't be bought' vs '(I need your love) I just wanna buy it' – and his eyebrow-raising 'You sure know a lot for a girl' line (for which I had in my mind's eye a picture of Bernard getting slapped), I have no issue with this song. It's terrific, both in its album form and the batch of US-label-commissioned remixes, the latter being thoughtfully executed and value-adding. From the heartbeat intro, to the mainline groove with driving synths and synth bass, Hooky's essential riffs, Dawn Zee and Beatrice Hatherley's (curiously robotic-sounding) backing, and the meter of Sumner's vocals, this is a solid slice of New Order dance.

It seems that given the numerous remixes commissioned, promo CD singles distributed and the fact that a digital single actually surfaced (exclusively on iTunes US), Warner Bros. US had designs on 'Guilt...' as a proper single, though they could've tried a little harder with its *artwork*. It's also possible that this release was purposefully specific to iTunes US in order to promote New Order's catalogue there (iTunes would've been barely two years old at the time).

Usually, I have nothing bad to say about any of the remixes. DJ Dan distinguishes himself with his emphasis on buildups, breakdowns and turning the buzz on the bass up to 11. Bill Hamel takes a different direction, with sweeps, space and a great vibe that uses Hooky's parts to great effect. It's really good, with a particularly well-executed middle breakdown, glitchy Sumner samples and a massive comeback. Listening to it again, I'd now put this in my all-time premier league of New Order remixes! MARK!'s 'True N.O.' versions take a bouncy progressive-house approach which is enjoyably different. Morel also successfully applies his 'Pink Noise' formula, with additional grooves and sequences that work well. Finally, Mac Quayle's mixes are also worthy interpretations – one of which was curiously included as a bonus track on the album's CD edition in the US only. It's all so promising and all so strange that these are largely lost to the wider New Order fan base.

'Turn' (Sumner, Hook, Morris, Cunningham)
Producers: New Order, Stephen Street

'Turn' has to be one of my all-time favourite rock/acoustic New Order songs. It is such a lovely track, with New Order's trademark melancholy and melody in full effect. With 'Turn', the band feels relaxed and at peace with their true nature; for once, eschewing questionable collaborations and ill-advised trips down the middle of the road. All members are in top form – Phil and Bernard wonderful on guitars (so many beautiful layers, riffs and textures), Peter's bass is terrific, and Stephen is faultless on drums. But there are very specific parts which make the song set up permanent camp in my consciousness: 1) the gorgeous chorus lyrics and Bernard's vocal performance: i.e., 'Turn your eyes from me/It's time for me to go/Across the hills and over the sea/I want you more than you know'; 2) the stunning moment when the bridge arrives at the chorus, right on the word 'Turn', where the guitars descend on the deep bass note; 3) the instrumental break, with its atmospherics and keys that follow the subtle tremolo-effected guitar melody. Stephen Street really earns his production credit on this song, and I can almost forgive him his trespasses elsewhere on the album (not including 'Morning Night And Day': another gem).

The inclusion of 'Turn' on the *Singles* compilation is interesting. It's a fantastic single-worthy song, to be sure, but pedantically not a single. Furthermore, it was included via a new edit by Street – something I felt was unnecessary because the original is perfectly fine as-is and not so long that cuts were required to service radio specifications, a 7", or similar. Street's new edit sounds *smoother*, with some refrains removed to shorten the length, and some adjustments in levels of various guitar parts. But it's neither here nor there, really, so I will always stick with the original. If only the album had finished here.

'Working Overtime' (Sumner, Hook, Morris, Cunningham)
Producers: New Order, Stephen Street

Part of me wants to rip into 'Working Overtime' because, frankly, I don't like it. But in noting the band members' collective love for the song, it has given me pause. Given all the imminent drama surrounding the band in 2005, and that this was to be the last track on the last album recorded by the three remaining original members (of a band founded on the influences of Bowie, The Stooges, Velvet Underground *et al.*), perhaps it's fitting and appropriate for them to rock out one last time, and who am I to deny them their tale of some 'piece of dirty trash ... he don't care ... working overtime ... don't need no one ... in trouble all the time', etc.. It's not all that far removed from the equally rocked-out sentiments in Joy Division's earliest recording 'At A Later Date': 'Working really tires me ... We try to get away ... drinking rotten beer

121

… I think i'll turn to crime', etc.. Or am I wishfully searching for a long arc to justify my argument?

'Working Overtime', chugs… 'Hey!'… it rolls… 'Hey!'… it distorts in all the right places… 'Hey!'… but it bores me senseless.

Jetstream (Single, 2005)
Personnel: Bernard Sumner, Peter Hook, Stephen Morris, Phil Cunningham, Ana Matronic
Record label: London Records
Original UK release date: 16 May 2005
Chart position: UK: 20
Refer to other details per *Waiting For The Sirens' Call* album and 'Jetstream' song entry above.

Waiting For The Sirens' Call (Single, 2005)
Personnel: Bernard Sumner, Peter Hook, Stephen Morris, Phil Cunningham
Record label: London Records
Original UK release date: 3 October 2005
Chart position: UK: 21
Refer to other details per *Waiting For The Sirens' Call* album and 'Waiting For The Sirens' Call' song entry above.

Guilt Is A Useless Emotion (Digital single, 2005)
Personnel: Bernard Sumner, Peter Hook, Stephen Morris, Phil Cunningham
Record label: Warner Bros. Records
Original US release date: 29 November 2005
Refer to other details per *Waiting For The Sirens' Call* album and 'Guilt Is A Useless Emotion' song entry above.

Recordings for Music From The Motion Picture Control (2007)
Personnel: Bernard Sumner, Peter Hook, Stephen Morris
Recorded late-2006; studio details unknown – probably Morris Farm, Rainow, UK
Producer: New Order
Record label: Warner Bros. Records
Original UK release date: 1 October 2007

'Exit' (Sumner, Hook, Morris, N. Curtis)
Leaving the cinema on my first viewing of *Control,* with its harrowing climax of a distraught Deborah Curtis running out into the street, it took me several hours to collect my thoughts on what I'd just watched. It's an incredible film that pulls no punches. And yet, knowing the story so well from so many sources, I thought I was prepared for it. That it was based on Debbie Curtis' book and directed by Anton Corbijn, meant we were always destined to get

intimate with the truth (as distinct from *24 Hour Party People*, where we got funky with the myth), and it would be uncomfortable and tragic.

Like you, dear reader, I've been emotionally shaped by the music of Joy Division and New Order – through their collective stories, their artfulness (by association with Factory and its command crew of savants), their independence, their individuality and their determination. 100 years from now, people will still be buying *Unknown Pleasures* t-shirts (and socks and tea towels). And I hope that in doing so, those fine folk will not just be sporting something with a cool design, but will continue to celebrate the works and the cultural impact of Curtis, Sumner, Hook, Morris, Gilbert, Cunningham, Chapman, Gretton, Wilson, Saville, Hannett, Erasmus and co..

Control is an incredible movie founded on incredible music – not only of Joy Division, but their influences and contemporaries (including Lou Reed, Buzzcocks, Bowie, Iggy, Roxy Music, Kraftwerk, etc.). It's a great soundtrack, made even more poignant by the inclusion of several new instrumental pieces by the remaining band members in their final recordings together as a group; recordings which could've so easily backed a 2007 incarnation of Joy Division had Curtis lived on, because in these new pieces I hear the echoes of tracks like 'The Eternal' and 'Auto-Suggestion'. We also know New Order (collectively and individually) have a terrific line in soundtrack work, and the *Control* pieces make clear connections to 'Soundtrack', 'Salvation' and 'Elegia'.

'Exit' is, for me, the first half of one overall work, with 'Hypnosis' being the second half. It's elegantly basic, with its three components of deep synth drones and washes, bass slides and bell melody being perfect in their simplicity, and the synthetic reverbed clicks/footsteps in the background sounding just like a Hannett field recording. It's this simplicity through which 'Exit' and 'Hypnosis' manage to conjure a sense of stark beauty – not unlike a bleak winter's scene, and I'm directly reminded of Kevin Cummins' classic photo of Joy Division on Epping Walk Bridge, and Charles Meecham's sleeve photo on their 'She's Lost Control'/'Atmosphere' 12".

'Hypnosis' (Sumner, Hook, Morris, N.Curtis)
Part II of the 'Exit'/'Hypnosis' split-combo, this piece continues the gentle ambient theme (with the same bell melody at its heart). But here, 'Exit''s bass slides and wave of strings are replaced with a heartbeat pulse, rumbles and flute tones, bookended with samples from the movie's hypnosis scene. Checking against Bernard's transcript of his actual hypnotising of the real Ian (as detailed in Sumner's *Chapter and Verse* autobiography), in the movie, Ian utters fictitious lines. Curtis' *actual* regression seems less poetic than the film makes out, but that's moviemaking, isn't it. Still, kudos to Bernard for trying something to help Ian with his illness, even though his throwaway quip, 'It would make a good party trick, if nothing else' speaks volumes about the immaturity, ignorance, stupidity etc. from the band's inner circle in respect to dealing with Ian's epilepsy.

The music is stark, ominous, even portentous, and totally fits as a soundtrack to *Control*. That the band, in this case, Sumner, Hook and Morris (although, interestingly, Ian and Debbie's daughter Natalie is listed as co-writer on the *Control* pieces) were able to make it happen, is what I find hard to get my head around. Recall your own youth, and now imagine (or relive, if it was indeed the case) a crushing tragedy during that time, and picture that part of your life being made into a movie with actors playing the part of you, your family and your mates, and to top it all off, you've been asked to provide the soundtrack to that same film. *How would you feel?* Would it give closure? Would it offer comfort? Would it just feel bizarre? I'm shaking my head in wonderment even as I write this. This is melancholy music for dark subject matter, as so much of Joy Division and New Order's music has always been.

'Get Out' (Sumner, Hook, Morris, N.Curtis)

This sounds so Joy Division. As the last recording from the original three, 'Get Out' takes me full circle – back through tracks like 'In A Lonely Place', 'Decades', 'I Remember Nothing' and even 'As You Said'. It's a stark piece, simple in instrumentation, beautiful in tone and melody, and a fitting final homage to who they were and what they sounded like: dark, spacious, thought-provoking, magnificent.

In more ways than one, the only thing missing was Ian Curtis. For three men that struggled to deal with the tragic loss of their friend and bandmate, they certainly honoured his legacy. They carried on. They made incredible music. They experimented. They looked forward (until it was alright to look back). They never (really) sold out. They succeeded. They f#%ked up. They cared. They made the most of it all … and I'm starting to sound like Paul Morley.

Control could've so easily been the full stop, because it all fell apart immediately after. My opinion (for what it's worth, because, quite frankly, none of us have any authority to cast aspersions on the internal legals, business dealings, politics, personal problems and creative differences between the members and management) is that Hooky probably carries the greatest regret from the sorry happenings of the mid-2000s and since. For fans, London Records kept some momentum going with the *Total* compilation, *Lost Sirens* and the flawed CD Collector's Editions, but one couldn't shake the depressing feeling that horses were being flogged and that what we'd hoped would never happen to New Order, had eventuated: a train wreck.

Lost Sirens (Album, 2013)

Personnel: Bernard Sumner, Peter Hook, Stephen Morris, Phil Cunningham
Recorded 2004 at Morris Farm, Rainow, UK; Real World Studios, Box, UK; St Catherine's Court, Bath, UK
Producers: Various (see track details)
Record label: Rhino Records

Original UK release date: 14 January 2013
Chart position: UK: 23

'I'll Stay with You' (Sumner, Hook, Morris, Cunningham)

Producers: New Order, Stephen Street

One school of thought has *Lost Sirens* emerging as an album of outtakes from the *Waiting For The Sirens' Call* sessions. Another has the band intentionally recording two albums' worth of material and reserving a set for a follow-up to *Waiting For The Sirens' Call*, to save time and effort. I'm inclined to believe the latter, because Stephen Morris said as much in statements at the time, but more so because some of the tracks on *Lost Sirens* are – in my opinion – superior to the lesser tracks on *WFTSC*. If it were the case that they'd only intended to record one album but found themselves feeling particularly productive, then a stronger track list for *Waiting For The Sirens' Call* might've looked something like this: 'Krafty', 'Waiting For The Sirens' Call', 'Who's Joe?', 'California Grass', 'I Told You So', 'Morning Night And Day', 'I'll Stay With You', 'Jetstream', 'Guilt Is A Useless Emotion', 'Turn', 'Recoil': with the other tracks available as bonuses on the singles. Still, the plans for the timely release of a follow-up LP were scuppered in the midst of peak legal nightmare, and it took eight years for *Lost Sirens* to emerge. That it did at all amidst such high drama was a credit to all concerned because there is some quality material on *Lost Sirens* (and some very mediocre, but that's par for the course by this time). I would also add that I really love the simple artwork of *Lost Sirens,* based as it was on Howard Wakefield's 30-year band anniversary stylings as used in *Clash* magazine, and some exclusive merchandise a few years earlier: infinitely superior to the *Waiting For The Sirens' Call* album artwork.

'I'll Stay With You' then. For me, it's the best song on the LP, and a great opening shot for an album that was, unfortunately, unable to sustain the quality. It was also a worthy inclusion on the 2016 reissue of *Singles*, even though it was never issued as a single – but then again, neither was 'Turn'. Opening with a cool (but brief) electronic intro, the song quickly morphs into what is effectively a classic New Order rock workout, rich with melody, hooks and sonic balance. Bernard does a really nice job with his vocal performance, particularly on his atypical scales in the choruses. The middle instrumental break is terrific, featuring all the key riffs, and there's a great additional bridge into the final chorus.

All in all, 'I'll Stay With You' is one of the top-drawer New Order rock tracks of the period. That there was ever a possibility in those dark days that it might've been truly *lost,* would've been a huge shame.

'Sugarcane' (Sumner, Hook, Morris, Cunningham)

Producers: New Order, Tore Johansson

I'm a bit grumpy about this song, which is, at best, a B-side. On the one hand, I enjoy Bernard's wake-up warning shot across the bow of superstardom –

speaking as the voice of experience to his younger contemporaries (or is it to his younger self?), with choice nuggets like 'Girls just wanna be with ya/Lawyers wanna deal with ya' and 'It's made you pretty vain with your perfect hair'. Also, the 'It's just another day in the life' refrain is nicely metered, and for me, is the best part of the song.

On the other hand, musically, 'Sugarcane' is cheap and nasty – cheesy funk over a disco beat, with heavy reliance on preset sounds (house piano, orchestra hits, and that truly god-awful flatulent synth bass sound used in Hooky's obvious absence). These sugary ingredients all come together in one of the most uninspiring instrumental breakdowns I can recall from New Order, which is normally an area where our heroes lift you into another realm altogether. Here it's a cloying mess, not unlike those ridiculous hipster donuts you see millennials queuing up for.

'Recoil' (Sumner, Hook, Morris, Cunningham)
Producers: Jim Spencer, New Order
Lost Sirens had lain largely dormant on my record shelf (despite its pleasing aesthetic) because I'd associated its release with such a grim period in the band's history. However, that said, in writing these reviews, I found myself re-evaluating it, even though I knew there were several sinkholes across its landscape.

Songs often have ideal settings, don't they? The other day I was driving up into the hills of the local hinterland with my better half, winding through country roads, the dappled sunlight coming through the forest canopy, the smell of recent rain etc., and – with 'Recoil' playing on the car stereo – it occurred to me that the song with its gorgeous piano, soporific lounge beats, Hooky's lovely meanderings, the subtle strings, Phil's smooth guitar work, and Bernard in full wistful/regret mode, was the perfect track for that moment. If ever you find yourself on an aimless afternoon drive to escape the city and clear your head, you'll find that 'Recoil' serves very nicely. It's as good as any of the strong album tracks recorded across the years.

'Californian Grass' (Sumner, Hook, Morris, Cunningham)
Producers: New Order, Stephen Street
Since the release of *Lost Sirens*, I've tried to convince myself to dislike this song. In hindsight, this was probably an autosuggestion that anything written by New Order involving wild horses, open plains, grocery stores or lawn on the West Coast, was destined to be dodgy. Grass, eh! – or are we talking *grass*? Anyway, 'Californian Grass' is quite a nice track, with much to like if given half a chance. In recent years, Bernard – by virtue of age or zeal – in several songs (and live performances) has opted to sing in a lower register, and here he croons the verses much deeper than usual. It's not disagreeable, particularly as he switches back and forth to his usual highs during the choruses, which have a tasteful vocal harmony layered in the mix.

Sonically, 'Californian Grass' seems to blend soft rock, the California sound, country, shoegaze and alternative pop – which is a potential recipe for disaster. But against all the odds, Sumner, Hook, Morris and Cunningham have made it work. For me, the song's success lies in New Order's innate alchemy for combining melody and melancholy, even from the most unlikely of elements. I'm also drawn to the organ loop used throughout, the subtle flourishes of guitar tone, Hooky's bass that signals and backs the choruses, and the beautifully layered guitars during the choruses. Stephen Street and the band did well here.

'Hellbent' (Sumner, Hook, Morris, Cunningham)
Producers: New Order, Stephen Street
Its inclusion on *Total* notwithstanding, 'Hellbent' – episode III in Bernard's *wotcha doin* B-grade horror trilogy – really does feel like a second-rate album leftover. Everything apart from its chorus and outro is hellbent on being pedestrian. The verses are lyrically and sonically devoid of any heart whatsoever. Hooky's performance is dialled-in, and not until Bernard opens into the chorus (with an apology) do we get some decent depth and melody to grab onto: and it's the song's saving grace.

There's half a good track in 'Hellbent', but that doesn't justify its appearance on a *best-of* compilation: not by a long shot.

'Shake It Up' (Sumner, Hook, Morris, Cunningham)
Producers: Mac Quayle, Stephen Street
My sister-in-law once got a chicken bone caught in her throat. She was fine, but what was allegedly a very nice meal, ended up with her in a state not unlike watching a cat cough up a fur ball. As I sit here listening to *Lost Sirens*, my brain is stuck on this image, because I feel like the album, at this point really needs a Heimlich manoeuvre.

Perhaps I'm being a little disingenuous, but 'Shake It Up' gets stuck in my craw for two reasons: 1) Bernard's 'wannas' and 'gottas' and the whole 'shake it up, YEAH!' palaver; 2) the tube/distortion effect applied to the guitar stabs, which make them sound like a mating toad, particularly as they come after an intro that offers such potential, suggesting a completely different song altogether is about to kick in. The choruses work fine, with Bernard's switching to a lower register and the 'Does it ever' callout. But the verses let the song down (again) because they sound like a lesser band's cheap attempt at trailer pop. The 'NO!' and 'HEY!' shouts are the point at which the chicken bones lodge themselves right in, and also, 'You coming all over like a piece of cake' must be the worst line I've ever heard on a Sumner-penned record!

And yet (as I've pointed out on more than a few occasions), there are all the elements of a much better song in here – the intro, the choruses, the rolling synth bass pattern, the under-utilised arpeggiating keyboard loop and the outro which features great strings and the synth bass to good effect. Fundamentally,

I think it's simply a production/time issue, and someone should've stood back, listened again and come at the mix differently.

Shaking up your life for a better tomorrow is a fine sentiment, made all the more potent and interesting given the state of the band at the time, and particularly at the time of the *Lost Sirens* release. But unfortunately, this song is not one where if I chew it slowly, it will go down better. The chicken stops here.

'I've Got a Feeling' (Sumner, Hook, Morris, Cunningham)
Producers: New Order, Stephen Street

This song starts so poorly that it was quite some time before I didn't immediately fast-forward it and eventually discover that, yet again, there was half a good song here, buried as it is in the chorus. But first, you must get past the intro, which is a challenge. To this day, I just can't stomach the clichéd 'wanna be's, 'can't get no's, 'they don't tell no's and 'we've gotta try-y-y-y-y-y's. There had already been enough *wannas* and *gonnas* deposited across *Get Ready*, *Waiting For The Sirens' Call* and *Lost Sirens* – but no more.

Years later, one day, whilst I had New Order loudly on random play, the turgid intro of 'I've Got A Feeling' began. Thinking, 'Oh no!', but being unable to reach the *next* button in time, the song had a chance to play through, and I was struck by its completely terrific chorus. For 30 seconds, I found myself lost in some great left-field rock, with Bernard in good singing form amidst some classic New Order guitar and bass; all brisk and well-produced. I particularly love the line 'Don't ask me why, but I've got to leave here' and how it's sung. Ignoring another crap verse, the last third of the track is similarly good, with the double-tracking of vocals, and Hooky's bass riffs. This song has real potential. But it would've required brutal revision, and – I fear – time, money, patience and enthusiasm had long run dry at Real World Studios.

I'm hard-pressed to recall another New Order song that's so yin and yang, and unfortunately for me, it's a lasting hallmark of *Lost Sirens*. Having said that, I've been pleasantly surprised at how much I've enjoyed a large part of the album, and I'll always be grateful to the band for releasing it.

It's Official, You're Fantastic: Music Complete +

Lost Sirens seemed to me upon its release in 2013 (eight years after being recorded), to be a closing curtain, and that the legacy of this once towering and majestic band was being picked at like a carcass. Peter Hook had hated the others enough to walk away from New Order in 2007 and claim that the band no longer existed, yet seemed content to journey with The Light, touring and releasing many live albums of Joy Division and New Order's works. Bernard, Stephen and Phil – having scratched an itch via Bad Lieutenant – were (re) joined by Gillian and Tom, releasing the *Troxy 2011* and *Bestival 2012* live performances, possibly as a statement of continuance of New Order as an ongoing entity, before bringing us to our knees with the promise of a new album and their signing to Mute. But after nearly 40 years of continuous creative endeavour, was it reasonable to expect that there was anything left in the tank?

Let's lay it out to this point. Original band (Joy Division) eschews a career with a major, to align with an untested and single-mindedly Mancunian new record label (Factory), with a manifesto of situationalism, superior design and risk-taking. Original band's lead singer dies from suicide at the peak of their powers. New band starts from absolute scratch, cutting off nearly all association with its back catalogue and previous incarnation, and no safe choices are made. New band forges a career at the leading edge of electronic/ rock, releasing some of the most seminal music of all time. Whilst with Factory, never do they follow anyone's lead. At the peak of their powers (again), the band's label and club, crumble around them, leaving them financially precarious and ending this singularly unusual music industry experiment. They sign to a London Records, and finish a new album under what can only be described as *difficult* conditions. It all gets too much, and the band folds – for a long while going their separate ways with solo projects, each of which is special in its own way. Not long after reforming for some gigs towards the end of the millennium, a key member must leave the band to care for family. Shortly afterwards, the band's manager – such a critical part of the *family* – dies. Against all expectation, the remaining band members come together to record a new album, with a new member coming on board for an extensive tour. Then a second album. It's a renaissance of sorts, but the songwriting is somewhat hit-and-miss. Key ingredients seem to be missing. Just as there is renewed peak interest in the Factory and Joy Division stories, and with two recent albums under their belt, several disasters befall the band, again: Tony Wilson dies, Gillian is diagnosed with breast cancer, and Hooky (who was already not dealing with the financial collapse of the Haçienda and other pressures) calls time on (his version of) the band. A legal quagmire ensues, lasting well over five years and causing untold damage to relations and reputations.

It is, it seems, the end of it all. Perhaps it should've, in fact, ended *there*. But then some remarkable things happened: 1) The band – and by that I mean mainly Sumner and Morris – decided that (contrary to what Peter

Hook claimed) New Order wasn't finished just yet; 2) Capitalising on the latent interest from the *24 Hour Party People an*d *Control* movies, the brand continued its commercial enterprise, including the *Glasgow* DVD, *Total, Lost Sirens,* and some Record Store Day releases; 3) Gillian was given the all-clear; 4) To honour their American collaborator Michael Shamberg, the band decided to reform, with Gillian returning after ten years, joined by Tom Chapman who'd played in Bad Lieutenant, to play some benefit gigs in Brussels and Paris. The positivity from this led to other gigs, which led to some live releases, which led to renewed hope; 5) The band signed to Mute. Don't underestimate the importance of this, because New Order were always an indie band needing an indie label (with means), ideally, fronted by passionate people. Daniel Miller's Mute Records was a perfect fit – the only fit, in my opinion. Above all, this gave Bernard, Stephen, Gillian, Phil and Tom space to breathe and be creative – with discerning ears on hand, and the likelihood of any campaign being handled smartly.

And so, the stage was set for the remarkable and wonderful triumph that is *Music Complete.* Did it deliver? Well, I wouldn't be writing this book if it didn't. It's fair to say that the album saved me from a musical oblivion of sorts. It was a renewal of hope, joy and passion, from a band that had been so important to me but had seemingly (and so disappointingly) smashed into the wall.

I love the way the *Music Complete* campaign has been managed. Of course, the music is brilliant, but also the presentation has been artful, the choice of singles great (and not necessarily obvious), the issuing of a companion album of extended versions (*Complete Music*) a fantastically-realised idea, the overall standard of remixing, strong, and live performances over the last decade have been joyous and a creative high. So yes, *Music Complete* has delivered, and the *new* New Order is magnificent.

Restless (Single, 2015)
Personnel: Bernard Sumner, Stephen Morris, Gillian Gilbert, Phil Cunningham, Tom Chapman
Record label: Mute Records
Original UK release date: 28 July 2015
Refer to other details per *Music Complete* album and 'Restless' song entry below.

Music Complete (Album, 2015) / *Complete Music* (Extended album, 2016)
Personnel: Bernard Sumner, Stephen Morris, Gillian Gilbert, Phil Cunningham, Tom Chapman
Recorded late-2014-May 2015 at 80 Hertz Studios, Manchester, UK; the band's various home studios.
Producer: New Order (except where indicated)
Record label: Mute Records

Original UK release date: Music Complete: 25 September 2015; Complete Music: 13 May 2016
Chart position: UK: 2

'Restless' (Sumner, Morris, Gilbert, Cunningham, Chapman)

'Restless' didn't connect with me immediately. It's good, but isn't among the album's strongest tracks. I reckon it was a very carefully-considered move to release this song first, ahead of other more-obvious candidates. I'm not sure if it's a Mute thing to do this, but I've seen it time and time again with Depeche Mode albums, for example, where the lead single is a bit challenging – e.g., 'Personal Jesus' (*Violator*), 'I Feel You' (*Songs of Faith and Devotion*), 'Barrel Of A Gun' (*Ultra*), etc.. These are songs that unbalance you and perhaps reset your expectations and presumptions about the albums, leaving room for greatness ahead.

My strongest impressions of 'Restless' are in the lyrics, with wise-man Bernard offering to the (restless) younger generations, solid first-person advice on need vs want in a changing world, where success and the cult of celebrity are all-consuming. The 'How much do you need?' question is a very a good one, and his 'It's not hopeless if you take less' line is spot-on. In fact, Sumner is in great form right across the album, with his observations borne from experience and the wisdom of age... to a dance beat. Musically, the highlights for me are in the beautiful chorus and bridge strings, Gillian's piano and the lovely guitar motifs. And can I say right now: Tom Chapman, welcome to New Order. Thanks for stamping your own mark on the band and album.

All of the *Music Complete* singles are supported by a clutch of high-quality remixes, not least of which are the band's own extended versions (of every album track) delivered on *Complete Music*. *I*n the case of 'Restless', the 'Extended Mix' really shines because it offers time and space with all of the beautiful riffs and tones, and it made me realise just how lovely this song is. Just listen to the breakdown from 6:15 and the subsequent rebuild to crescendo in the final minutes. Terrific. The Agoria versions are good – in particular, the 'Agoria Dub' from the *Music Complete Remix EP*. The 'xxxy Build Up Mix' has a darker edge with some deep bass tones underpinning a new rolling drum program, top-end bleep patterns and filtered arpeggios. It's very good actually, and second only to the 'RAC Mix': the best of the remixes, in my opinion. This version is excellent, with some nicely-effected vocal loops, reverb, phasing and depth in the production. The only remix that unfortunately misses the mark is 'Andrew Weatherall's Remix', which never escapes its main (and strangely muted) acid pattern.

'Singularity' (Sumner, Morris, Gilbert, Cunningham, Chapman)

Producer: Tom Rowlands

One of the great things about *Music Complete* is the diversity in the electronic tracks – calling those of us of a certain generation (X?) back to the dance floors

131

of the disco, club, field and festival. 'Singularity' – as to be expected, being the techno/big-beat production lovechild of The Chemical Brothers and New Order – is a muscular track, to be sure. It's stamped with the imprimatur of Tom Rowlands' programming – incessant brain-drilling mid-range loops, noisy chattering sequences, brash flares of synth, cacophonous highs followed by drop-downs to pure techno, and most importantly, exquisite blending with traditional rock elements such as Chapman's bass and those huge rock-drum bridges (I assume performed by Morris rather than programmed). Bernard is in absolute top form with his songwriting and vocal performance. And the lines 'For lost souls who can't come home/For friends not here/We shed our tears' is up there in my list of all-time favourite Sumner lyrics.

The 'Extended Mix' of 'Singularity' – unlike other extended version from *Complete Music* – loses some of the urgency and shape-shifting that you get with the original. Although, having said that, it's nice to hear some of the details in this more spacious mix. 'Erol Alkan's Stripped Mix' has a nice clarity with its emphasis on the buzzing sequencer loop as its backbone, but Bernard's vocal sounds too isolated and *down the hall, a*nd the bridges are too discordant. 'Alkan's Extended Rework' follows similar lines but is re-edited more effectively. The 'Liars Remix' is a curious beast, taking aim at a glitchy dubstep target, to reasonable effect. Mark Reeder certainly took his time putting his own stamp on the band for which he's been such a long-time colleague and friend. His 'Duality Remix' (and 'Edit') honours the original, but replaces several of the Chemicals' signature noisy-but-good core sequences with his own – in particular, with his alternative synth-bass programming. I particularly like Reeder's 'Individual Remix', which takes this approach a step further and has an entirely reworked core of clean electronic sequences. Excellent. And finally, James Zeiter's remixes are fantastic, with his eponymous 'Remix' (and associated 'Dub') a high-BPM driving techno gem, with lots of lengthy analogue FX builds, airs and washes, rubbery bass, buzzing filters and subtle drum shifts. I also want to point out that James has also had an extensive role in the remastered Definitive Editions of the New Order albums. Having had a little input myself into the early discussions around archive and inclusions, I can tell you that James (and all those involved in the projects) have done and are doing New Order fans a painstakingly-researched, deeply-considered, carefully-crafted and stunningly-realised service.

'Plastic' (Sumner, Morris, Gilbert, Cunningham, Chapman)

It's official, 'Plastic' is fantastic. Here's why: New Order produced it. By themselves. No Chemical Brothers. No Stuart Price. No Stephen Street. No John Leckie. No Jim Spencer. No Steve Osborne. No Flood. No Steven Hague. No Arthur Baker. None of 'em. Collaborations are nice, but *they* are the pioneers. 'Plastic' is not a track needing a helpful hand from some upstart to give it kudos with the masses and cachet with the critics. It's first-class wondrously-realised dance music delivered straight to you by Sumner, Morris, Gilbert, Cunningham and Chapman.

It was very specifically 'Plastic', which made me realise that New Order was back. Not back in the sense of a recurring bout of Covid, but back in the sense of a restoration of primacy. It's such a fantastic electronic dance track, drenched as it is in the DNA of 'Blue Monday', 'Bizarre Love Triangle', 'Round & Round' and 'Vanishing Point' – laser-sharp, super-clear, bass-heavy, perfectly padded, and synth-rich, with an instrumental breakdown and rebuild that has the sequences detuning and tumbling over each other in a way that just blows my mind. 'Plastic' sits easily in my top-5 tracks of all time from my favourite band.

I just love the wry take on celebrity worship that Bernard shares on 'Plastic', and how it all gets unexpectedly turned around in the outro, with some harsh truths about the superficial. Sumner nails his vocal, but it's made sublime with Dawn Zee and co. on backing vocals, providing those perfect emphases on 'special', 'iconic', 'focus', 'you don't want it' and 'attention'. She and Denise Johnson (RIP) are superb backing vocalists for Bernard.

Should it have been a single? Yes and no. Certainly, it seems such an obvious choice for being singled out, remixed, edited etc., but when I think about it, there's a certain purity in 'Plastic' remaining an album-only track, supported only by an equally terrific 'Extended Version' (one of the best on *Complete Music*). Like 'Vanishing Point' on *Technique*, 'Plastic' is perfect just the way it is and can't be bettered, so why try harder. Furthermore, it illustrates just how strong *Music Complete* is – that Mute was spoilt for choice, and a track like 'Plastic' wasn't required as a single. Amazing, really, and very Factory-like in its perversity.

The 'Extended Mix' is a total joy – restructured and stretched in all the right places, emphasising those Moroder-esque sequences to remind us where the band's earliest disco influences lay, whilst stamping their own signature darker EBM and alternative flavours all over it. I love how the original's outro vocals are brought forward midway into the track to signpost – after much-vocoded intoxication – a revised extended instrumental closing. Just when the original version closes on panning ambience, the extended version decides to go around the block a few more times. What a brilliant album this is. What a brilliant band they are.

'Tutti Frutti' (Sumner, Morris, Gilbert, Cunningham, Chapman)

One of the greatest qualities of *Music Complete* is its diversity. Just look at the quad of tracks that is 'Singularity', 'Plastic', 'Tutti Frutti' and 'People On The High Line' – surely one of the finest sequences of tracks across any of their albums, and all of them electronic but uniquely different in style. But is this because the band was particularly exploring brave new territory in 2015? No, I don't think so. For so long, New Order delivered right at the pointy edge, and there's no denying how peerless so much of the band's first decade of output was, but I'm not sure I really want New Order at this stage in their career to be forging new sub-genres of electronic music. I'm just super-happy to see them clearly having fun again, creating in their own context and at their own pace, whilst embracing and extending their legacy, freed from many of the pressures that had an impact on their output and activities since *Republic*.

This lifting of stress from New Order's collective shoulders is beautifully realised in 'Tutti Frutti' – surely one of the friskiest tunes in their canon, from its unabashed disco stomp, to Giacomo Cavagna's girl-slaying Italianisms, to Bernard's own dusky croaks, to La Roux's lovely backing vocals, and most of all, the layers-upon-layers of gorgeous bells, synths and strings (the latter by Joe Duddell and the Manchester Camerata). At about the four-minute mark, the blending of La Roux's backing chorus into the acoustic guitar melody that arcs over the mix and into the elegant violin flurries, is just wonderful. The whole song resonates in a rich tone and melody that suggests some serious input from Gillian – so sorely missing from New Order's writing process since 1998.

An obvious choice as a single, 'Tutti Frutti' is also quite well-served by remixes. The 'Extended Mix' on *Complete Music* is excellent, and distinguishes itself from the album version by maintaining the beat and emphasising all the signature sounds in its extended instrumental sections. Hot Chip took their time, given they'd already collaborated with Bernard five years earlier. But, to be frank, I'm not overly excited with their remix. It's a little too *burbling*, which is a shame, because I really rate Hot Chip as a band. 'Tom Trago's Crazy Days Remix' has a smooth lounge quality in its backing, but the way he's chopped Bernard's vocals is really irritating. The 'Tom Rowlands Remix' takes three minutes to get going, separately trying out various ideas, as distinct from using them to build up the track, which tends to drop away rather than hit a higher gear. The 'Richy Ahmed Remix' offers an interesting take on matters, but it's largely a complete rewrite (albeit actually quite good as a stand-alone piece of tech house), with only some vocal samples taken from the original, that don't really work in context. The 'Hallo Halo Remix' is excellent, featuring a distinctive updated backbone driven by a swing beat and revised bass line (with a nice detune at the end of every four bars) and a proper cutup of the vocal samples. However, my favourite is the 'Takkyu Ishino Remix' from the digital *Music Complete Remix EP* and Japan-only 12". The vocal samples are used really well (sounding quite dry, until they're synthetically harmonised later in the mix) in this slightly insane reworking, which I can only describe as neo-acid. It's a terrific mix of a terrific track.

'People On The High Line' (Sumner, Morris, Gilbert, Cunningham, Chapman)

This is a good time to discuss the playing of bass guitar in New Order. Peter Hook: Salfordian. Irreplaceable. Original. Unique, with a body of peerless work that will be remembered forever. I'm very sad at the way his part of the band's story left the road, smashed through the fence and went over the cliff. But I'm also happy he's doing his own thing, touring and celebrating that history. By his own published admissions, he was struggling with a range of issues, and like any human being in challenging circumstances, he may not have made the right decisions, said the right things or acted in his own best interests. But the water seems to have largely passed under the bridge now, which I hope is true, and good on Hooky for developing with The Light what is a must-see live experience. Without him, there was no Joy Division and no New Order, but it's certainly *not* the case that without him, New Order was finished.

Tom Chapman: French. Accomplished. Funky. Chapman isn't Hook, but neither is Hook, Chapman. What Tom has managed to do brilliantly is find his own place in the band (initially under tremendous scrutiny) and help create a new incarnation of the group. And what *Music Complete* lays out so clearly, is that New Order since 2011 is its own thing, with five fully-fledged members firing on all cylinders. New Order without Hooky is 100% awesome, just as it was with him.

It's 'People On The High Line' (one of the band's favourites on the album) that so clearly stamps Chapman's distinctive mark on proceedings. What a joyous party this is, opening with chopped-up percussive bass, electronic drum shots and woozy guitar slides, leading directly into some pure top-shelf funk, with Chic-esque guitar riffs, a disco pattern complete with handclaps, and a wonderful bass groove the likes of which I can't recall from any New Order song before. This leads directly into a great snare roll heralding a happy house-piano sequence that rolls in and around more of Chapman's glorious slap-and-pick bass (with those cheeky high emphases), heralding über-cheese snare shots (with the echo turned up to 11) that feed into Bernard's opening verse. Also working particularly well here are La Roux's backing vocals, which rise and dip harmonically higher and lower than Bernard's at different stages. It's a really great vocal production, as are the lyrics 'I'll keep trying/It's all gonna be alright' and 'I'm a shadow of a man without your love'. I love both the sentiment and performances from Sumner and La Roux.

There are lots of remixes! The 'Claptone Remix' opening drum pattern is very familiar, and I'm trying to place it. Nevertheless, I quite like its new repeating synth bassline, although dropping most of Chapman's performance is sacrilegious given that it's so integral to the original. The 'Purple Disco Machine Remix' offers a more-robust disco stomp with particular sequences and riffs from the original, including (just) the 'It's all gonna be alright' vocal line on repeated loop. The 'LNTG Can't Get Any Higher Remix' emphasises La Roux's vocals, bringing them much further forward in the mix along with the funk guitar, though the way it's looped gives an overly-staccato feel. Planet Funk present quite a different interpretation, pitching Bernard's vocal into a different key and building a new track around it. There's some great atmosphere created, with all those tuneful bells, motifs and great progressions. Really interesting. Hybrid's mix is also great, with their progressive structure and core grooves, which have a great driving quality. Their 'Armchair Mix' strips all the drum and bass out of their main remix, except for a background heartbeat, leaving just vast washes of atmosphere, ambience and tone in a great secondary offering.

135

'Stray Dog' (Sumner, Morris, Gilbert, Cunningham, Chapman)

Music Complete is such a fascinating album. It's the most diverse album since *Brotherhood* – covering killer dance tracks, quality rock songs, slow ones, fast ones, and left-field numbers like 'Stray Dog', which for me hark back to the likes of 'Angel Dust', 'Murder' and 'Mesh'. And unlike the vocalist collaborations on *Get Ready* and *Waiting For The Sirens' Call* – which were more miss than hit – just how good is it that the band was able to dial-in one of their all-time biggest influences from back in the Warsaw/Joy Division days: namely Iggy Pop FFS!

Few call it out as one of the highlights on the album, but I really like 'Stray Dog', starting with Iggy's signature growl, which sounds like he's gargling on coffee granules while soaking in cheap tequila... in a dust storm... with rattlesnakes – perfect, really for telling Bernard's poetic tale of unconditional love and secrets to happiness, and perfect for naming a beer. I freely admit, though, to having Googled 'grimpen mire'.

Musically, 'Stray Dog' is terrific, building up from its moody nightscape intro through unusually effected bass guitar and percussion, distant electronic tones and riffs, descending guitars and a lovely synth-bass sequence. It's beautifully produced and rich with texture and melody. Using Iggy via a spoken-word performance works a treat. The 'lover vs supplier' lines lead into a thumpingly-good instrumental break, with Phil and Bernard on storming guitars, backed with Morris' excellent (as always) drumming. The final minute and a half – heralded by Iggy's growling and hissing – holds some lovely synths and strings from Gillian.

The 'Extended Mix' holds true to the original in atmosphere and instrumentation. But as with everything on *Complete Music,* the reshuffling of layers and levels allows us to come at the track from a different direction. The industrial loop, which leads the track and provides a tonal backbone, works well. The overall mix seems more spacious, and you get some isolation of key parts – e.g., Chapman's sliding bass riff, and Stephen's percussion and programming (the electronic nature of which is dialled right up) – but I think the track's storytelling quality is lost a little in the alternative programming of the 'Extended Mix'.

'Academic' (Sumner, Morris, Gilbert, Cunningham, Chapman)

Completely and utterly wonderful, and there it sits, like 'Plastic', unblemished by its non-issue as a single. Primarily Phil Cunningham and Tom Chapman's baby, 'Academic' is perfect in its guitar melodies and riffs, lyrics and vocal performance, and most importantly, richness and depth in its production. Other highlights are in the driving percussion and bass line, the gorgeous vocal harmonies and the many additional flourishes held back until the extended outro – a quality you find with quite a few tracks on this album, like a reserve of riches being shared out. I'm quite fond of the 'Extended Mix' as well, isolating as it does a more electronic core around the synth bass and strings.

We also have Mark Reeder's supreme 'Akademix' from the *Music Complete Remix EP* (from which his 'Academixxx' was edited for the *Electronic Sound* magazine 7"), which itself was an unexpected treat when it came out on digital platforms in 2017. A fantastic version, delivering a full set of vocals, a dark-disco core sequence, flares of guitar feedback and the main guitar riff coming in and out of the reverb, with added depth in the synth layers.

Seven tracks into *Music Complete*, and nothing had yet to drop below bloody amazing; four of which were as good as you can get! So, what makes a great New Order song? Can the qualities be distilled KLF-style into a checklist for success and emulation? No, because New Order's has been a singularly unique, tragic, triumphant and mad journey of places, people and situations that has influenced their art.

'Nothing But A Fool' (Sumner, Morris, Gilbert, Cunningham, Chapman)

This song is difficult to pin down. On the one hand, it contains one of my all-time favourite chorus lyrics from Bernard, featuring classic Sumner reflections on relationships, sung sensitively but rendered angelic courtesy of Dawn Zee and Denise Johnson, and emphasised with beautiful strings, Chapman's driving bass and a choice drumming performance from Morris. 'If you can hold her in your hands/Don't ever let her drift away'. Beautiful.

Unfortunately, and in jarring opposition to the above sentiments, I find the verses flat and uninspiring, with more than a nod to similarly-lumpen tracks on the London-era albums. The song starts like a sequel to 'Stray Dog', but the atmosphere established by the textured guitars in the first minute feels immediately vacuumed out of the song when it drops down into the ponderous verse lyrics, instrumentation and performance. 'Nothing Like A Fool' feels like two songs spliced together – one a bit tired, and one remarkable, and it's that dichotomy that challenges me here.

Luckily, we have a couple of extended mixes offering the potential for redress. Although the (original) 'Extended Mix' doesn't stray very far from the album version, 'Extended Mix Two' on *Complete Music* is excellent, going a long way to improving the track's overall *architecture*. I like the way the intro and verse instrumentation are allowed to play out for longer and with greater emphasis on low-end strings and Chapman's bass, offering a much better progression into Bernard's verses. In fact, the strings are far more prominent throughout the mix – which I love: particularly around the seven-minute mark. The Manchester Camerata did a lovely job, and they're given some space here to spread their wings. The only real negative is that the backing vocals are less prominent in the mix, which is a shame.

The existence of updated (version two) extended mixes of 'Nothing Like A Fool' and 'Superheated' on *Complete Music* is quite interesting, illuminating the band's desire to continue shaping these tracks into their best form. In both cases, the band was 100% right in doing so, and kudos to Mute for supporting

New Order's artistic freedom, because I'm not sure London Records would've supported the same.

'Unlearn This Hatred' (Sumner, Morris, Gilbert, Cunningham, Chapman, Rowlands)

Producee: Tom Rowlands

The Chemical Brothers are remarkable and hugely important, contributing more than a few tracks into my must-haves. Their collaborations and productions, more often than not, are equally awesome, and with respect to New Order, you'd have to agree that 'Here To Stay' and 'Singularity' are right up there in the band's canon of greats, for which I'm in awe of Tom Rowlands.

Having said that, I can't connect to the same degree with 'Unlearn This Hatred'. Why? Because – 'Heartache' (repeat), 'I'm your automatic lover' (What? And I thought Bernard was a 'jetstream lover' anyway), the quirky intro loop with the brash synth quickly becomes irritating, the snare sound used throughout is really dry and abrupt, and there's very little bottom-end in the mix until the brief instrumental break.

There are still a few gems in the pan, such as the overall sentiment of unlearning hatred, the harmony effect used over the 'make a sign' chorus vocal lines, the melodic reverbed bell riff in the intro, the instrumental break and its bass sequence variation, and the way the track ends. And so, it was these elements that I looked for in its companion 'Extended Mix'. But I found this one – of all those on *Complete Music* – to be the least reinterpreted from its original: which was disappointing and a lost opportunity. Can someone please get hold of the stems and have a crack at an 'Extended Mix Two'?

'The Game' (Sumner, Morris, Gilbert, Cunningham, Chapman)

'For life is good, and it is special ... For this is life and it's immortal'. Bernard's musings on 'The Game' (of life?) are some of his most determinedly-optimistic in-the-face-of-it-all lyrics yet – an angle he's been developing for some time, and, given the life he's led, one that's heartwarming and quite moving.

I love 'The Game' in particular for the lyrics and chorus instrumentation. The segue from (the glitchiness and high energy of) the main sequence, down to (the majesty and grandeur of) the chorus is a real highlight, as is the panorama of percussion from Stephen, and the gorgeous strings, guitar tones and layer upon layer of atmosphere. The guitars leading into the closing instrumental break are also sublime. Full marks to Sumner and Cunningham here.

The 'Extended Mix' is just as good – the way it opens quietly on the first verse, and into a beautifully-stretched instrumental intro where you can take in all the programming subtleties. In fact, the restructuring applied in this mix offers lots of new detail right across the board. If I have one (very minor) quibble, it's that some of the grandiosity of the original's choruses is missing, mainly because of the absence of the strings.

Mark Reeder takes 'The Game' to a whole new level with his 'Spielt Mit Version' (from which there also exists a 'Spielt Mit Stella Polaris Edit'), which is simply beautiful – the pianos, bass, the space and depth, the vocal layering, the keeping to a slow tempo throughout, and the strings! This version is a perfect example of why a remix doesn't have to be an up-tempo dance number. It can be a rolling storm of dark elegance. Reeder understands wonderfully well that less can be so much more, and this version is easily in my list of best New Order remixes.

'Superheated' (Sumner, Cunningham, Chapman, Flowers)
Producers: New Order, Stuart Price
5 June 2016. Sydney – the last night of New Order's four-night residency at the Sydney Opera House for the *Vivid* event. Last night's set was with the Australian Chamber Orchestra, but tonight is just the band. These will remain my favourite ever gigs, not only for the sublime setlist and performances in a remarkable location, but also because of the full access Andy and Rebecca provided on both nights. It was wonderful to chat to everyone – band, management, and others who'd made the trip, including Paul Morley. Serendipitously, our seats for the final show were right beside Kevin Cummins (one of the greatest rock photographers of all time), with whom we struck up a great conversation and who left me with an indelible memory from the final night – the band's encore featured (as expected) 'Blue Monday' and 'Love Will Tear Us Apart'. But what to end on; what to mark the completion of four nights of triumphant New Order and Joy Division classics? What to have ringing in our ears as we depart the cavernous glory of Jørn Utzon's iconic Opera House? What career-defining celebration can top those two preceding songs, and take us from ecstasy to delirium? To the opening strains of 'Superheated', I look over and catch Cummins shaking his head and expressing none-too-softly, 'F#%king hell Bernard!'.

A bit of an anti-climax, I agree. But is it really that bad? Bernard Sumner flies under the radar as a writer of love songs, and on a good day, he can write a cracking one, usually involving regret, yearning, heartache and lament: all quality ingredients. And when combined with New Order's classic alt-indie-electronic backings, all is well. Having said that, I'm not convinced that 'Superheated''s Bryan-Adams-meets-Robbie-Williams in a Mills & Boon bake-off (to the ultra-cliched tones of harp and chimes) is what we were looking for. I choose to blame Brandon Flowers and Stuart Price for this travesty. Although, who are we to deny Flowers' closure in working with the group that inspired his own band back in 2001? – even though the shläger is dialled up to 11 as we weep over makeup, photographs, kisses, anger, blame, desire and leaving. Pass the tissues and chocolate.

But there's still enough in this cheese fondue to suggest great possibility. Sumner and Flowers complement each other vocally. Their performances are tastefully produced, and the core instrumentation and programming are perfectly okay: particularly in the synth bass and strings, which are very Pet Shop Boys-esque. These parts just needed another's ears, and yet, the original 'Extended Mix' didn't make the grade either. I'm so glad they went back (well, Richard X anyway) and had another go, because, of all the restructures on *Complete Music*, the 'Extended Mix Two' gets the Most-Improved Award – particularly for its smooth extended intro and lovely breakdown/rebuild. The harps and chimes are rendered innocuous, and we're left with some smartly reprogrammed synth-pop that richly deserves admiration.

Kevin, you were probably right in your assessment on that blustery evening in Sydney. But in a funny way, the echoing strains of 'Now that it's over' seemed just fine for a band closing a remarkable gig in 2016, as distinct from 35 years earlier when the group would more likely skulk off stage, leaving the sequencers running – different needs for different times, but both effective in their way. Still, I enjoyed your reaction and the discussion afterwards. Your work is much appreciated; we've all seen New Order through your eyes.

Music Complete is wonderful, but is it their best album? No. But it's a damn remarkable album that renewed my faith in my favourite band when I thought all hope was gone. Of course, it's a new version of the band without Peter Hook but is no less valid. New Order now is sublime. It is evolved. Matured. Fine-tuned. The return of Gillian, the incorporation of Tom, and the signing to Mute, have all given the band – dare I say it – greater class. They've been touring solidly since, with many of the gigs exceptional. And, in my estimation, the *NOMC15* and $\sum$*(No,12k,Lg,17Mif)* live albums are two of their finest.

Tutti Frutti (Single, 2015)
Personnel: Bernard Sumner, Stephen Morris, Gillian Gilbert, Phil Cunningham, Tom Chapman, La Roux
Record label: Mute Records
Original UK release date: 20 October 2015
Refer to other details per *Music Complete* album and 'Tutti Frutti' song entry above.

Singularity (Single, 2016)
Personnel: Bernard Sumner, Stephen Morris, Gillian Gilbert, Phil Cunningham, Tom Chapman
Record label: Mute Records
Original UK release date: 3 February 2016
Refer to other details per *Music Complete* album and 'Singularity' song entry above.

People On The High Line (Single, 2016)
Personnel: Bernard Sumner, Stephen Morris, Gillian Gilbert, Phil Cunningham, Tom Chapman, La Roux
Record label: Mute Records

Original UK release date: 21 June 2016
Refer to other details per *Music Complete* album and 'People On The High
Line' song entry above.

Recording for STUMM433 (Compilation, 2019)
Personnel: Bernard Sumner, Stephen Morris, Gillian Gilbert, Phil Cunningham,
Tom Chapman
Recorded at about 4:30 p.m. on 28 August 2018 at soundcheck at The Anthem,
Washington, D.C., USA
Producer: New Order
Record label: Mute Records
Original UK release date: 4 October 2019

'4'33"' (Cage)
I'm not really one for devoting a lot of energy to esoteric forms of music and
the theory of sound, and I don't particularly circulate among the devotees of
avant-garde, where there seems to be just as much air-kissing as there is serious
contemplation of the void. That said, in my travels with electronic music
over the years, I have built up a lot of respect for those who have dedicated
themselves to expanding our horizons and shaking the foundations of what we
classify as art and music.

Mute's *STUMM433* compilation (of its bands and artists offering their take on
John Cage's challenge of four minutes and 33 seconds' silence-as-performance)
is truly thought-provoking, particularly because of Mute's through this release
wonderfully supporting charities involved in tinnitus: something suffered by
many fans and practitioners of music alike. Unfortunately, they never get to
hear 4'33" of pure silence.

It's fascinating to hear the 58 different interpretations of Cage's call to not
perform, though I thought Cage's intent was for the piece to be the sound
of the performer *not* performing for four minutes and 3 seconds – i.e.,
instruments down but on stage (or in the studio), rather than a recording at
a bus station or park: unless of course, the band brought their instruments
to the bus station or park to not play them. Oh dear. Anyway, I enjoy that this
project brought together bands as diverse as Laibach, Erasure, A Certain Ratio,
Cabaret Voltaire, Einstürzende Neubauten, and New Order, and unified them
in the same sonic context. New Order's contribution sounds to my ears like a
heavily air-conditioned and cavernous wooden-floored warehouse, with people
occasionally walking by, doors being closed and a bag of crisps being shuffled.
I was secretly hoping to hear '4'33"' from New Order's studio on the Morris
farm, with all their gear switched on and humming but no one home, and a
single window open to the outside to catch a sheep bleating or a tank rolling
past. But I think that would be too intentional.

The *STUMM433* box set is a bold statement, containing exactly four hours, 23
minutes and 54 seconds of *something*. Though what that is, I'll never be 100%

sure. I've listened to it once. I doubt I'll listen to it again. But it has made me pause and think on deeper things. If I ever meet Daniel Miller, he'll get my nod of approval, but an air kiss is unlikely.

Be A Rebel (Single, 2020)
Personnel: Bernard Sumner, Stephen Morris, Gillian Gilbert, Phil Cunningham, Tom Chapman
Recorded late-2014-May 2015 at 80 Hertz Studios, Manchester, UK, and the band's various home studios. Finalised in 2020.
Producers: New Order, Bernard Sumner
Record label: Mute Records
Original UK release date: 8 September 2020

'Be A Rebel' (Sumner, Morris, Gilbert, Cunningham, Chapman)
The last few years have been a nightmare, haven't they? In another time and place (Sydney on 11 March 2020, to be precise (Seems so long ago now)), you'd have found me at the Hordern Pavilion with my brother and one of my best mates, enjoying the experience of their first-ever New Order gig. It was a cracking set, and in hindsight, we were damn lucky to be there, because the preceding gigs in Japan had already been cancelled, and only one of the two scheduled Melbourne gigs went ahead: all because of the rapidly changing Covid-19 situation. The band just managed to evacuate the country on 15 March before the borders were closed, and then all hell broke loose everywhere as we well know. I had a beer with Andy Robinson the day before the Sydney gig, where we discussed a bunch of things, including publishing this book, the box sets, and the band's concerns around performing-vs-cancelling. Decisions were being made on an hourly basis, and I'm forever grateful that they came all the way to Australia for just two gigs whilst the walls came tumbling down around them.

Later that year, around the time New Order was to have originally toured the US (with the Pet Shop Boys – delayed until September 2022), the band posted a cryptic teaser on social media, but little did we expect a new single:

> In tough times, we wanted to reach out with a new song. We can't play live for a while, but music is still something we can all share together. We hope you enjoy it… until we meet again.
> Bernard Sumner

This is apparently an outtake from *Music Complete* (I didn't know there were any), for which Bernard finished the vocals, and final adjustments were facilitated through file-sharing amongst the band members whilst in Covid isolation. Just how creatively rich was the *Music Complete* recording process, for a song like 'Be A Rebel' to not make the original final cut! In my opinion, it's stronger than 'Unlearn This Hatred', and easily on par with 'Nothing But A

Fool'. It's a perfectly fine piece of electronic pop, with lots of strings, punchy synth bass and Bernard singing his observations on life (and apparently directed to his son, which, if you listen carefully, offer quite a special message). Lines like 'For this world can be a dangerous place/But it's all we've got and it's quite a lot' seem to nail the world as it was in 2020/2021. I really love Bernard's vocal on 'Be A Rebel'. It sounds like a performance from his boyish younger self, and it combines beautifully with some lovely melody lines across the synths and keys.

A brief excerpt of the song in the ads for the New Order/Adidas SPZL campaign heralded what's become a much-extended release campaign, delivering numerous remixes and must-have physical issues which shone some welcome light over these dark Covid years. This 'Adidas' version subsequently released on digital platforms as the one-shot 'Renegade Spezial Edit', teased at a really interesting new take (from Bernard himself) that was fully realised on the 12". Bernard's 'Renegade' mixes are fantastic, highlighting and extending the synth-bass sequences, keys and strings in all the right places, and the excellent vocoding/FX of his vocal. Also great is Chapman's bass – brought to the front in the mix's (long and glorious) instrumental second half, which just keeps layering, dropping and rebuilding. The 'Instrumental Mix' is far from token, putting Bernard's superb musical production in the spotlight, with the lush synths backing the verses and choruses given clear air to shine. Morris' 'T34 Mix' (Is it possible to have a favourite tank?) is also terrific, with a tightly-looped intro which then – daiquiri in hand – heads straight to the dance floor, emphasising a new house beat, riffs and textures, whilst keeping all the main melodies and vocal performance intact: as all good remixes should. The 12" of these mixes – with its *dove-grey* pressing and lovely packaging – was a highlight release of 2020.

But wait, there's more! Spread out over numerous subsequent digital releases, and then collated onto the CD single and a second vinyl release, the excellent 2x12" *Be A Rebel (Remixes)* issue, are the following. The 'Paul Woolford Remix Edit' – fine but not startling, but a subsequent New Order edit of his mix has some extended instrumental sequences, effects and retro flourishes (circa 'True Faith'), which really enhance Woolford's approach. The 'Maceo Plex Remix' does nothing for me, the best part being the isolated *Blade Runner*-esque tones at around the one-minute mark. But they herald an irritating pitch shift and back-masking of Bernard's vocal. Mark Reeder's 'Dirty Devil Remix' once again shows how it should be done, reshaping around a classic 'Plastic'-like dance core, and I love the new depth and urgency in the chord sequence that underpins the main melody. Super programming. His 'Cheeky Devil Remix' (available only on his superb *Subversiv-Dekadent* compilation) offers a cruisy alternative. JakoJako has basically written a completely new song with Bernard's vocal laid over it. Having said that, it has quite a nice ambient vibe that reminds me of Orbital and System 7. Similarly, the 'Melawati Remix' is another completely new instrumental, albeit with a darker, glitchy, cinematic quality, and using repeats of a few pitched-down 'Take a look at yourself' samples. Effective, but it's not 'Be A Rebel'. Last but not least, who else but Arthur Baker to close the many 'Be A Rebel' remixes on offer. He's gone for an uplifting and joyous extended pop mix, with some great additional backing vocals. Part of the New Order story since 1983, Arthur still manages to land a great mix nearly 40 years later.

Music is the stuff of life. And even if it's not a 'True Faith' or a 'Temptation', 'Be A Rebel' is a great tune, which in the space of four minutes, made 2020 just that little bit better. Bring on the remaining Definitive Boxes, their return to gigs (as we speak), and hopefully even more new music.

(The Best Of) New Order?

So, dear reader, I've been (over)sharing my heartfelt impressions on each and every New Order song, along with what I hope is interesting context and some useful facts. As with most things in this band's orbit, I can't guarantee 100% truth, but I've made every effort to be as accurate as possible.

What are New Order's best songs? I've collated my own favourites into a corresponding Spotify playlist for your convenience at https://spoti.fi/3ejLVNT, and you can visit my blog for my personal ratings. If I were to pick just three, they would be 'All Day Long', 'Your Silent Face' and 'Temptation'. My favourite albums are *Power Corruption And Lies*, *Technique* and *Music Complete*. Favourite three remixes – 'Confusion' ('Koma and Bones Version'), 'True Dub' and 'Waiting For The Sirens' Call' ('Planet Funk Remix'). Again, visit the blog for an expanded list. Best compilation: *Singles*. Best single: 'True Faith'. Best live album: ∑*(No,12k,Lg,17Mif) New Order + Liam Gillick: So it goes.* Best artwork: *Low-life*. Best video clip: 'Regret'. Best autobiography (to date)? Stephen's.

I hope we share many of the same thoughts on this remarkable catalogue of music, and I very much hope we beg to differ on just as many because I'd sure enjoy the debate.

Afterword

New Order (whether it be Sumner/Hook/Morris, Sumner/Hook/Morris/Gilbert, Sumner/Hook/Morris/Cunningham or Sumner/Morris/Gilbert/Cunningham/ Chapman) have produced in no uncertain terms some of the most incredible music of the last 40 years – a unique vision of alternative electronic rock forged in Manchester and exported to the world, connecting with the alternative-minded and the club-centric, the football fan and the artist, the boffin and the aesthete. I'm in there somewhere, as I expect are all of you.

Their journey has been astonishing – the genesis of Warsaw, the beauty and permanence of Joy Division, the rise (and fall) of Factory Records, the assimilation of New York, the rise (and fall) of The Haçienda, the modernity of Peter Saville, the revitalisation of Manchester, their top-class manager(s), BeMusic, Electronic, Revenge, The Other Two, Monaco, Bad Lieutenant, their tragic losses, their unholy messes, their remarkable resilience. And... finally... when New Order hang up their boots to permanently embrace the easy life, may they meander in their sailing ships and career about the countryside in their armoured personnel carriers until they drop. Because, frankly, they've earned it giving us so much astounding, magnificent music.

Index of Song Versions and Remixes

This index lists all studio versions and remixes of every New Order song as reviewed in this book, cross-referenced with the sources listed in the discography, which appears further below.

'Ceremony'
- Original version: 'Ceremony' 7", 12" [#1/#3], Singles / Total compilations.
- Re-recorded version: 'Ceremony' 12" [#2], Substance / International / Retro compilations.

'In A Lonely Place'
- Edited version: B-side of 'Ceremony' 7".
- Full version: B-side of 'Ceremony' 12" [#1/#2/#3], Substance (non-LP editions only) / Retro compilations.

'Homage'
- Movement album (Definitive Edition Extras bonus CD only).

'Are You Ready For This?'
- Movement album (Definitive Edition Extras bonus CD only).

'Procession'
- 'Procession' 7", 1981-1982 / Substance (non-LP editions only) / Retro / Singles compilations.

'Everything's Gone Green'
- Edited version: B-side of 'Procession' 7", Singles compilation.
- Full version: 'Everything's Gone Green' 12", CDS, 1981-1982 / Substance / Retro compilations.
- Dave Clarke Mix: Rest Of compilation, B-side of New State Recordings 12" [#4].
- Cicada Remix: B-side of 'Waiting For The Sirens' Call' 7" [#2].

'Dreams Never End'
- Peel Session: The Peel Sessions (1981) release.
- Movement album, Retro compilation.

'Truth'
- Peel Session: The Peel Sessions (1981) release.
- Movement album.

'Senses'
- Peel Session: The Peel Sessions (1981) release.
- Movement album.

'Chosen Time'
- Movement album.

'ICB'
- Peel Session: The Peel Sessions (1981) release.
- Movement album.

'The Him'
- Movement album.

'Doubts Even Here'
- Movement album.

'Denial'
- Movement album.

'Cries And Whispers'
- B-side of 'Everything's Gone Green' 12", CDS, Substance (non-LP editions only) / Retro compilations.

'Mesh'
• B-side of 'Everything's Gone Green' 12", CDS, 1981-1982 / Substance (CS edition only) compilations.

'Temptation'
• Edited version: 'Temptation' 7", Singles / Total compilations.
• Full version: 'Temptation' 12", 1981-1982 / Retro compilations.
• 1987 version: Substance compilation, 'Touched By The Hand Of God' CDS.
• 1998 version: Retro compilation (limited-edition bonus CD only).
• CJ Bolland Mix: Rest Of compilation.
• Secret Machines Remix: B-side of 'Waiting For The Sirens' Call' 7" [#1].

'Hurt'
• Edited version: B-side of 'Temptation' 7".
• Full version: B-side of 'Temptation' 12", 1981-1982 compilation.
• Edited 12" version: Substance compilation.

'Video 5-8-6'
• In edited parts: Feature Mist / Touch.Sampler compilations.
• 'Video 5-8-6' 12", CDS.

'Turn The Heater On'
• The Peel Sessions (1982) release.

'Too Late'
• The Peel Sessions (1982) release.

'Ode To Joy'
• Merry Xmas From The Haçienda And Factory Records 7" flexi, Ghosts Of Christmas Past (Remake) compilation (2CD edition only).

'Rocking Carol'
• Merry Xmas From The Haçienda And Factory Records 7" flexi, Ghosts Of Christmas Past (Remake) compilation (2CD edition only).

'Blue Monday'
• 'Blue Monday' 12", B-side of 'BlueMonday-1995' 12" [#2], Substance / International / Retro / Singles / Total compilations.
• 'The Beach': B-side of 'Blue Monday' 12", Substance compilation (non-LP editions only).
• 'Blue Monday 1988' (by John Potoker) edited version: 'Blue Monday 1988' 7", CDS, CDV, Best Of / Singles compilations.
• 'Blue Monday 1988' (by John Potoker) full version: 'Blue Monday 1988' 12", CDS, CDV, New State Recordings 12" [#10], Best Remixes (digital) compilation.
• 'Blue Monday 1988 Dub' (by John Potoker): 'Blue Monday 1988' CDV, Brotherhood (Collector's Edition).
• 'Beach Buggy' (by Michael Johnson) edited version: B-side of 'Blue Monday 1988' 7".
• 'Beach Buggy' (by Michael Johnson) full version: 'Blue Monday 1988' CDS, B-side of 12".
• Hardfloor Mix (aka Hardfloor Remix): 'BlueMonday-95' 12" [#1], CS, CDS [#1], Rest Of compilation, B-side of New State Recordings 12" [#10].
• Hardfloor Dub: 'Blue Monday-95' CDS [#2].
• Andrea Mix (by Jam & Spoon): 'BlueMonday-95' CDS [#1], 12" [#1].
• Manuela Mix (by Jam & Spoon): 'BlueMonday-95' CDS [#1], B-side of 12" [#1], Retro compilation.
• Plutone Mix: 'BlueMonday-95' CDS [#2], 12" [#2].
• Plutone Dub: EU promo-only 12".
• Starwash Mix: 'BlueMonday-95' CDS [#2], 12" [#2].
• Brain Mix (aka Corleone Mix): EU promo-only 12".

'Age Of Consent'
• Power Corruption And Lies album.
• Howie B. Remix: Rest Of compilation.
'We All Stand'
• Peel Session: The Peel Sessions (1982) release.
• Power Corruption And Lies album.
'The Village'
• Power Corruption And Lies album.
'5-8-6'
• Peel Session: The Peel Sessions (1982) release.
• Power Corruption And Lies album.
'Your Silent Face'
• Power Corruption And Lies album, Retro compilation.
• Evening Session: In Session release.
'Ultraviolence'
• Power Corruption And Lies album.
'Ecstasy'
• Power Corruption And Lies album.
'Leave Me Alone'
• Power Corruption And Lies album, Retro compilation.
'Confusion'
• Edited version: 'Confusion' 7", Singles [2016] compilation.
• Full version: 'Confusion' 12", Retro compilation.
• 'Confused Beats': A-side of 'Confusion' 12".
• Instrumental: B-side of 'Confusion' 12", Substance compilation (non-LP editions only).
• Rough Mix: B-side of 'Confusion' 12".
• Rough Mix edited version: Singles [2005] compilation.
• 1987 version: Substance / International compilations.
• Dub 1987: 'Touched By The Hand Of God' CDS.
• Alternative Mix (by Mark Quail and Peter Daou): 'Confusion (Remix)' 12".
• Essential Mix (by Lenny D and Victor Simonelli): A-side of 'Confusion (Remix)' 12".
• Trip 1-Ambient Confusion (by Lenny D and Victor Simonelli): A-side of 'Confusion (Remix)' 12".
• Accapella: B-side of 'Confusion (Remix)' 12".
• Con-om-fus-ars-ion Mix (by Omar Santana): B-side of 'Confusion (Remix)' 12".
• Confused Ooh-Wee Dub (by Omar Santana): B-side of 'Confusion (Remix)' 12".
• Pump Panel Reconstruction Mix: Rest Of compilation, New State Recordings 12" [#4].
• Koma And Bones Version (edit): 'Confusion (Remixes '02)' CDS.
• Koma And Bones Vocal Version (aka Koma & Bones Vocal Mix): 'Confusion (Remixes '02)' 12" [#1], on the Retro compilation.
• Koma & Bones Remix: New State Recordings 12" [#3].
• Electroclash Version (edit – by Larry Tees): 'Confusion (Remixes '02)' CDS.
• Larry Tees Electroclash Mix: B-side of 'Confusion (Remixes '02)' 12" [#1].
• Accapella And Parts: B-side of 'Confusion (Remixes '02)' 12" [#1].
• Outputs Nu-Rocktro Version (edit): 'Confusion (Remixes '02)' CDS.
• Outputs Nu-Rocktro Version: 'Confusion (Remixes '02)' 12" [#2].
• Arthur Bakers 2002 Version (edit): 'Confusion (Remixes '02)' CDS.
• Arthur Bakers 2002 Version: B-side of 'Confusion (Remixes '02)' 12" [#2].
• Asto Dazed Mix (edit): 'Confusion (Remixes '02)' CDS.
• Asto Dazed Mix: B-side of 'Confusion (Remixes '02)' 12" [#2].

'Thieves Like Us'
• Edited version: 'Thieves Like Us' 7", Singles / Total compilations.
• Full version: 'Thieves Like Us' 12", Substance / Best Of / International compilations, B-side of the New State Recordings 12" [#11].
• Instrumental Edit: B-side of 'Shell-Shock' 7".
• Instrumental: B-side of 'Murder' 12", Substance compilation (non-LP editions only).
'Lonesome Tonight'
• Edited version: B-side of 'Thieves Like Us' 7".
• Full version: B-side of 'Thieves Like Us' 12", Substance (non-LP editions only) / Retro compilations.
'Murder'
• 'Murder' 12", Substance compilation (non-LP editions only).
'The Perfect Kiss'
• Low-life album, Best Of / International / Retro / Singles [2005] compilations.
• Edited version: 'The Perfect Kiss' 7", Singles [2016] compilation.
• US edited version: Total compilation.
• Full version: 'The Perfect Kiss' 12", Low-life album (CS only).
• Edited 12" version: Substance compilation.
• Live Take Recorded At Video Shoot (aka Live Version From The Perfect Kiss Video): Retro (limited-edition bonus CD only) / Best Remixes (digital) compilations.
• 'The Kiss of Death' (edit): B-side of 'The Perfect Kiss' 7".
• 'The Kiss of Death': B-side of 'The Perfect Kiss' 12", Low-life album (CS only), Substance compilation (non-LP editions only).
• 'Perfect Pit': B-side of 'The Perfect Kiss' 12", Low-life album (CS only).
'Love Vigilantes'
• Low-life album.
'This Time Of Night'
• Low-life album.
'Sunrise'
• Low-life album, Retro compilation.
'Elegia'
• Low-life album, Retro compilation.
• Full Version: Retro compilation (limited-edition untitled bonus CD only), Low-life album (Definitive Edition Extras bonus CD only).
'Sooner Than You Think'
• Low-life album, Retro compilation.
'Sub-Culture'
• Low-life album.
• Remix (by John Robie) edited version: 'Sub-Culture' 7", Singles compilation.
• Remix (by John Robie) full version: 'Sub-Culture' 12".
• Remix (by John Robie) edited 12" version: Substance compilation.
• 'Dub-Vulture' (by John Robie) edited version: B-side of 'Sub-Culture' 7".
• 'Dub-Vulture' (by John Robie) full version: B-side of 'Sub-Culture' 12", Substance (CS edition only), New State Recordings 12" [#12].
'Face Up'
• Low-life album.
'Shell-Shock'
• Edited version: 'Shell-Shock' 7", Best Of / Singles compilations.
• Full version: 'Shell-Shock' 12".
• Edited 12" version: Substance / International / Retro compilations, B-side of New State Recordings 12" [#11].

- Soundtrack version: Pretty In Pink (Original Motion Picture Soundtrack)
- 'Shellcock' (aka Dub Version): B-side of 'Shell-Shock' 12" as before, Substance (CS edition only).

'State Of The Nation'
- Edited version: 'State Of The Nation 7", Singles compilation.
- Full version: 'State Of The Nation' 12", Substance / Best Remixes (digital) compilations.

'Shame Of The Nation'
- Edited version: B-side of the 'State Of The Nation 7".
- Full version: B-side of the 'State Of The Nation' 12", Substance compilation (non-LP editions only), B-side of the New State Recordings 12" [#12].

'Paradise'
- Brotherhood album.
- Robert Racic Remix: Retro compilation.
- Peel Session: In Session release.

'Weirdo'
- Brotherhood album.

'As It Is When It Was'
- Brotherhood album.

'Broken Promise'
- Brotherhood album, Retro compilation.

'Way Of Life'
- Brotherhood album.

'Bizarre Love Triangle'
- Brotherhood album, Retro / Singles [2005] compilations.
- Remix (by Shep Pettibone) edited version: 'Bizarre Love Triangle' 7", Total / Singles [2016] compilations.
- Remix (by Shep Pettibone) full version (aka Shep Pettibone Remix, aka Shep Pettibone Extended Dance Mix): 'Bizarre Love Triangle' 12", on the Substance / International / Retro / Best Remixes (digital) compilations, New State Recordings 12" [#8].
- 'Bizarre Dub Triangle' (by Shep Pettibone) edited version: B-side of the 'Bizarre Love Triangle' 7".
- 'Bizarre Dub Triangle' (by Shep Pettibone) full version (aka 'I Don't Care' on US editions): B-side of the 'Bizarre Love Triangle' 12", Substance (CS edition only).
- 'Bizarre Love Triangle-94' (by Stephen Hague): Best Of compilation.
- Armand Van Helden Mix: Rest Of compilation.
- Richard X Remix edited version: B-side of 'Waiting For The Sirens' Call' 7" [#3].
- Richard X Remix full version: New State Recordings 12" [#11].

'All Day Long'
- Brotherhood album, Retro compilation.

'Angel Dust'
- Brotherhood album.
- 'Evil Dust': 'True Faith' CDV, Brotherhood (Collector's Edition).

'Every Little Counts'
- Brotherhood album, Retro compilation.

'True Faith'
- Edited version: 'True Faith' 7", CDV, Total / Singles [2016] compilations.
- Full version: 'True Faith' 12" [#1], Substance / International / Retro / Singles [2005] compilations.

- Remix (by Shep Pettibone, aka Morning Sun Extended Remix and Shep Pettibone Remix): 'True Faith' 12" [#2], CDV, 'Nineteen63' CDS [#2], Rest Of / Best Remixes (digital) compilations, B-side of the New State Recordings 12" [#8].
- 'True Dub' (by Shep Pettibone, aka Alternate Faith Dub): B-side of 'True Faith' 12" [#2].
- 'TrueFaith-94' (by Mike 'Spike' Drake & Stephen Hague) edited version (aka Radio Edit): 'TrueFaith-94' 7", CS, CDS.
- 'TrueFaith-94' (by Mike 'Spike' Drake & Stephen Hague) full version (aka The 94 Remix): 'TrueFaith-94' CDS, B-side of 12", Best Of compilation.
- Perfecto Radio Edit (by Paul Oakenfold and Steve Osbourne): 'TrueFaith-94' CDS, B-side of 7", CS.
- Perfecto Mix (by Paul Oakenfold and Steve Osbourne): 'TrueFaith-94' 12", CDS.
- Sexy Disco Dub (by Paul Oakenfold and Steve Osbourne): A-side of 'TrueFaith-94' 12".
- The TWA Grim Up North Mix: 'TrueFaith-94' CDS, B-side of 12".
- Peel Session: In Session release.
- Morel's Extra Dub: 'True Faith' (US 2001) 2x12".
- Philip Steir Dub: B-side of 'True Faith' (US 2001) 2x12".
- Morel's Pink Noise Club Mix: B-side of 'True Faith' (US 2001) 2x12".
- Pink Noise Morel Edit: Retro compilation (limited-edition untitled bonus CD only).
- Philip Steir Re-Order Mix: C-side of 'True Faith' (US 2001) 2x12".
- Morel's Calling Shifty Dub: D-side of 'True Faith' (US 2001) 2x12".
- King Roc Remix: New State Recordings 12" [#9].
- Eschreamer Dub (by Tall Paul): Brotherhood (Collector's Edition).

'1963'
- Full version: B-side of 'True Faith' 7", 12" [#1], Substance compilation.
- '1963-94' (by Mike 'Spike' Drake & Stephen Hague, aka 94 Album Version): 'Nineteen63' CDS [#1], CS, Best Of compilation.
- Edit of '1963-94' (as '1963'): Singles [2005] compilation.
- 95 Arthur Baker Radio Remix: 'Nineteen63' CDS [#1], CS, Retro / Singles [2016] compilations.
- 95 Arthur Baker Remix: 'Nineteen63' CDS [#2].
- Joe T. Vanelli Dubby Mix: 'Nineteen63' 12" [#1/#3], CDS [#1].
- Joe T. Vanelli Light Mix: B-side of 'Nineteen63' 12" [#1], A-side of 12" [#3].
- Lionrock Full Throttle Mix: 'Nineteen63' 12" [#2], CDS [#1], B-side of 12" [#3].
- Lionrock Sparse N' Fast Mix: B-side of 'Nineteen63' 12" [#2].
- Lionrock M6 Sunday Morning Mix: B-side of 'Nineteen63' 12" [#2/#3].

'Touched By The Hand Of God' (Sumner/Hook/Morris/Gilbert)
- Salvation! soundtrack.
- Remix (by Arthur Baker) edited version: 'Touched By The Hand Of God' 7", Best Of / Singles compilations.
- Remix (by Arthur Baker) full version (aka Twelve Inch Mix): 'Touched By The Hand Of God' 12", CDS, International compilation, Brotherhood (Collector's Edition).
- Remix Version (by Arthur Baker): Salvation! soundtrack (EU Interphon CD-issue only).
- 'Touched By The Hand Of Dub' (by Arthur Baker) edited version: B-side of 'Touched By The Hand Of God' 7".
- 'Touched By The Hand Of Dub' (by Arthur Baker) full version: B-side of 'Touched By The Hand Of God' 12".
- Biff & Memphis Remix: Rest Of compilation.
- Peel Session: In Session release.

'Salvation Theme'
• On the Salvation! soundtrack.
'Let's Go'
• Salvation! Soundtrack, Retro compilation, Low-life (Collector's Edition).
• 'Let's G…': Retro compilation (limited-edition untitled bonus CD only).
• Re-recorded version (aka 'Let's Go (Nothing For Me)'): Best Of (US-only editions) / Retro compilations, '1963' CDS [#2].
'Sputnik'
• Salvation! soundtrack.
'Skullcrusher'
• Salvation! soundtrack.
'Fine Time'
• Edited version: 'Fine Time' 7", CDS, Best Of / Singles / Total compilations.
• Full version: 'Fine Time' 12" [#1], CDS, Technique album, Retro compilation.
• 'Fine Line': B-side of 'Fine Time' 12" [#1].
• Silk Mix (by Steve 'Silk' Hurley, aka Steve 'Silk' Hurley Remix): 'Fine Time' CDS, 12" [#2], Retro / Best Remixes (digital) compilations, B-side of New State Recordings 12" [#8], Technique (Collector's Edition).
• Messed Around Mix (by Steve 'Silk' Hurley): 'Fine Time' CDS, B-side of 12" [#2].
'Don't Do It'
• 'Fine Time' CDS, B-side of 7", B-side of 12" [#1].
'All The Way'
• Technique album.
'Love Less'
• Technique album.
'Round & Round'
• Technique album, Retro compilation.
• Remix (by Stephen Hague) edited version (aka Seven Inch): 'Round & Round' 7", CDS [#1], International / Singles compilations.
• Remix (by Stephen Hague) full version (aka Twelve Inch): 'Round & Round' 12" [#1], CDS [#1], Technique (Collector's Edition), Best Remixes (digital) compilation.
• Club Mix (by Ben Grosse and Kevin Saunderson): 'Round & Round' 12" [#2/#3], CDS [#2].
• Detroit Mix (by Kevin Saunderson, aka Kevin Saunderson Remix): 'Round & Round' CDS [#2], B-side of 12" [#2/#3], A-side of New State Recordings 12" [#8].
• Twelve Inch Mix (by Ben Grosse): 'Round & Round' CDS [#2], B-side of 12" [#3].
• 'Round & Round-94' (by Stephen Hague): Best Of compilation.
'Best & Marsh'
• Edited version (aka Seven Inch): 'Round & Round' CDS [#1], B-side of 7".
• Full version (aka Theme From Best & Marsh): B-side of 'Round & Round' 12", Retro compilation (limited-edition untitled bonus CD only), Technique (Collector's Edition).
'Guilty Partner'
• Technique album.
'Run'
• Technique album, Best Of / Singles [2005] compilations.
• 'Run 2' (by Scott Litt) edited version: 'Run 2' 7", 12", Singles [2016] compilation.
• Extended Version (by Scott Litt): A-side of 'Run 2' 12", Technique (Collector's Edition).
'MTO'
• B-side of 'Run 2' 7", 12".

- Minus Mix (by Mike 'Hitman' Wilson): B-side of 'Run 2' 12", Technique (Collector's Edition).

'Mr Disco'
- Technique album.

'Vanishing Point'
- Technique album, Best Of compilation.
- Instrumental Making Out Mix: 'Round & Round' CDS [#1], Technique (Collector's Edition).

'Dream Attack'
- Technique album.

'The Happy One'
- Edited sections (aka 'Intermede Musical No 1-6'): Substance 1989 (video) / Palatine Lane compilations.

'World In Motion'
- 'World In Motion' 7", 12" [#1], CS, CDS, CDS [2002], Best Of / Singles / Total compilations.
- Subbuteo Mix (by Graeme Park and Mike Pickering): 'World In Motion' CDS [#1], 12" [#2], Retro compilation.
- Subbuteo Dub (by Graeme Park and Mike Pickering): A-side of 'World In Motion' 12" [#2].
- Carabinieri Mix (by Andy Weatherall and Terry Farley): B-side of 'World In Motion' 12" [#2], Technique (Collector's Edition), Best Remixes (digital) compilation.
- No Alla Violenza Mix (by Andy Weatherall and Terry Farley): 'World In Motion' CDS, CDS [2002], B-side of 12" [#2].

'The B-Side'
- B-side of 'World In Motion' 7", 12" [#1], CS, CDS [#1].

'Regret'
- Republic album, International / Retro / Total compilations.
- The 7" Inch Version: 'Regret' 7", CS, CDS, Best Of / Singles compilations.
- The NewOrder Mix: B-side of 'Regret' 7", CS, CDS.
- Fire Island Mix (by Terry Farley and Pete Heller): 'Regret' 12", CDS, Rest Of compilation.
- Junior Dub Mix (by Terry Farley and Pete Heller): A-side of 'Regret' 12", CDS.
- Sabres Slow 'N' Low (by Sabres of Paradise – Andrew Weatherall, Gary Burns, and Jagz Kooner): B-side of 'Regret' 12", Retro compilation.
- Sabres Fast 'N' Throb (by Sabres of Paradise – Andrew Weatherall, Gary Burns, and Jagz Kooner): B-side of 'Regret' 12".
- Tocadisco Remix: B-side of New State Recordings 12" [#9].
- Tocadisco Dub: B-side of New State Recordings 12" [#9].

'World' / 'World (The Price Of Love)'
- Republic album.
- 'World (The Price Of Love)' The Radio Edit: 'World (The Price Of Love)' 7", CS, CDS [#1], Best Of / Singles compilations.
- Perfecto Edit: B-side of 'World (The Price Of Love)' 7", CS, CDS [#1].
- Perfecto Mix: 'World (The Price Of Love)' 12" [#1], 2x12" [#2], CDS [#1], Rest Of / Best Remixes (digital) compilations.
- Sexy Disco Dub (by Perfecto – Paul Oakenfold & Steve Osbourne): A-side of 'World (The Price Of Love)' 12" [#1], B-side of 2x12" [#2], CDS [#1].
- Brothers In Rhythm Mix: B-side of 'World (The Price Of Love)' 12" [#1], C-side of 2x12" [#2, CDS [#2].

- Brothers Dubstrumental (by Brothers In Rhythm): C-side of 'World (The Price Of Love)' 2x12" [#2], CDS [#2].
- World In Action Mix (by K-Klass): B-side of 'World (The Price Of Love)' 12" [#1], D-side of 2x12" [#2], CDS [#2].
- The Pharmacy Mix (by K-Klass): D-side of 'World (The Price Of Love)' 2x12" [#2].
- The Pharmacy Dub (by K-Klass): 'World (The Price Of Love)' CDS [#2].
- 'World (The Price Of Dub)' (by Brothers In Rhythm): B-side of 'Ruined In A Day' 12" [#1/#2].

'Ruined In A Day'
- Republic album.
- The Radio Edit: 'Ruined In A Day' CS, CDS [#1], Best Of / Singles compilations.
- The Ambient Mix (by Booga Bear): 'Ruined In A Day' CDS [#1].
- The Sly & Robbie Radio Edit: 'Ruined In A Day' CDS [#2].
- The Bogle Mix (by Sly & Robbie and Handel Tucker, aka 12 Inch Bogle Mix): 'Ruined In A Day' 12" [#1/#2], CS, CDS [#2].
- The Live Mix (by Sly & Robbie and Handel Tucker): A-side of the 'Ruined In A Day' 12", CS, CDS [#2].
- The Dance Hall Groove (by Sly & Robbie and Handel Tucker): 'Ruined In A Day' CDS [#2].
- Rhythm Twins Dub (by Sly & Robbie and Handel Tucker): 'Ruined In A Day' CDS [#2].
- Reunited In A Day Remix (by K-Klass): B-side of the 'Ruined In A Day' 12" [#1/#2], CDS [#1], Rest Of / Best Remixes (digital) compilations.
- Reunited In A Day Instrumental (by K-Klass): B-side of the 'Ruined In A Day' 12" [#2].

'Vicious Circle'
- The New Order Mix: 'Ruined In A Day' CS.
- Mike Haas Mix: 'Ruined In A Day' CDS [#1].

'Spooky'
- Republic album, 'Spooky' CDS [#1], B-side of 12" [#1], CS.
- Edit of album version: Singles [2005] compilation.
- Minimix (by Fluke, aka Fluke Edit): 'Spooky' CDS [#1], CS, Singles [2016] compilation.
- Magimix (by Fluke): 'Spooky' 12" [#1], CDS [#1], CS, Rest Of compilation.
- Moulimix (by Fluke): B-side of 'Spooky' 12" [#1], CDS [#1], CS.
- Out Of Order Mix (by Paul van Dyk): 'Spooky' CDS [#2], 12" [#2], Best Remixes (digital) compilation.
- Stadium Mix (by Tony Garcia): B-side of 'Spooky' 12" [#2], CDS [#2].
- New Order In Heaven (by Paul van Dyk): A-side of 'Spooky' 12" [#2], CDS [#2].
- Boo! Dub Mix (by Tony Garcia): B-side of 'Spooky' 12" [#2], CDS [#2].
- Stadium Instrumental (by Tony Garcia): 'Spooky' CDS [#2].
- Nightstripper Mix (by Peter Daou and Tony Garcia): 'Nineteen63' CDS [#2].

'Everyone Everywhere'
- Republic album, Retro compilation.

'Young Offender'
- Republic album.

'Liar'
- Republic album.

'Chemical'
- Republic album.

'Times Change'
• Republic album.
'Special'
• Republic album.
'Avalanche'
• Republic album.
'Brutal'
• The Beach (Motion Picture Soundtrack), Retro compilation.
'Crystal'
• Get Ready album, A-side of 'Here To Stay' 12" [#1], International / Retro compilations.
• Edited version: 'Crystal' CDS [#1], DVD, Singles / Total compilations.
• Digweed & Muir 'Bedrock' Radio Edit: 'Crystal' CDS [#2].
• Digweed & Muir 'Bedrock' Mix: 'Crystal' 12" [#1].
• Digweed & Muir 'Bedrock' Mix Edit: 'Crystal' CDS [#1].
• Digweed & Muir 'Bedrock' Dub: B-side of 'Crystal' 12" [#1].
• Lee Coombs Remix: 'Crystal' CDS [#2], 12" [#2], New State Recordings 12" [#3].
• Lee Coombs Remix edited version: Retro compilation.
• Lee Coombs Dub: B-side of 'Crystal' 12" [#2].
• John Creamer & Stephane K Intro Remix: 'Crystal' 12" [#3].
• John Creamer & Stephane K Main Remix Edit: 'Crystal' CDS [#2].
• John Creamer & Stephane K Main Remix: B-side of 'Crystal' 12" [#3], Best Remixes (digital) compilation.
'Behind Closed Doors'
• 'Crystal' CDS [#1], DVD.
'60 Miles An Hour'
• Get Ready album, International compilation.
• Radio Edit: '60 Miles An Hour' CDS [#1], DVD, Singles compilation.
• Supermen Lovers Remix: '60 Miles An Hour' CDS [#2].
'Sabotage'
• '60 Miles An Hour' CDS [#1], DVD.
'Turn My Way'
• Get Ready album.
'Vicious Streak'
• Get Ready album.
'Primitive Notion'
• Get Ready album.
'Slow Jam'
• Get Ready album, Retro compilation.
• Evening Session: In Session release.
'Rock The Shack'
• Get Ready album.
• Evening Session: In Session release.
'Someone Like You'
• Get Ready album.
• Futureshock Vocal Remix: '60 Miles An Hour' CDS [#2], 'Someone Like You' 12" [#1], B-side of New State Recordings 12" [#5].
• Futureshock Strip Down Mix: B-side of 'Someone Like You' 12" [#1].
• Gabriel + Dresden 911 Vocal Mix: A-side of 'Someone Like You' 12" [#1].
• Gabriel + Dresden Voco-tech Dub: B-side of 'Someone Like You' 12" [#1].
• James Holden Heavy Dub: '60 Miles An Hour' CDS [#2], 'Someone Like You' 12" [#2], New State Recordings 12" [#2].

- Funk D'Void Remix: '60 Miles An Hour' CDS [#1], B-side of 'Someone Like You' 12
  [#2], B-side of New State Recordings 12" [#2].
'Close Range'
- Get Ready album.
- Evening Session: In Session release.
'Run Wild'
- Get Ready album, Retro compilation.
- Steve Osborne Original Mix: Retro compilation (limited-edition untitled bonus CD
  only).
'Here To Stay'
- Radio Edit: 'Here To Stay' CDS [#1/#2], DVD, International / Singles compilations.
- Full Length Vocal: 'Here To Stay' 12" [#1/#2], CDS [#1].
- Extended Instrumental: B-side of 'Here To Stay' 12" [#2], Retro compilation.
- Felix Da Housecat – Thee Extended Glitz Mix: B-side of 'Here To Stay' 12" [#1], CDS
  [#2], DVD, New State Recordings 12" [#7], Best Remixes (digital) compilation.
- The Scumfrog – Dub Mix: B-side of 'Here To Stay' 12" [#1], CDS [#2].
'Player In The League'
- 'Here To Stay' CDS (#1).
'Such A Good Thing'
- 'World In Motion' CDS [2002], Retro compilation (limited-edition untitled bonus CD
  only).
'Vietnam'
- War Child – Hope compilation.
'Soundtrack'
- On The Peter Saville Show Soundtrack.
'Krafty'
- 'Krafty' CDS [#1], Waiting For The Sirens' Call album.
- Single Edit: 'Krafty' CDS [#1], 12" [#1], Singles / Total compilations.
- The Glimmers 12" Extended Mix: A-side of 'Krafty' 12" [#1], CDS [#2], C-side of (US)
  2x12" [#2].
- The Glimmers Dub Version: B-side of 'Krafty' 12" [#1], B-side of (US) 2x12" [#2],
  B-side of New State Recordings 12" [#6].
- Phones Reality Remix: B-side of 'Krafty' 12" [#1], CDS [#2], A-side of (US) 2x12" [#2].
- Andy Green Remix: 'Krafty' CDS [#2].
- Re-Edit Of Album Version (by Rich Costey): 'Krafty' CDS [#2].
- Riton Re-Dub Remix (aka Riton Remix): D-side of 'Krafty' (US) 2x12" [#2], New State
  Recordings 12" [#6].
- Morel's Pink Noise Vocal: 'Krafty' (US) 2x12" [#2].
- Morel's Pink Noise Dub Mix: D-side of 'Krafty' (US) 2x12" [#2].
- DJ Dan Vocal: B-side of 'Krafty' (US) 2x12" [#2], Best Remixes (digital) compilation.
- DJ Dan Dub: 'Jetstream' (US) CDS [#3].
- Eric Kupper Club Remix: C-side of 'Krafty' (US) 2x12" [#2].
- The Passengerz Revolution Club Mix: 'Jetstream' (US) CDS [#3].
- Japanese Version: Waiting For The Sirens' Call album (Japanese-only CD edition).
'Who's Joe?'
- Waiting For The Sirens' Call album.
'Hey Now What You Doing'
- Waiting For The Sirens' Call album.
'Waiting For The Sirens' Call'
- Waiting For The Sirens' Call album.

- Rich Costey Radio Edit: 'Waiting For The Sirens' Call' 7" [#1], Singles compilation.
- Rich Costey Mix: 'Waiting For The Sirens' Call' CDS.
- Band Mix: 'Waiting For The Sirens' Call' 7" [#2].
- Jacknife Lee Remix edited version: 'Waiting For The Sirens' 7" [#3].
- Jacknife Lee Remix full version: 'Waiting For The Sirens' CDS.
- Planet Funk Remix: New State Recordings 12" [#1].
- Asle Dub: B-side of New State Recordings 12" [#1].
- Filterheadz Remix: B-side of New State Recordings 12" [#4].

'I Told You So'
- Waiting For The Sirens' Call album.
- Stuart Price's Remix (aka Crazy World Mix): B-side of New State Recordings 12" [#12], Lost Sirens album.

'Morning Night And Day'
- Waiting For The Sirens' Call album.

'Dracula's Castle'
- Waiting For The Sirens' Call album.

'Jetstream'
- Waiting For The Sirens' Call album, 'Jetstream' CDS [#2].
- Radio Edit: 'Jetstream' CDS [#1], 12" [#1], Singles compilation.
- Jacques Lu Cont Remix: A-side of 'Jetstream' 12" [#1], CDS [#2], (US) 2x12" [#2], (US) CDS [#3].
- Jacques Lu Cont Dub: B-side of New State Recordings 12" [#6].
- Richard X Remix (Edit): 'Jetstream' CDS [#1].
- Richard X Remix: B-side of 'Jetstream' 12" [#1], CDS [#2], B-side of (US) 2x12" [#2], (US) CDS [#3], Best Remixes (digital) compilation.
- Tom Neville Remix: Jetstream CDS [#2], B-side of 12" [#1], C-side of (US) 2x12" [#2], (US) CDS [#3].
- Tom Neville Remix Dub (aka Tom Neville Dub): A-side of (US) 'Jetstream' 2x12" [#2], B-side of New State Recordings 12" [#6].
- Arthur Baker Remix: 'Jetstream' CDS [#2], C-side of (US) 2x12" [#2], (US) CDS [#3], A-side of New State Recordings 12" [#11].
- Phela Vocal Remix (by Pete Heller): New State Recordings 12" [#5].
- Pete Heller Remix (Phela Dub): D-side of (US) 'Jetstream' 2x12" [#2], (US) CDS [#3].

'Guilt Is A Useless Emotion'
- Waiting For The Sirens' Call album, 'Guilt Is A Useless Emotion' (US) Digital, CDS [#1/#2].
- DJ Dan Club Mix Edit: 'Guilt Is A Useless Emotion' (US) CDS [#2].
- DJ Dan Club Mix: 'Guilt Is A Useless Emotion' (US) Digital, CDS [#1].
- DJ Dan Mixshow: 'Guilt Is A Useless Emotion' (US) CDS [#1].
- Bill Harnel Vocal Mix Edit: 'Guilt Is A Useless Emotion' (US) CDS [#2].
- Bill Harnel Vocal Mix: 'Guilt Is A Useless Emotion' (US) Digital, CDS [#1].
- MARK!'s True N.O. Vox Edit (by Mark Picchiotti, aka Blueplate Vox Edit): 'Guilt Is A Useless Emotion' (US) CDS [#2].
- MARK!'s True N.O. Vox (by Mark Picchiotti): 'Guilt Is A Useless Emotion' (US) Digital, CDS [#1].
- MARK!'s True N.O. Dub (by Mark Picchiotti): 'Guilt Is A Useless Emotion' (US) CDS [#1].
- Morel's Pink Noise Mix Edit (by Richard Morel): 'Guilt Is A Useless Emotion' (US) CDS [#2].

- Morel's Pink Noise Mix (by Richard Morel): 'Guilt Is A Useless Emotion' (US) Digital, CDS [#1].
- Morel's Pink Noise Dub (by Richard Morel): 'Guilt Is A Useless Emotion' (US) CDS [#1].
- Mac Quayle Extended: 'Guilt Is A Useless Emotion' (US) Digital, CDS [#1].
- Mac Quayle Vox (aka Mac Quayle Vocal Mix): Waiting For The Sirens' Call album (US-only CD edition).

'Turn'
- Waiting For The Sirens' Call album.
- Edit (by Stephen Street): Singles compilation.

'Working Overtime'
- Waiting For The Sirens' Call album.

'Exit'
- Music From The Motion Picture Control.

'Hypnosis'
- Music From The Motion Picture Control.

'Get Out'
- Music From The Motion Picture Control.

'I'll Stay with You'
- Lost Sirens album, Singles [2016] compilation.

'Sugarcane'
- Lost Sirens album.

'Recoil'
- Lost Sirens album.

'Californian Grass'
- Lost Sirens album.

'Hellbent'
- Lost Sirens album, Total compilation.

'Shake It Up'
- Lost Sirens album.

'I've Got A Feeling'
- Lost Sirens album.

'Restless'
- Music Complete album.
- Single Version: 'Restless' CDS, Digital.
- Extended Mix: A-side of Music Complete Box Set 12"s, Complete Music album.
- Extended 12" Mix: 'Restless' 12", CDS, Digital.
- Agoria Remix: B-side of 'Restless' 12", CDS, Digital.
- Agoria Dub: Music Complete Remix EP (digital).
- xxxy Build Up Mix: 'Restless' CDS, Digital.
- RAC Mix: 'Restless' CDS, Digital.
- Andrew Weatherall Remix: B-side of 'Restless' 12", CDS, Digital.

'Singularity'
- Music Complete album.
- Single Edit: 'Singularity' CDS, Digital.
- Extended Mix: B-side of Music Complete Box Set 12"s, 'Singularity' 12", CDS, Digital, Complete Music album.
- Erol Alkan's Stripped Mix: 'Singularity' CDS, Digital.
- Erol Alkan's Extended Rework: B-side of 'Singularity' 12", Digital.
- Mark Reeder's Duality Remix Edit: 'Singularity' CDS, Digital.
- Mark Reeder's Duality Remix: 'Singularity' Digital.

- Mark Reeder's Individual Remix: A-side of 'Singularity' 12", Digital.
- JS Zeiter Remix: 'Singularity' CDS, Digital.
- JS Zeiter Dub: B-side of 'Singularity' 12", Digital.
- Liars Remix: 'Singularity' Digital.

'Plastic'
- Music Complete album.
- Extended Mix: C-side of Music Complete Box Set 12"s, Complete Music album.

'Tutti Frutti'
- Music Complete album.
- Single Version: 'Tutti Frutti' CDS, Digital.
- Extended Mix: D-side of Music Complete Box Set 12"s, Complete Music album.
- Extended 12" Mix: 'Tutti Frutti' 12" [#1/#2].
- Extended 12" Mix Two: 'Tutti Frutti' CDS, Digital.
- Hot Chip Remix Vinyl Edit: B-side of the 'Tutti Frutti' 12" [#1].
- Hot Chip Remix: 'Tutti Frutti' CDS, Digital.
- Tom Trago's Crazy Days Remix: 'Tutti Frutti' CDS, Digital.
- Richy Ahmed Remix: 'Tutti Frutti' CDS, Digital.
- Hallo Halo Remix: 'Tutti Frutti' CDS, Digital.
- Tom Rowlands Remix: 'Singularity' CDS, Digital.
- Takkyu Ishino Remix: B-side of (JP) 'Tutti Frutti' 12" [#2], Music Complete Remix EP (digital).

'People On The High Line'
- Music Complete album.
- Extended Mix: E-side of Music Complete Box Set 12"s, B-side of the 'People On The High Line' 12", CDS, Digital, Complete Music album.
- Richard X Video Mix: 'People On The High Line' 7".
- Richard X Radio Edit: 'People On The High Line' CDS, Digital.
- Claptone Radio Edit: B-side of 'People On The High Line' 7".
- Claptone 12" Remix: 'People On The High Line' 12", CDS, Digital.
- LNTG Can't Get Any Higher Remix (by Late Night Tuff Guy): 'People On The High Line' CDS, Digital.
- Planet Funk Remix: 'People On The High Line' CDS, Digital.
- Hybrid Remix: 'People On The High Line' CDS, Digital.
- Hybrid Armchair Remix: 'People On The High Line' CDS, Digital.
- Purple Disco Machine Remix: Music Complete Remix EP (digital).

'Stray Dog'
- Music Complete album.
- Extended Mix: F-side of Music Complete Box Set 12"s, Complete Music album.

'Academic'
- Music Complete album.
- Extended Mix: G-side of Music Complete Box Set 12"s, Complete Music album.
- Mark Reeder's Academix: Music Complete Remix EP (digital).

'Nothing But A Fool'
- Music Complete album.
- Extended Mix: H-side of Music Complete Box Set 12"s.
- Extended Mix Two: Complete Music album.

'Unlearn This Hatred'
- Music Complete album.
- Extended Mix: I-side of Music Complete Box Set 12"s, Complete Music album.

'The Game'
• Music Complete album.
• Extended Mix: J-side of Music Complete Box Set 12"s, Complete Music album.
• Mark Reeder Spielt Mit Version: Music Complete Remix EP (digital).
'Superheated'
• Music Complete album.
• Extended Mix: K-side of Music Complete Box Set 12"s.
• Extended Mix Two: Complete Music album.
'4'33"'
• STUMM433 compilation.
'Be A Rebel'
• 'Be A Rebel' 12" [#1], CDS, Digital [#1/#2/#7].
• Edit: 'Be A Rebel' CDS, Digital [#1/#7].
• Renegade Spezial Edit (by Bernard Sumner): 'Be A Rebel' CDS, Digital [#2/#7], C-side of 2x12" [#2].
• Bernard's Renegade Mix (by Bernard Sumner): 'Be A Rebel' 12" [#1], CDS, Digital [#3/#7].
• Bernard's Renegade Instrumental Mix (by Bernard Sumner): B-side of 'Be A Rebel' 12" [#1], CDS, Digital [#3/#7].
• Stephen's T34 Mix (by Stephen Morris): B-side of 'Be A Rebel' 12" [#1], CDS, Digital [#3/#7].
• Paul Woolford Remix Edit: 'Be A Rebel' Digital [#4].
• Paul Woolford Remix New Order Edit: 'Be A Rebel' 2x12" [#2], CDS, Digital [#7].
• Maceo Plex Remix: B-side of 'Be A Rebel' 2x12" [#2], CDS, Digital [#4/#7].
• Bernard's Outlaw Mix (by Bernard Sumner): C-side of 'Be A Rebel' 2x12" [#2], CDS, Digital [#4/#7].
• Mark Reeder's Dirty Devil Remix: D-side of 'Be A Rebel' 2x12" [#2], CDS, Digital [#5/#7].
• JakoJako Remix: A-side of 'Be A Rebel' 2x12" [#2], CDS, Digital [#7].
• Melawati Remix: B-side of 'Be A Rebel' 2x12" [#2], CDS, Digital [#7].
• Arthur Baker Remix: D-side of 'Be A Rebel' 2x12" [#2], CDS, Digital [#6/#7].

Core Release Discography

This is a discography of New Order's main UK singles, albums, and compilations, along with key reissues, and some miscellaneous, promotional & non-UK releases where there is unique content or format. Note, however, that it does not list *every* live or radio version, limited edition, radio/DJ-promo, label-advance, non-UK pressing, or general reissue, because there are many such artefacts. There are also many New Order remixes which appear outside the core catalogue; some considered official, and many which are unofficial (e.g., on white labels).

To detail every possible source of New Order music would require its own lengthy book, so your best source of discographic information is Discogs.

Singles
'Ceremony'
• 7": March 1981 – Factory FAC 33
• 12" [#1]: March 1981 – Factory FAC 33 [green sleeve]. Remastered & reissued 8 March 2019.
• 12" [#2]: September 1981 – Factory FAC 33 [cream/blue sleeve]. Remastered & reissued 8 March 2019.
• 12" [#3]: 16 April 2011 – Rhino Records FAC 33 [RSD issue]
'Procession'
• 7": September 1981 – Factory FAC 53 [9 different sleeves]
'Everything's Gone Green'
• 12": December 1981 – Factory Benelux (BL) FBNL 8. Remastered & reissued 15 March 2019 – Factory Benelux FBN 8.
• CDS: 1990 – Factory Benelux (BL) FBN 8CD
'Temptation'
• 7": 10 May 1982 – Factory FAC 63. Remastered & reissued 18 April 2009 – Warner / Rhino Records FAC 63 [RSD issue]
• 12": 10 May 1983 – Factory FAC 63. Remastered & reissued 22 March 2019.
'Blue Monday'
• 12": 7 March 1983 – Factory FAC 73. Remastered & reissued 22 March 2019.
'Confusion'
• 7": 22 August 1983 – Factory 7FAC 93 [radio promo]
• 12": 22 August 1983 – Factory FAC 93. Remastered & reissued 2 October 2020.
'Thieves Like Us'
• 7": April 1984 – Factory FAC 103 [radio promo]
• 12": April 1984 – Factory FAC 103. Remastered & reissued 2 October 2020.
'Murder'
• 12": May 1984 – Factory Benelux (BL) FBN 22. Remastered & reissued 2 October 2020.
'The Perfect Kiss'
• 7": 12 May 1985 – Factory FAC 123-7
• 12": 12 May 1985 – Factory FAC 123. Remastered & reissued 27 January 2023.
'Sub-Culture'
• 7": 28 October 1985 – Factory FAC 133
• 12": 28 October 1985 – Factory FAC 133. Remastered & reissued 27 January 2023.
'Shell-Shock'
• 7": 17 March 1986 – Factory FAC 143
• 12": 17 March 1986 – Factory FAC 143. Remastered & reissued 27 January 2023.

'State Of The Nation'
• 7": 15 September 1986 – Factory FAC 153
• 12": 15 September 1986 – Factory FAC 153
'Bizarre Love Triangle'
• 7": 5 November 1986 – Factory FAC 163-7
• 12": 5 November 1986 – Factory FAC 163
'True Faith'
• 7": 20 July 1987 – Factory FAC 183/7
• 12" [#1]: 20 July 1987 – Factory FAC 183
• 12" [#2]: September 1987 – Factory FAC 183R
• CDV: August 1988 – Factory FACDV 183
'Touched By The Hand Of God'
• 7": 7 December 1987 – Factory FAC 193/7
• 12": 7 December 1987 – Factory FAC 193
• CDS: 7 December 1987 – Factory FACD 193
'Blue Monday 1988'
• 7": April 1988 – Factory FAC 73R-7
• 12": April 1988 – Factory FAC 73R
• CDS: April 1988 – Factory FACD 73R
• CDV: April 1988 – Factory FACDV 73R
'Fine Time'
• 7": 28 November 1988 – Factory FAC 223-7
• 12" [#1]: 28 November 1988 – Factory FAC 223
• 12" [#2]: December 1988 – Factory FAC 223R
• CDS: 28 November 1988 – Factory FACD 223
'Round & Round'
• 7": 27 February 1989 – Factory FAC 263/7
• 12" [#1]: 27 February 1989 – Factory FAC 263
• 12" [#2]: April 1989 – Factory FAC 263R
• 12" [#3]: April 1989 – Factory FAC 263DJ [DJ promo]
• CDS [#1]: 27 February 1989 – Factory FACD 263
• CDS [#2]: April 1989 – Factory FACD 263R
'Run 2'
• 7": 28 August 1989 – Factory FAC 273/7 [radio promo]
• 12": 28 August 1989 – Factory FAC 273
'World In Motion'
• 7": 21 May 1990 – Factory FAC 293/7
• 12" [#1]: 21 May 1990 – Factory FAC 293
• 12" [#2]: June 1990 – Factory FAC 293R
• CS: 21 May 1990 – Factory FAC 293C
• CDS [#1]: 21 May 1990 – Factory FACD 293
'Confusion (Remix)'
• 12": July 1990 – Minimal Records (US) QAL-249
'Regret'
• 7": 5 April 1993 – London Records NUO1
• 12": 5 April 1993 – London Records NUOX1
• CS: 5 April 1993 – London Records NUOMC1
• CDS: 5 April 1993 – London Records NUOCD1
'Ruined In A Day'
• 12" [#1]: 21 June 1993 – London Records NUOX2

163

- 12" [#2]: 21 June 1993 – London Records NUOXDJ2 [DJ promo]
- CS: 21 June 1993 – London Records NUOMC2
- CDS [#1]: 21 June 1993 – London Records NUOCD2
- CDS [#2]: 28 June 1993 – London Records NUCDP2

'World (The Price Of Love)'
- 7": 5 April 1993 – London Records 857240.7
- 12" [#1]: 23 August 1993 – London Records NUOX3
- 2x12" [#2]: 23 August 1993 – London Records NUOXDJ3 [DJ promo]
- CS: 23 August 1993 – London Records NUOMC3
- CDS [#1]: 23 August 1993 – London Records NUOCD3
- CDS [#2]: 23 August 1993 – London Records NUCDP3

'Spooky'
- 12" [#1]: 6 December 1993 – London Records NUOX4
- 12" [#2]: 13 December 1993 – London Records NUXXDJ4 [DJ promo]
- CS: 6 December 1993 – London Records NUOMC4
- CDS [#1]: 6 December 1993 – London Records NUOCD4
- CDS [#2]: 13 December 1993 – London Records NUCDP4

'TrueFaith-94'
- 7": 7 November 1994 – London Records NUO5
- 12": 7 November 1994 – London Records NUOX5
- CS: 7 November 1994 – London Records NUOMC5
- CDS: 31 October 1994 – London Records NUOCD5

'Nineteen63'
- 12" [#1]: 1994 – London Records NUOXDJ6 [DJ promo]
- 12" [#2]: 1994 – London Records NUXXDJ6 [DJ promo]
- 12" [#3]: 9 January 1995 – London Records NUOX6
- CS: 9 January 1995 – London Records NUOMC6
- CDS [#1]: 9 January 1995 – London Records NUOCD6
- CDS [#2]: 16 January 1995 – London Records NUCDP6

'BlueMonday-95'
- 12" [#1]: 26 July 1995 – London Records NUOX7
- 12" [#2]: 26 July 1995 – London Records 850041.1
- CS: 26 July 1995 – London Records NUOMC7
- CDS [#1]: 26 July 1995 – London Records NUOCD7
- CDS [#2]: 26 July 1995 – London Records 850041.2

'Video 5-8-6'
- 12": 15 September 1997 – Touch Tone7.1
- CDS: 15 September 1997 – Touch Tone7

'True Faith' (2001)
- 2x12": 2001 – Qwest Records (US) PRO-A-100663

'Crystal'
- 12" [#1]: 13 August 2001 – London Records NUOX8
- 12" [#2]: 13 August 2001 – London Records NUOXX8
- 12" [#3]: 13 August 2001 – London Records NUOXXX8
- CS: 13 August 2001 – London Records NUOMC8
- CDS [#1]: 13 August 2001 – London Records NUOCD8
- CDS [#2]: 13 August 2001 – London Records NUCDP8
- DVD: 13 August 2001 – London Records NUDVD8

'60 Miles An Hour'
- CDS [#1]: 19 November 2001 – London Records NUOCD9

- CDS [#2]: 19 November 2001 – London Records NUCDP9
- DVD: 19 November 2001 – London Records NUDVD9
'Someone Like You'
- 12" [#1]: 17 December 2001 – London Records NUOX10
- 12" [#2]: 17 December 2001 – London Records NUOXX10
'Confusion (Remixes '02)'
- 12" [#1]: 2002 – Whacked Records (US) WACKT002
- 12" [#2]: 2002 – Whacked Records (US) WACKT002RE
- CDS: 2002 – Whacked Records (US) WACKT002CD
'Here To Stay'
- 12" [#1]: 15 April 2002 – London Records NUOX11
- 12" [#2]: 15 April 2002 – London Records NXDJ11
- CDS [#1]: 15 April 2002 – London Records NUOCD11
- CDS [#2]: 15 April 2002 – London Records NUCDP11
- DVD: 15 April 2002 – London Records NUDVD11
'World In Motion'
- CDS [#2]: 3 June 2002 – London Records NUOCD12
'Krafty'
- 12" [#1]: 7 March 2005 – London Records NUOX13
- 2x12" [#2]: March 2005 – Warner Bros. Records (US) 0-42800
- CDS [#1]: 7 March 2005 – London Records NUOCD13
- CDS [#2]: 7 March 2005 – London Records NUCDP13
'Jetstream'
- 12" [#1]: 16 May 2005 – London Records NUOX14
- 2x12" [#2]: June 2005 – Warner Bros. Records (US) 0-42813
- CDS [#1]: 16 May 2005 – London Records NUOCD14
- CDS [#2]: 16 May 2005 – London Records NUCDP14
- CDS [#3]: 12 July 2005 – Warner Bros. Records (US) 42813-2
'Waiting For The Sirens' Call'
- 7" [#1]: 3 October 2005 – London Records NUO15V1
- 7" [#2]: 3 October 2005 – London Records NUO15V2
- 7" [#3]: 3 October 2005 – London Records NUO15V3
- CDS: 3 October 2005 – London Records NUOCD15
'Guilt Is A Useless Emotion'
- CDS [#1]: 3 November 2005 – Warner Bros. Records (US) PRO-CDR-101687 [promo only]
- CDS [#2]: 16 November 2005 – Warner Bros. Records (US) PRO-CDR-101687-2 [promo only]
- Digital: 29 November 2005 – Warner Bros. Records (US) [iTunes only]
'Restless'
- Digital: 28 July 2015 – Mute Records IMUTE541
- 12": 6 October 2015 – Mute Records 12MUTE541
- CDS: 6 October 2015 – Mute Records CDMUTE541
'Tutti Frutti'
- Digital: 20 October 2015 – Mute Records
- 12" [#1]: 11 December 2015 – Mute Records 12MUTE542
- 12" [#2]: 11 December 2015 – Mute Records (JP) 12JMUTE542
- CDS: 11 December 2015 – Mute Records CDMUTE542
'Singularity'
- Digital: 3 February 2016 – Mute Records

- 12": 25 March 2016 – Mute Records 12MUTE545
- CDS: 25 March 2016 – Mute Records CDMUTE545

'People On The High Line'
- Digital: 21 June 2016 – Mute Records
- 7": 29 July 2016 – Mute Records MUTE553 [shaped]
- 12": 29 July 2016 – Mute Records 12MUTE553
- CDS: 29 July 2016 – Mute Records CDMUTE553

'Be A Rebel'
- Digital [#1]: 8 September 2020 – Mute Records I1MUTE619
- Digital [#2]: 14 October 2020 – Mute Records I2MUTE619
- Digital [#3]: 13 November 2020 – Mute Records IMUTE619
- Digital [#4]: 16 December 2020 – Mute Records R1MUTE619
- Digital [#5]: 5 March 2021 – Mute Records R2MUTE619
- Digital [#6]: 4 May 2021 – Mute Records R3MUTE619
- Digital [#7]: 27 August 2021 – Mute Records IRMUTE619
- 12" [#1]: 13 November 2020 – Mute Records 12MUTE619
- 12" [#2]: 27 August 2021 – Mute Records R12MUTE619
- CDS: 27 August 2021 – Mute Records CDMUTE619

Albums
Movement
- LP: 13 November 1981 – Factory FACT 50. Remastered and reissued (as LP+2CD+DVD Box Set Definitive Edition) 5 April 2019 – Warner Music 0190295662882.
- CS: 1985 – Factory FACT 50C
- CD: 1986 – Factory FACD 50. Remastered & reissued (as 2CD Collector's Edition) 6 October 2008 – London Records / Rhino Records 2564693694. See also Definitive Edition above.

Power Corruption And Lies
- LP: May 1983 – Factory FACT 75. Remastered and reissued (as LP+2CD+2DVD Box Set Definitive Edition) 2 October 2020 – Warner Music 0190295659158.
- CS: December 1986 – Factory FACT 75C
- CD: 1986 – Factory FACD 75. Remastered & reissued (as 2CD Collector's Edition) 29 September 2008 – London Records / Rhino Records 2564693698. See also Definitive Edition above.

Low-life
- LP: 13 May 1985 – Factory FACT 100. Remastered and reissued (as LP+2CD+2DVD Box Set Definitive Edition) 27 January 2023 - Warner Music 0825646253012.
- CS: 13 May 1985 – Factory FACT 100C
- CD: October 1985 – Factory FACD 100. Remastered & reissued (as 2CD Collector's Edition) 29 September 2008 – London Records / Rhino Records 2564693700. See also Definitive Edition above.

Brotherhood
- LP: September 1986 – Factory FACT 150
- CS: September 1986 – Factory FACT 150C
- CD: September 1986 – Factory FACD 150. Remastered & reissued (as 2CD Collector's Edition) 29 September 2008 – London Records / Rhino Records 2564693699.

Technique
- LP: 30 January 1989 – Factory FACT 275
- CS: 30 January 1989 – Factory FACT 275C

- DAT: 30 January 1989 – Factory FACT 275D
- CD: 30 January 1989 – Factory FACD 275. Remastered & reissued (as 2CD Collector's Edition) 29 September 2008 – London Records / Rhino Records 2564693697.

Republic
- LP: 3 May 1993 – London Records 828 413.1. Remastered & reissued 24 September 2015 – Rhino Records 0825646072231.
- CS: 3 May 1993 – London Records 828 413.4
- CD: 3 May 1993 – London Records 828 413.2

Get Ready
- LP: 27 August 2001 – London Records 8573896211. Remastered & reissued 24 September 2015 – Rhino Records 0825646071043.
- CS: 27 August 2001 – London Records 8573896214
- CD: 27 August 2001 – London Records 8573896212

Waiting For The Sirens' Call
- 2LP: 28 March 2005 – London Records 2564622021. Remastered & reissued 24 September 2015 – Rhino Records 0825646071968.
- CD: 28 March 2005 – London Records 2564622022

Lost Sirens
- LP: 14 January 2013 – Rhino Records 2564662715
- CD: 14 January 2013 – Rhino Records 2564653448

Music Complete
- 2LP: 25 September 2015 – Mute Records STUMM390
- CD: 25 September 2015 – Mute Records CDSTUMM390
- 2LP+6x12" Box Set: 6 November 2015 – Mute Records BXSTUMM390

Complete Music
- 2CD: 13 May 2016 – Mute Records LCDSTUMM390

Compilations
1981-1982
- EP: 1982 – Factory (US) FACTUS 8
- CD: 1989 – PolyGram (CA) 830408-2

Substance 1987
- 2LP: 17 August 1987 – Factory FACT 200
- 2CS: 17 August 1987 – Factory FACT 200C
- 2CD: 17 August 1987 – Factory FACD 200
- 2DAT: 17 August 1987 – Factory FACT 200D

Substance 1989
- VHS: September 1989 – Factory FACT 225
- LD: 21 May 1991 – Virgin Vision (JP) TELP 42036

(The Best Of) NewOrder
- 2LP: 21 November 1994 – London Records 828580.1
- CS: 21 November 1994 – London Records 828580.4
- CD: 21 November 1994 – London Records 828580.2
- VHS: 1994 – PolyGram Video (DE) 6337303
- LD: 25 Jan 1995 – PolyGram Video (JP) POLD 1011

(The Rest Of) NewOrder
- 2LP: 21 August 1995 – London Records 828657.1
- CS: 21 August 1995 – London Records 828657.4
- CD: 21 August 1995 – London Records 828657.2

International
- CD [#1]: 4 November 2002 – London Records 0927492262
- 2CD [#2]: 4 November 2002 – London Records 5050466144522 [limited edition]

Retro
- 4CD: 9 December 2002 – London Records 0927494992. Initial release with bonus 5th CD.

Best Remixes
- Digital: 21 June 2005 – Warner Bros. Records

A Collection
- DVD: 19 September 2005 – Warner Music Vision 034970484-2

Singles
- 2CD: 3 October 2005 – London Records 2564626902. Remastered & revised
- 2CD: 9 September 2016 – Rhino Records 0825646069637.
- 4LP: 9 September 2016 – Rhino Records 0825646069620

Total (From Joy Division To New Order)
- CD: 6 June 2011 – Rhino Records 5052498647958
- 2LP: 29 November 2018 – Warner Music 0190295663841

Music Complete: Remix EP
- Digital: 7 April 2017 – Mute Records RISTUMM390

Live and Radio Session Releases
Taras Shevchenko
- VHS: August 1983 – Factory FACT 77
- BETA: August 1983 – Factory FACT 77

Pumped Full Of Drugs
- VHS: August 1986 – Factory FACT 177
- BETA: August 1986 – Factory FACT 177
- LD: 21 August 1985 – Columbia (JP) 78C58-6098
- DVD: December 2001 – Columbia (JP) COBY-4138

Academy
- VHS: April 1989 – Palace PVC 3019M

The Peel Sessions (1982 session)
- EP: September 1986 – Strange Fruit SFPS 001. Remastered & reissued 29 August 2020 – BBC 0190295303433.
- CS: 1987 – Strange Fruit SFPSC 001
- CD: March 1988 – Strange Fruit SFPSCD 001

The Peel Sessions (1981 session)
- EP: 16 November 1987 – Strange Fruit SFPS 039
- CD: September 1988 – Strange Fruit SFPSCD 039
- CS: 1989 – Strange Fruit SFPSC 039

Peel Sessions (combined)
- LP: 1990 – Strange Fruit SFRLP 110
- CS: 1990 – Strange Fruit SFRMC 110
- CD: 1990 – Strange Fruit SFRCD 110. Reissued 2000 – Strange Fruit SFRSCD 095.

BBC Radio 1 **Live In Concert**
- LP: 10 February 1992 – Windsong International WINLP 011
- CS: 10 February 1992 – Windsong International WINMC 011
- CD: 10 February 1992 – Windsong International WINCD 011. Reissued 2000 – Strange Fruit SFRSCD 093.

3 16
- DVD: May 2001 – Warner Music Vision 8573848022

5 11
- DVD: December 2002 – Warner Music Vision 0927493662
In Session
- CD: 12 April 2004 – Strange Fruit SFRSCD 128
Live In Glasgow
- 2DVD+CD: 2 June 2008 – Warner Music Entertainment 5051442846829
Live At The London Troxy (10 December 2011)
- 2CD: 21 December 2011 – Abbey Road Live Here Now
- Digital: 21 December 2011 – Abbey Road Live Here Now
Live At Bestival 2012
- 2CD: 5 July 2013 – Sunday Best Recordings SBESTCD60
- Digital: 5 July 2013 – Sunday Best Recordings
NOMC15
- 3LP: 16 June 2017 – Live Here Now LHN018LP
- 2CD: 16 June 2017 – Live Here Now LHN018CD
- Digital: 16 June 2017 – Live Here Now
∑(No,12k,Lg,17Mif) New Order + Liam Gillick: So It Goes..
- 3LP: 12 July 2019 – Mute STUMM450
- 2CD: 12 July 2019 – Mute CDSTUMM450
- Digital: 12 July 2019 – Mute
Education Entertainment Recreation
- 3LP: 7 May 2021 – Warner Music 0190295211646
- 2CD: 7 May 2021 – Warner Music 0190295048112
- BLU+2CD Box Set: 7 May 2021 – Warner Music 0190295375973
- Digital: 7 May 2021 – Warner Music

Miscellaneous
Merry Xmas From The Haçienda And Factory Records (incl. 'Ode To Joy' and 'Rocking Carol')
- Flexi 7": December 1982 – Factory FAC 51B
Feature Mist (incl. 'Video 5-8-6' [parts 1+3])
- CS: 1 December 1982 – Touch T01
Discreet Campaigns (incl. 'Sunrise – Instrumental Rough Mix')
- CS: 1985 – Rorschach Testing Product ROR 1
Pretty In Pink (Original Motion Picture Soundtrack) (incl. 'Shell-Shock')
- LP: 1986 – A&M Records (US) SP-3901
- CS: 1986 – A&M Records (US) CS-3901
- CD: 1986 – A&M Records (US) CD-3901
Salvation! (Original Soundtrack) (incl. 'Touched By The Hand Of God', 'Salvation Theme', 'Sputnik', 'Let's Go', and 'Skullcrusher')
- LP: February 1988 – Les Disques Du Crépuscule (BL) TWI 774 / Interphon (DE) IPLP 2012-32
- CD: February 1988 – Les Disques Du Crépuscule (BL) TWI 774-2 / Interphon (DE) IPCD 2022-36
Palatine Lane (incl. 'Intermede Musical No 1-6')
- CDS: January 1992 – Factory FAC 303
New Order Story
- VHS: November 1993 – PolyGram Video 087134-3
- LD: 1993 – Polygram Video (JP) POLD 1007/8
- DVD: 19 September 2005 – Warner Music Vision 034970485-2

Touch. Sampler (incl. 'Video 5-8-6' [part 2])
* CD: 1997 – Touch T_Zero_2
The Beach (Motion Picture Soundtrack) (incl. 'Brutal')
* CS: 21 February 2000 – London Records 4344310794
* CD: 21 February 2000 – London Records 4344310792
The Peter Saville Show Soundtrack (incl. 'Soundtrack')
* CD: June 2003 – London Records SAVILLE 1
War Child – Hope (incl. 'Vietnam')
* CD: April 2004 – London Records 5046658462
New State Recordings 12x12" Campaign
* 12" [#1]: 27 February 2006 – New State Recordings NSER007 incl. remixes of 'Waiting For The Sirens' Call'.
* 12" [#2]: 27 February 2006 – New State Recordings NSER008 incl. remixes of 'Someone Like You'.
* 12" [#3]: 27 February 2006 – New State Recordings NSER009 incl. remixes of 'Confusion', and 'Crystal'.
* 12" [#4]: 27 February 2006 – New State Recordings NSER010 incl. remixes of 'Confusion', 'Everything's Gone Green', and 'Waiting For The Sirens' Call'.
* 12" [#5]: 27 February 2006 – New State Recordings NSER011 incl. remixes of 'Jetstream', and 'Someone Like You'.
* 12" [#6]: 27 February 2006 – New State Recordings NSER012 incl. remixes of 'Krafty', and 'Jetstream'.
* 12" [#7]: 27 February 2006 – New State Recordings NSER014 incl. remixes of 'Here To Stay', and 'Jetstream'.
* 12" [#8]: 27 February 2006 – New State Recordings NSER015 incl. remixes of 'Bizarre Love Triangle', 'Round & Round', 'True Faith', and 'Fine Time'.
* 12" [#9]: 27 February 2006 – New State Recordings NSER016 incl. remixes of 'True Faith', and 'Regret'.
* 12" [#10]: 27 February 2006 – New State Recordings NSER017 incl. remixes of 'Blue Monday'.
* 12" [#11]: 27 February 2006 – New State Recordings NSER018 incl. remixes of 'Bizarre Love Triangle', 'Jetstream', 'Shell-Shock', and 'Thieves Like Us'.
* 12" [#12]: 27 February 2006 – New State Recordings NSER019 incl. remixes of 'Sub-Culture', 'State Of The Nation', and 'I Told You So'.
Music From The Motion Picture Control (incl. 'Exit', 'Hypnosis', and 'Get Out')
* CD: 1 October 2007 – Warner Bros. Records 5051442447828
Ghosts Of Christmas Past (Remake) (incl. 'Ode To Joy', and 'Rocking Carol')
* 2CD: 30 November 2015 – Les Disques Du Crépuscule TWI 158 CD
STUMM443 (incl. 4'33")
* 5LP: 4 October 2019 – Mute Records STUMM433
* 5CD: 4 October 2019 – Mute Records CDSTUMM433

Above: Stephen Morris, 6 Apr 2014, Lollapalooza, São Paulo, Brazil.

Below: Tom Chapman, 16 Jun 2016, Glastonbury UK.

Further Reading

Aizlewood, J., *Decades Joy Division and New Order* (Palazzo Editions Ltd, 2021)
Cummins, K., *Joy Division* (Random House Inc., 2010)
Cummins, K., *New Order* (Random House Inc., 2015)
Cummins, K., *Joy Division: Juvenes* (Octopus, 2021)
Curtis, D., *Touching From a Distance* (Faber & Faber, 2014)
Curtis, I., *So This is Permanence – Joy Division Lyrics and Notebooks* (Faber & Faber, 2014)
Edge, B., *New Order + Joy Division – Pleasures and Wayward Distractions* (Omnibus Press, 1984)
Flowers, C., *New Order + Joy Division* (Omnibus, 2012)
Gretton, R., *One Top Class Manager* (www.1topclassmanager.co.uk, 2008)
Hook, P., *The Haçienda – How Not To Run A Club* (Simon & Schuster UK, 2009)
Hook, P., *Unknown Pleasures – Inside Joy Division* (Simon & Schuster UK, 2013)
Hook, P., *Substance – Inside New Order* (Simon & Schuster UK, 2016)
Middles, M., *Factory – The Story of the Record Label* (Ebury Publishing, 2011)
Middles, M., *From Joy Division to New Order – The True Story of Anthony H. Wilson and Factory Records* (Virgin, 2002)
Morley, P., *From Manchester with Love – The Life and Opinions of Tony Wilson* (Faber & Faber, 2021)
Morley, P., *Joy Division – Piece by Piece* (Plexus Publishing, 2015)
Morris, S., *Record Play Pause – Confessions of a Post-Punk Percussionist: Volume I* (Little, Brown Book Group, 2019)
Morris, S., *Fast Forward – Confessions of a Post-Punk Percussionist: Volume II* (Little, Brown Book Group, 2020)
Nolan, D., *Bernard Sumner – Joy Division, Electronic and New Order Versus the World* (Independent Music, 2007)
Nolan, D., *Tony Wilson – You're Entitled to an Opinion But The High Times and Many Lives of the Man Behind Factory Records and The Haçienda* (John Blake, 2010)
Nice, J., *Shadowplayers – The Rise and Fall of Factory Records* (Quarto Publishing Group UK, 2011)
Ott, C., *Joy Division's Unknown Pleasures* (Bloomsbury Publishing, 2004)
Reade, L., *Mr Manchester and the Factory Girl – The Story of Tony and Lindsay Wilson.* ISBN 9780859658751
Robertson, M., *Factory Records – The Complete Graphic Album* (Thames & Hudson, 2007)
Savage, J., *The Haçienda Must be Built!* (International Music Publications, 1992)
Savage, J., *This Searing Light, the Sun and Everything Else – Joy Division: The Oral History* (Faber & Faber, 2019)
Sharp, C., *Who Killed Martin Hannett? The Story of Factory Records' Musical Magician* (Aurum, 2007)
Sumner, B., *Chapter and Verse – New Order, Joy Division and Me* (Transworld, 2014)
Thompson, D., *True Faith – An Armchair Guide to New Order – Joy Division, Electronic, Revenge, Monaco and the Other Two* (Helter Skelter, 2005)
Wilson, A. H., *24 Hour Party People – What the Sleeve Notes Never Tell You* (4 Books, 2002)

On Track series
Alan Parsons Project – Steve Swift 978-1-78952-154-2
Tori Amos – Lisa Torem 978-1-78952-142-9
Asia – Peter Braidis 978-1-78952-099-6
Badfinger – Robert Day-Webb 978-1-878952-176-4
Barclay James Harvest – Keith and Monica Domone 978-1-78952-067-5
The Beatles – Andrew Wild 978-1-78952-009-5
The Beatles Solo 1969-1980 – Andrew Wild 978-1-78952-030-9
Blue Oyster Cult – Jacob Holm-Lupo 978-1-78952-007-1
Blur – Matt Bishop – 978-178952-164-1
Marc Bolan and T.Rex – Peter Gallagher 978-1-78952-124-5
Kate Bush – Bill Thomas 978-1-78952-097-2
Camel – Hamish Kuzminski 978-1-78952-040-8
Caravan – Andy Boot 978-1-78952-127-6
Cardiacs – Eric Benac 978-1-78952-131-3
Eric Clapton Solo – Andrew Wild 978-1-78952-141-2
The Clash – Nick Assirati 978-1-78952-077-4
Crosby, Stills and Nash – Andrew Wild 978-1-78952-039-2
The Damned – Morgan Brown 978-1-78952-136-8
Deep Purple and Rainbow 1968-79 – Steve Pilkington 978-1-78952-002-6
Dire Straits – Andrew Wild 978-1-78952-044-6
The Doors – Tony Thompson 978-1-78952-137-5
Dream Theater – Jordan Blum 978-1-78952-050-7
Electric Light Orchestra – Barry Delve 978-1-78952-152-8
Elvis Costello and The Attractions – Georg Purvis 978-1-78952-129-0
Emerson Lake and Palmer – Mike Goode 978-1-78952-000-2
Fairport Convention – Kevan Furbank 978-1-78952-051-4
Peter Gabriel – Graeme Scarfe 978-1-78952-138-2
Genesis – Stuart MacFarlane 978-1-78952-005-7
Gentle Giant – Gary Steel 978-1-78952-058-3
Gong – Kevan Furbank 978-1-78952-082-8
Hall and Oates – Ian Abrahams 978-1-78952-167-2
Hawkwind – Duncan Harris 978-1-78952-052-1
Peter Hammill – Richard Rees Jones 978-1-78952-163-4
Roy Harper – Opher Goodwin 978-1-78952-130-6
Jimi Hendrix – Emma Stott 978-1-78952-175-7
The Hollies – Andrew Darlington 978-1-78952-159-7
Iron Maiden – Steve Pilkington 978-1-78952-061-3
Jefferson Airplane – Richard Butterworth 978-1-78952-143-6
Jethro Tull – Jordan Blum 978-1-78952-016-3
Elton John in the 1970s – Peter Kearns 978-1-78952-034-7
The Incredible String Band – Tim Moon 978-1-78952-107-8
Iron Maiden – Steve Pilkington 978-1-78952-061-3
Judas Priest – John Tucker 978-1-78952-018-7

Kansas – Kevin Cummings 978-1-78952-057-6
The Kinks – Martin Hutchinson 978-1-78952-172-6
Korn – Matt Karpe 978-1-78952-153-5
Led Zeppelin – Steve Pilkington 978-1-78952-151-1
Level 42 – Matt Philips 978-1-78952-102-3
Little Feat – 978-1-78952-168-9
Aimee Mann – Jez Rowden 978-1-78952-036-1
Joni Mitchell – Peter Kearns 978-1-78952-081-1
The Moody Blues – Geoffrey Feakes 978-1-78952-042-2
Motorhead – Duncan Harris 978-1-78952-173-3
Mike Oldfield – Ryan Yard 978-1-78952-060-6
Opeth – Jordan Blum 978-1-78-952-166-5
Tom Petty – Richard James 978-1-78952-128-3
Porcupine Tree – Nick Holmes 978-1-78952-144-3
Queen – Andrew Wild 978-1-78952-003-3
Radiohead – William Allen 978-1-78952-149-8
Renaissance – David Detmer 978-1-78952-062-0
The Rolling Stones 1963-80 – Steve Pilkington 978-1-78952-017-0
The Smiths and Morrissey – Tommy Gunnarsson 978-1-78952-140-5
Status Quo the Frantic Four Years – Richard James 978-1-78952-160-3
Steely Dan – Jez Rowden 978-1-78952-043-9
Steve Hackett – Geoffrey Feakes 978-1-78952-098-9
Thin Lizzy – Graeme Stroud 978-1-78952-064-4
Toto – Jacob Holm-Lupo 978-1-78952-019-4
U2 – Eoghan Lyng 978-1-78952-078-1
UFO – Richard James 978-1-78952-073-6
The Who – Geoffrey Feakes 978-1-78952-076-7
Roy Wood and the Move – James R Turner 978-1-78952-008-8
Van Der Graaf Generator – Dan Coffey 978-1-78952-031-6
Yes – Stephen Lambe 978-1-78952-001-9
Frank Zappa 1966 to 1979 – Eric Benac 978-1-78952-033-0
Warren Zevon – Peter Gallagher 978-1-78952-170-2
10CC – Peter Kearns 978-1-78952-054-5

Decades Series

The Bee Gees in the 1960s – Andrew Mon Hughes et al 978-1-78952-148-1
The Bee Gees in the 1970s – Andrew Mon Hughes et al 978-1-78952-179-5
Black Sabbath in the 1970s – Chris Sutton 978-1-78952-171-9
Britpop – Peter Richard Adams and Matt Pooler 978-1-78952-169-6
Alice Cooper in the 1970s – Chris Sutton 978-1-78952-104-7
Curved Air in the 1970s – Laura Shenton 978-1-78952-069-9
Bob Dylan in the 1980s – Don Klees 978-1-78952-157-3
Fleetwood Mac in the 1970s – Andrew Wild 978-1-78952-105-4
Focus in the 1970s – Stephen Lambe 978-1-78952-079-8
Free and Bad Company in the 1970s – John Van der Kiste 978-1-78952-178-8

Genesis in the 1970s – Bill Thomas 978178952-146-7
George Harrison in the 1970s – Eoghan Lyng 978-1-78952-174-0
Marillion in the 1980s – Nathaniel Webb 978-1-78952-065-1
Mott the Hoople and Ian Hunter in the 1970s – John Van der Kiste
978-1-78-952-162-7
Pink Floyd In The 1970s – Georg Purvis 978-1-78952-072-9
Tangerine Dream in the 1970s – Stephen Palmer 978-1-78952-161-0
The Sweet in the 1970s – Darren Johnson from Gary Cosby collection 978-1-78952-139-9
Uriah Heep in the 1970s – Steve Pilkington 978-1-78952-103-0
Yes in the 1980s – Stephen Lambe with David Watkinson 978-1-78952-125-2

On Screen series

Carry On... – Stephen Lambe 978-1-78952-004-0
David Cronenberg – Patrick Chapman 978-1-78952-071-2
Doctor Who: The David Tennant Years – Jamie Hailstone 978-1-78952-066-8
James Bond – Andrew Wild – 978-1-78952-010-1
Monty Python – Steve Pilkington 978-1-78952-047-7
Seinfeld Seasons 1 to 5 – Stephen Lambe 978-1-78952-012-5

Other Books

1967: A Year In Psychedelic Rock – Kevan Furbank 978-1-78952-155-9
1970: A Year In Rock – John Van der Kiste 978-1-78952-147-4
1973: The Golden Year of Progressive Rock 978-1-78952-165-8
Babysitting A Band On The Rocks – G.D. Praetorius 978-1-78952-106-1
Eric Clapton Sessions – Andrew Wild 978-1-78952-177-1
Derek Taylor: For Your Radioactive Children – Andrew Darlington
978-1-78952-038-5
The Golden Road: The Recording History of The Grateful Dead – John Kilbride 978-1-78952-156-6
Iggy and The Stooges On Stage 1967-1974 – Per Nilsen 978-1-78952-101-6
Jon Anderson and the Warriors – the road to Yes – David Watkinson
978-1-78952-059-0
Nu Metal: A Definitive Guide – Matt Karpe 978-1-78952-063-7
Tommy Bolin: In and Out of Deep Purple – Laura Shenton 978-1-78952-070-5
Maximum Darkness – Deke Leonard 978-1-78952-048-4
Maybe I Should've Stayed In Bed – Deke Leonard 978-1-78952-053-8
The Twang Dynasty – Deke Leonard 978-1-78952-049-1

and many more to come!

Would you like to write for Sonicbond Publishing?
We are mainly a music publisher, but we also occasionally publish in other
genres including film and television. At Sonicbond Publishing we are always
on the look-out for authors, particularly for
our two main series, On Track and Decades.

Mixing fact with in depth analysis, the On Track series examines the
entire recorded work of a particular musical artist or group. All genres are
considered from easy listening and jazz to 60s soul to 90s pop, via rock and
metal.

The Decades series singles out a particular decade in an artist or group's
history and focuses on that decade in more detail than may be allowed in
the On Track series.

While professional writing experience would, of course, be an advantage,
the most important qualification is to have real enthusiasm and knowledge
of your subject. First-time authors are welcomed, but the ability to write well
in English is essential.

Sonicbond Publishing has distribution throughout Europe and North
America, and all our books are also published in E-book form. Authors will
be paid a royalty based on sales of their book.
Further details about our books are available from
www.sonicbondpublishing.com. To contact us, complete the contact form
there or email info@sonicbondpublishing.co.uk